The Challenge of a Bilingual Society in the Basque Country

Edited by

Pello Salaburu and Xabier Alberdi

Current Research Series No. 9

Center for Basque Studies
University of Nevada, Reno

Published in conjunction with the University of the Basque Country
UPV/EHU

Universidad   Euskal Herriko
del País Vasco   Unibertsitatea

Current Research
Selections of the ongoing work done by the faculty of the University of the
Basque Country (UPV/EHU), www.ehu.es

Editorial Committee
Amaia Maseda (Chair, University of the Basque Country, UPV/EHU), Arantza
Azpiroz (University of the Basque Country, UPV/EHU), Javier Echeverría (Uni-
versity of the Basque Country, UPV/EHU, and Ikerbasque), Jon Landeta (Uni-
versity of the Basque Country, UPV/EHU), Sandra Ott (UNR), Joseba Zulaika
(UNR), Santos Zunzunegui (University of the Basque Country, UPV/EHU)

Current Research Series No. 9
Center for Basque Studies
University of Nevada, Reno
Reno, Nevada 89557
http://basque.unr.edu

Library of Congress Cataloging-in-Publication Data

The challenge of a bilingual society in the Basque country / edited by Pello
Salaburu and Xabier Alberdi.
    p. cm. -- (Current research series ; no. 9)
 "Published in conjunction with the University of the Basque Country UPV/
EHU."
 Summary: "Collection of articles by Basque academics on Basque language and
its relations to bilingual society"--Provided by publisher.
 Includes bibliographical references and index.
 ISBN 978-1-935709-30-5 (pbk. : alk. paper) 1. Basque language--Social
aspects. 2. Bilingualism--Spain. 3. Bilingualism--France. I. Salaburu
Etxeberria, Pello. II. Alberdi, Xabier.

PH5024.75C48 2012
499'.92--dc23

2012035033

Contents

Introduction

PELLO SALABURU and XABIER ALBERDI,
the University of the Basque Country (UPV/EHU)

Some non-Indo-European languages survive in Europe, but the only one of these in the western half of the continent is Euskara (the Basque language).[1] It is, according to every study and despite the fact that the oldest testimonies in Euskara are only two thousand years old, a language that was used in the region prior to the invasions of Indo-European peoples with other cultures and other languages six thousand years ago. The Basque language, spoken by half a million people, is not related to any other language in the world. It is, therefore, atypical and unique from that perspective.

This language has survived through centuries, even though it has not enjoyed—until quite recently and only in one part of the Basque Country— the stable recognition of being a coofficial language recognized by the public administration. It has been preserved despite enormous difficulties and in constant competition with much more powerful languages. Even though 25 percent of the population speaks it today, it has suffered a significant decline in use through the centuries.

Following the death of the dictator Francisco Franco in 1975, the major changes that took place in one area of the Basque Country—what is termed the Comunidad Autónoma del País Vasco-Euskal Autonomia Erkiedgoa (CAPV-EAE, the Autonomous Community of the Basque Country), in Spain—led to a completely new situation: Euskara became, together with Spanish, a language officially recognized by law, and the rights of Basque-speakers were protected through various regulations in different social spheres. In the space of a few years, Euskara went from being a language spoken mostly in rural areas to being used in the media, at university, and in the offices of the Basque government. In short, it became a "visible" language in a modern society.

---

1. In this work the terms "Euskara" and "Basque" will be used equally to refer to the Basque language.

In the current work we present some of the features that characterize a modern bilingual society. We begin by defining what is understood by "the Basque Country," a term loaded with enormous social, cultural, and political connotations that has led to major confusion: Chapter 1 explains these problems and explores their causes. Official recognition of a language by the public authorities is only possible if the necessary legislative changes take place so that its speakers see their rights protected in practice, and this often poses new problems and unforeseen situations. As chapter 2 explains, bilingual societies end up devising their own regulations in order to facilitate and develop social coexistence. Because Euskara is a non-Indo-European language it follows that it has certain features that differentiate it completely from its neighboring languages, as explained in chapter 3. Despite being a language spoken in a reduced space and with not so many speakers, the complex terrain of the region, its administrative division into two different states as well as into several regional administrations, and the lack of a single written code that might help to structure the form of the language has meant that many local dialects and forms of speech have been preserved, as examined in chapter 4. Chapter 5 addresses precisely the history of a unique achievement: the development of a standard written code that in the few decades of its brief existence has been extraordinarily successful. It studies the specific form of that model and its bases. Chapter 6 provides ample information about the sociolinguistic situation of the language: speakers, use, spheres of use, people's attitudes toward it, and so on. Basque society has demonstrated a clear preference for its children being educated through the medium of Euskara at school. The survival of Spanish is guaranteed for a number of reasons but parents also want Euskara, one of the Basque community's main signs of identity, to be learned and used. Chapter 7 explains how education is organized from a linguistic perspective. Chapter 8 addresses an issue of great interest from a neurological point of view: the description of certain features of the brain in bilingual people. The application of empirical laboratory techniques to people who use languages as differently structured as Spanish and Basque has led to the emergence of new fields of study in these sciences. Finally, chapter 9 focuses on certain aspects of Basque literature: the spread of the language into education, the media, the translation of texts, and the public administration has had the natural consequence of an unprecedented boom in written literature in the Basque language, with the works of Basque authors now being systematically translated into other languages.

The authors of these chapters are professors at the Universidad del País Vasco/Euskal Herriko Unibertsitatea (UPV/EHU, the University of the Basque Country) and have widespread experience in research on the Basque language from different perspectives. Basque society is a bilingual society— in the French part Euskara and French are spoken and in the Spanish part

Euskara and Spanish are apoken—in which two languages are used and all speakers are guaranteed basic rights in the CAPV-EAE and parts of Navarre. This is a new situation in Basque history: a history that, for good or bad, is still being written by its protagonists—the inhabitants of the Basque Country. We are lucky on this occasion to be direct witnesses and conscious protagonists of that history, something that is quite unusual in the history of languages.

1

A Nation in Search of a Name: Cultural Realities, Political Projects, and Terminological Struggles in the Basque Country

Ludger Mees, the University of the Basque Country (UPV/EHU)

"*Izena duenak badu izana*": this well-known Basque saying means that a name has an existence of its own, words are not neutral and, consequently, by controlling words we are also able to modulate meanings. In Basque history, few words or concepts have been as strongly contested as those concerning the naming of the Basque people or country. Throughout history, even before the birth of Basque nationalism in the late nineteenth century, while over a dozen proposals for naming the Basque Country have been formulated, none of them have been established on a permanent basis: these include *Euskal Herria, Eskual Herria, Euskalerria, Euskaria, Euskeria, Vasconia, Euzkadi, Euskadi, País Vasco, País Vasco-Navarro, Pueblo Vasco, Pays Basque*, and *Bizkaia* (García-Sanz, Iriarte, and Mikelarena 2002). Considering the diversity of these names, writer Bernardo Atxaga has compared this situation with that of an archipelago made up of a large number of islands where, nevertheless, access between them is not always easy. To break with this lack of communication, and to establish a semantic link between the different parts of the Basque Country, Atxaga suggests replacing the standard *Euskal Herria* with *Euskal Hiria*. The concept of *hiria* ("city" or *polis*) introduced a new civic dimension into the definition of the country, thereby harmonizing the ethnic and/or linguistic dimensions and adapting the definition to the needs of a modern, open, and heterogeneous society in order to include the different sectors of which it is composed (www.atxaga.org/blog/17). Other contemporary writers, such as Pedro Ugarte, are more skeptical when contemplating the future of a

* This article is part of a research project financed by the Spanish Ministry of Science and Innovation (ref. HAR 2011-24387), in the framework of a Group Research Project of the UPV/EHU (ref. GIU 11/21). For more information about this research see Granja, Pablo, Mees, and Casquete 2012, and Mees 2012

project such as the Basque Country that still has no name: "The little country is still a very complicated place. How can it not be if we still don't even know what it's called? And this intrinsic problem is also, unfortunately, the source of its infeasibility" (*El País*, 24 Jul, 2010). This does not in any way suggest a new form of postmodern skepticism. Sixty years before, the French Basque cleric, writer, and philosophy teacher, Etienne Salaberry, did not question the viability of the Basque Country but rather the need—however impossible—to decide upon one of the different names used to describe it. Salaberry championed a flexible laissez-faire attitude toward this subject as long as the fact that "we remain brothers" was always remembered, regardless of the word chosen. However, it appears that Salaberry himself was not entirely convinced of the feasibility of his own proposal. He knew that the background to the controversy was highly significant given that, in his opinion, the use of one name or another would enable "a kind of psychoanalysis of our deepest tendencies" to be carried out (*Gernika* 18, Jan–Mar 1952).

In fact, more than an individual or collective kind of psychoanalysis, the dispute over the name is a good reflection of the struggle for power in the Basque Country; a struggle characterized primarily by the emerging nationalism and its concomitant need to mark its territory and establish a political profile of its own and, later, among the different sectors of nationalism in the battle for hegemony.

The Origins

Two concepts that have been a significant part of the controversy since the end of the nineteenth century right up to the present are those of Euskal Herria and Euskadi, and their different spelling variants (for example, Eskual Herria and Euzkadi). Clearly, one of the factors that helps to explain why it is so difficult to find a univocal place name for the Basque Country (or the Basque people) is the fact that, historically, its territory has never been one political administrative entity with features proper to a state and with clearly defined borders. Sancho el Mayor's Kingdom of Pamplona in the eleventh century was not a modern state in this sense. The kingdom also covered non-Basque territories as well as exercising a more indirect influence over the French Basque part.

Although this represented a political and administratively divided country, a process of "ethnogenesis", in Anthony D. Smith's words, soon began with the appearance of a name being one of the "first visible signs of collective similarity and difference" (Smith 2009, 46). The marker of this "similarity" and "difference" was language; Euskara or the Basque language. The name Euskal Herria literally referred to the people who spoke this language, to the "land of those who speak Basque." The first references to this name appear in a manuscript written between 1564 and 1567 by Juan Pérez de Lazarraga: "*çegayti eusquel errian dira heder guztioc dotadu*" ("on why Euskal Herria has been endowed with all these beauties") (www.gipuzkoakultura.net). Not long afterward (1571), Joanes Leizarraga used the same term in his translation of the New Testament: "*bat bederac daqui Euskal herrian quasi etche batetic bercera-ere minçatzeco manerán cer differentiá eta diuersitatea den*" ("everyone knows that in Euskal Herria different ways of speaking are evident almost from one house to another") (www.euskomedia.org/PDFAnlt/mono/leizarraga/leizarraga_biblia.pdf). Nonetheless, neither of these texts offers any indication as to who formed part of this Euskal Herria and where exactly they lived. A people existed with certain linguistic characteristics, but a territory had not yet been established. This would appear almost a century later in *Gero*, the literary work by Pedro Axular, parish priest of the small French Basque town of Sara (Sare), who spelled out the names of the seven Basque territories on either side of the border (www.axularnet.com/web/gero.html).[1]

This definition of the country through language was consolidated not only within the territory but also had some success beyond it. Wilhelm von Humboldt was responsible for presenting the particular case of the Basque people and their language at international forums. Despite the political and administrative fragmentation which existed in the early nineteenth century, Humboldt bestowed sufficient importance on the indigenous language to define the Basque people as a nation. Nevertheless, as an astute analytical observer of the Basque situation, Humboldt was aware of the terminological problem. The German scholar lamented the "division" of the "unfortunate Basque nation"; a division that was highly problematic for anyone who wanted to find a common name for all Basque people: "There is not one single name that is used unanimously by the French, the Spanish, and the German people" (Humboldt 1904, 224).

However, the Basque scholars who followed Humboldt soon took up the term Euskal Herria. From among the many testimonies that we could cite from the international bibliography to substantiate the natural use of the concept of Euskal Herria throughout the nineteenth century to define an ethno-linguistic community on both sides of the Pyrenees, it is worth including here a translated citation from the prestigious encyclopedia *Deutsches Staats-Wörterbuch* (German State Dictionary) of 1857: "The language spoken by the Basque people is called *Euscara, Eskuara,* or *Esquera* by those people themselves. In line with this, their country is called *Euscalerria* and the local name for the people themselves is *Euscal-dunac.*" It is

---

1. Their common denominator was the fact that the Basque language is spoken or was spoken in all of them.

interesting to see that this very definition introduced the idea that some inhabitants of the Basque Country, particularly those in the French territories, are no longer "Basque" since they have lost their indigenous language (Bluntschli and Brater 1857, 665).

However, in the nineteenth-century Europe of liberalism, romanticism, and nationalism, it is not surprising that the linguistic differential would acquire more political connotations by becoming a key element in the definition of a nationality that called for some kind of self-governance. Another key element in this was the *fueros* (Spain) and *fors* (France)—charters granting the Basque provinces significant degrees of politico-administrative decision-making authority—that were abolished in the French part with the late eighteenth-century French Revolution, and on the other side of the Pyrenees as a result of the nineteenth-century Carlist Wars. As already noted, at an international level, Humboldt was already one step ahead insofar as he conferred a more political sense to the concept of "Bizkaian" by referring to the Basque people with the term "nation" or "nationality". After the last Carlist War of 1876, in the Basque Country itself *fuerismo* (a movement created to lobby for reinstating the *fueros*) was responsible for disseminating the idea of an ethno-cultural community with the right to recover the self-governance that had been lost with the abolition of the *foral* laws (Rubio Pobes 2003). Out of this context, a new impulse toward the use of classical concepts emerged. Thus, the Asociación Euskara de Navarra (Euskara Association of Navarre), created in 1878, called on the solidarity of the Basque people of the Old Kingdom along with their brothers from Araba, Gipuzkoa, and Bizkaia. Meanwhile, the *Sociedad Euskalerria* (Basque Country Society), founded at the end of 1876 did the same from Bilbao, although it should be noted that in the discourse of both organizations, references to the Basque people of Iparralde (the northern Basque Country) were merely symbolic (Corcuera Atienza 2006, 67–110). The proliferation of the use of the concept Euskal Herria continued up to the end of the nineteenth century, both in the Basque Country as well as among Basque groups of the diaspora in the Americas. Thus, the magazine *Euskal-Herria* was founded in 1880 in Donostia-San Sebastián and in 1898 the weekly *Eskual Herria* was published for the first time in Baiona (Bayonne). Moreover, with the publication of the magazines *Californiako Eskual Herria* (Los Angeles 1893–1898) and *La Platako Eskual Herria* (Buenos Aires, 1889) in the Americas, toward the end of the nineteenth century it could be argued, just as a report from Euskaltzaindia (the Royal Academy of the Basque Language) does, that "as well as appearing in the name of entities, the use of Euskal Herria is normal, regardless of the ideological framework posed" (Euskaltzaindia 2004, 480). Turning once again to the terminology used by Smith, this conceptual proliferation is almost certainly an indicator of the advancing process of ethnogenesis that had led to the creation of a "sense of distinctive ethnic identity."[2] It is worth recalling that this identity was articulated mainly in terms of cultural and linguistic parameters, even though references to the *fueros* and to self-governance had introduced connotations that were clearly political, yet still compatible with the political and administrative framework of the Spanish Monarchy.

The Sudden Appearance of Sabino Arana and Euzkadi

The spectacular emergence of Basque political nationalism at the end of the century introduced significant changes to the semantic field (Larronde 1977; Pablo, Mees, and Rodríguez Ranz 1999; Corcuera 2006). Sabino Arana's Basque nationalism was born out of an intensive and violent process of socioeconomic modernization. His radical nature and initial separatist discourse were primarily a consequence of the severity with which modernization had transformed the economic, social, cultural, and political structures of Bizkaia and Gipuzkoa over the course of just a few years. But this was also the result of the need to take control of a public space by being distinct from the other political powers that, from Carlism to *fuerismo* and even republicanism, had raised the flag of the *fueros* in one way or another. Within this context, the need emerged to launch not only a political message that was clear and distinctive, but also to do so by wrapping that message up semantically in a way that was strikingly original. This is how the concept of Euzkadi—initially written with a "z" by its inventor Arana–emerged; a concept that was called upon from this point onward to compete with the traditional Euskal Herria.

The invention and propagation of the word Euzkadi did not come about without some contradictions, even though Arana's arguments were entirely coherent at all times with regard to his political thinking. In any case, Arana did not waste too much time on this subject, given that he only really needed one single in-depth article in order to put forward his proposal. It did not matter that previously he preferred the term Euskaria to refer to the Basque Country in its entirety, and that, even after the creation of Euzkadi, he would continue to use this term on certain occasions. Moreover, his initial *Bizkai-tarrismo* (a Bizkaia-centric form of nationalism) is the reason why he was to dedicate so much more attention to the history of this Basque territory than to the Basque Country as a whole, and that his idea of brotherhood among all Basques would be subordinated to the demand for the specific autonomy of each one of the territories in the future confederation. The statutes of the first

---

2. "Only when a collective proper name is conferred on a population, highlighting the unity of its parts, and only when it becomes widely accepted by the members of the population, can a sense of distinctive ethnic identity begin to emerge" (Smith 2009, 46).

nationalist association, the Euzkeldun Batzokija, expressed this idea clearly: "A free Bizkaya in a free Euskeria" (*Bizkaitarra* 10, 24 May, 1894).

This provincial vision, however, would be subjected to differences in emphasis and corrections throughout the last years of the decade. Insofar as Basque nationalism stepped out of the fiefdom of Bilbao and Bizkaia in order to win over an audience in the other Basque territories, the maintenance of the *Bizkaitarrista* discourse on its own would have represented an obstacle in the way of expanding the nationalist movement. Because of this, Arana increasingly focused his analysis on aspects that had been marginalized up until then, concentrating more on the national dimension of the Basque race and, consequently, on the confederation of the territories. Given that race was the principal marker of difference that characterized a nation for the founder of the EAJ-PNV (Basque and Spanish acronyms for the Basque Nationalist Party), a concept such as Euskal Herria, based, above all, on linguistic criteria, could not be of any use. Nor did the prospect of locating the initial focus and nationalist fiefdom in a sociolinguistic environment as Hispanicized as Bilbao appear to be particularly attractive in terms of measuring membership of the nation with the criteria of linguistic knowledge and usage when a significant part of the early nationalists no longer knew Euskara.

We cannot be certain about the exact moment in time when Sabino Arana invented the word Euzkadi, but we can provide details of its first appearance in the public domain: he used it for the first time in 1896, the year his book *Lecciones de ortografía del euskera bizkaino* (Lessons in orthography of Bizkaian Euskara) was published, and whose last page includes the word "Euzkadi" above the coat of arms with the six Basque territories. One year later it appeared again in a new, lesser-known work written in Basque, *Umiaren lenengo Aizkidia* (First children's companion) (Corcuera 2006, 220; Arana 1965, 982). But it was not until 1901 that his famous article titled "Euzko" appeared, in which he laid the foundations and explained the content of this new word, as well as the reasons that had led to his inventing it (Pagola 2005, 152–55). In point of fact, he did this in the first edition of a new magazine called *Euzkadi*, where he reached the following conclusion:

> Euzkelerria, formed by Euzkel and erri (people), can only mean the people of Euzkera, whether the families who comprise it are Basque or not. An area of Basque-speaking gypsies is Euzkelerria; whereas, by contrast, a significant proportion of the Spanish-speaking population in Bizkaya, Araba and Navarre is not. . . . What I set out to prove has been established: that in Euzkera today, Basque does not have a name, nor do the entirety of its race, its people and its land (*Euzkadi* 1, March 1901).

The debate was thus established. The journal, *Euskalduna*, the voice of the moderate sector of Basque nationalism, took under a month to challenge

Arana's suggestion,; rejecting it as fanciful: "Only those of us who live tranquilly in Euskalerria can be called Euskaldunes (Basque speakers), and do not go to live in countries that, like Euskadi, appear more like regions taken out of legends, populated by mythological beings, than the places where the most traditional people live, work, think and pray" (*Euskalduna* 176, April 7, 1901).

Clearly, this critique cannot be understood without taking into account the context in which this initial form of Basque nationalism found itself, marked by a struggle for control of the party between two competing sectors; the moderate sector on the one hand, and the radical one on the other. The premature death of the leader and founder in 1903, as well as his immediate elevation to the status of national hero worshipped by all, boosted his terminological proposal that was becoming increasingly accepted in the different sectors of the nationalist collective. Few critical voices remained within this collective prepared to challenge the term Euzkadi. One of the exceptions was Arturo Campión, who, as a well-known intellectual and a man with ideas close to moderate Basque nationalism, although not a member of the party, dared to reopen the controversy just four years after the death of the *Master*.

Campión recovered the argument about the artificial creation of the neologism Euzkadi, which was unknown to most Basque people and, therefore, not suitable in terms of encouraging them to identify it with their country. He was immediately contested by Luis de Eleizalde, one of the foremost intellectuals of Basque nationalism, who defended Sabino's proposal (Euzkadi 9, January 1907).

This debate in 1907, which continued in the daily press and other editions of the magazine *Euzkadi*, was probably the last internal controversy about the name of the country before the Spanish Civil War (1936–1939). In fact, the growth of Basque nationalism and the cult of its founder would silence critics. There was no longer any doubt that the Country of the Basques was Euzkadi, and the leadership of the party acknowledged this when they gave this name to the new nationalist nationalist daily newspaper whose first edition came out on February 1, 1913. Finally, years after his death, Sabino Arana had won the battle over the name, even though this victory would lead to another problem: that of the absolute identification of the term Euzkadi with Basque nationalism; something that was a clear obstacle in terms of recovering the wide consensus that there had been concerning the concept of Euskal Herria up until the late nineteenth century. If Arana invented Euzkadi in order to set himself apart from other political alternatives, these alternatives were now tempted to recoup the traditional name in order to distance themselves from Basque nationalism. The motion of the Catholic-Foralist minority in the City

Council of Iruñea-Pamplona was highly significant in this sense, insofar as, in 1932, it opposed the use of the name *Euzkadi* in the draft statutes of autonomy prepared by the provincial governments. Instead, the Catholic Foralists advocated the exclusive use of the term "Euskalerria" (García-Sanz, Iriarte, and Mikelarena 2002, 89).

Possibly in order to avoid potential disagreements concerning questions of identity and terminology, the draft Basque autonomy statute voted on in 1933 retained the ambiguity of the 1932 text by treating both terms as synonymous: "Araba, Gipuzkoa, and Bizkaia . . . agree to constitute themselves, within the Spanish state, in an autonomous political and administrative nucleus that will be called 'País Vasco' in Spanish and 'Euskalerria' or 'Euzkadi' in Basque" (Escudero and Villanueva 1976, 210–34). Later, the definitive text of 1936 sought a similar balance by completely replacing the concept of Euzkadi in Spanish, which only spoke of the "País Vasco" (Basque Country). The Basque version, by contrast, no longer mentioned *Euskalerria* and spoke only about *Euzkadi* (Castells 1976, 129–54; Granja 2008).

Among the left-wing groups, the Communist Party (PCE by its Spanish acronym)—pushed along by Stalin's pro-nationalities politics–was to take the most important steps toward the new terminology. Between 1933 and 1937 its newspaper was called *Euskadi Roja* (Red Euskadi), and in its last year its spelling was changed: *Euzkadi Roja*, like the party itself, was founded in 1935 with the official name of the Communist Party of Euskadi, and in the Spanish Civil War it became known as the Communist Party of Euzkadi. The socialists, despite being more reticent, created the Socialist Central Committee of Euzkadi during the civil war. It is difficult to know the reason why the PCE wrote the beginning of the word with an "s" while the socialists remained faithful to Arana's spelling with a "z." In general, the "z" had always symbolized a closeness and faithfulness to the founder of the EAJ-PNV, whose successors still use the "z" even today (in the term "Euzkadi Buru Batzarra" or governing committee of the party), even though Euskaltzaindia settled the contentious spelling some time ago. In fact, in January 1920, after consulting a report put together by its president, Resurrección María de Azkue, members of the academy voted on the spelling of all words derived from the *eusk/euzk* root. Arana had wanted the root of the word *eguzki* (sun) to be in the word *euz*, as further proof of the sun worshipping that, in his opinion, was practiced by the ancient Basque people. Azkue, however, rejected Arana's etymological theory as "too obscure" and "not particularly credible" ["*gauza ilunegia ta agiantz andirik ez duena*"]. After also finding this same word according to its particular etymology in *Bizkaia* ["be-Euzko-di-a" = "all the Basque people down below"], and given that Bizkaia/Vizcaya was written with "z" in both

Basque and in Spanish, the correct spelling for all derivates of *euzk*, according to the founder of the EAJ-PNV, was that with a "z."[3] Nevertheless, neither Azkue nor the majority of academics were convinced by this. In his report, the president of Euskaltzaindia admitted how difficult it was to reach a consensus: "As on many other matters, we Basques go about our business without being able to reach a mutual understanding on the subject of how to spell our own language" ["*Euskaldunok, beste gauza askotan bezela, gure izkuntza onen idazkeran ere elkar ezin uruturik gabiltza*"]. His strongest argument in favor of retaining the s lay in the fact that Sabino Arana had been the first to break with a broad consensus, given that no other author had thought to write the derivatives of *eusk* with a "z." Azkue found a wide majority in favor of his proposal: with eight votes against two, the academics decided to keep the classic "s" (*Euskera* 1, no. 1, 1920, 61–65; *Euskera* 1, no. 2, 1920, 14–19; Pagola 2005, 152–61).

After all this, even though the members of Euskaltzaindia had supported his verdict decisively, this still did not put an end to the confusion about how to write the word *Euskadi* because there were still adherents to Arana's spelling, even within the left-wing parties such as the CPE. To explain this attitude, it could be suggested that the formation of the Basque government in 1936, with the communist Juan Astigarrabía being a minister in *Lehendakari* (President) José Antonio Aguirre's first cabinet, along with the assumption of independence, were contributory factors that brought the CPE closer to the EAJ-PNV and also, therefore, led them to adopt the spelling of Euzkadi with a "z." In the case of the socialists, it is clear that the reason for using the "z" had nothing to do with a proximity to Arana but, instead, was probably due to institutional loyalty, given that the official name of the autonomous Basque Country was Euzkadi with a "z." This practice was also accepted by the heterodox nationalism of EAE-ANV (Basque and Spanish acronyms for Basque Nationalist Action) that had accepted the Arana "z" without any problems since its foundation in 1930, as reflected in its founding manifesto. The *Manifiesto de San Andrés* defined "the fundamental ideological basis" of the new party as "the affective and efficient affirmation of the national personality of the Basque Country, called Euzkadi in Basque, Euskalerria traditionally, and Vasconia in the Latin languages (Pablo, Granja, and Mees 1998, 91). In any

---

3. Thus, Xabier Zabaltza insists that Arana actually invented the word Euzkadi explaining it in his famous article of 1901 with the reference to *eguzki* (and not to that which, in Arana's opinion, was its authentic and true root) so as not to "impose a spelling and a national name whose foundations lay in its etymology of 'Bizkaia' on the non-Bizkaian Basques . . . Sabino Arana created the name that gave the Basque nation an image of and a likeness to his own homeland. Deep down, the founder of nationalism never ceased to be a *Bizkaitarra*" (1997, 79). Nevertheless, as Inés Pagola (2005, 155) also recalls, Arana used the same argument in his etymology of other words, such as that of Gipuzkoa that is also written with a "z" in both languages.

case, and in summary, it can be observed that the indisputable leadership of the first *Lehendakari*, Aguirre, as well as the hegemony of the EAJ-PNV in the governments of war and exile, ended up consolidating the use not only of the *ikurriña* as the official Basque flag, but also of the name Euzkadi as the name for the Basque Country among the non-nationalist left (Mees 2006). Thus, the experience shared by Basque nationalists and followers of the Popular Front (the coalition of center and left-wing political parties that came to power in the 1936 general elctions) in the trenches, in the resistance, and in exile, forged a symbolic universe common to both nationalists and the left, removing the neologism *Euzkadi* from the unique preserve of the *jeltzale* (members of the EAJ-PNV) and, in practice, stripping it of the racial connotations with which it had been created.

The Return of Euskal Herria

Nonetheless, the debate about the naming of the Basque Country was not over. During the Franco regime (1939–75), and logically given that the term *Euzkadi* already referred, in a sense, to those who had lost the war and continued to oppose the dictatorship, the term Euskal Herria underwent a notable revival in the circles closest to the regime. Thus, to cite a few examples, in 1948, the traditionalist academic Francisco Elías de Tejada defended his alternative at all costs in opposition to the term Euzkadi and in favor of Euskalerria:

> The nationalist wave sought a more endearing name and came across *Euzkadi*, which aimed to add a political nuance to the sense of a Basque state. . . . I prefer Euskaleria, Hispanicized as Euskalerría. This is the word of the romantic poets and the ancestral dreamers: to find the substantive form without detaining oneself over adjectival motivations. It has a sense of a common land but without immediate political dimensions. And, above all, it expresses what is most essential to the Basque communities: the fact that they are not recognized as a state, their peculiarly simple psychology, their lack of interest in deploying high-profile figures; in a word, their primitivism. In the glorious parade of popular varieties of Spanishness, the Basques are the gray note that contrasts with Andalusian red and the seriously black Castilian (Elías de Tejada 1948, 100–1).

Almost twenty years later, the magazine *¿Qué pasa?*, with extreme right-wing views and linked to the most fundamentalist sectors of the regime, published an article by the Carlist Pilar Roura Garisoain from Navarre, in which the author unequivocally declared that "I love EUSKAL-ERRIA and all that it means for those of us born in this land who also share the blood of the mysterious and thousand-year-old *Euskaldun* race." Euskal Herria was a concept based on an "authentic foral regionalism" of lands whose Basqueness increased in proportion to the extent that it provided human resources to the great Spanish fatherland:

> Carlism is like Euskal-Erria, tenacious, firm and rebellious when that which is untouchable is threatened: the religion of our elders, the homeland (that some Basque people mistakenly wanted to make so small, reducing it to a mere plot, forgetting that the Basques were never more Basque than when they offered men to Spain and to the world; saints, warriors, seafarers of immortal fame), the fundamental liberties of the law and the recognition of a HEAD, responsible before God and before all men, who could be called nothing other than KING, because neither Spain nor *Vasconia*—one of the most beautiful daughters of Spain—deserve less given their distinction and nobility (*¿Qué Pasa?* 190, Aug 19, 1967).

For the Franco regime and the circles closest to it, Euskal Herria was thus a politically loaded concept that described a region, and even a race, of Spain; one proud of its traditions and customs and a net contributor to the greatness of the Spanish nation. It was a cultural and regionalist concept, devoid of any particularist political connotations. It was absolutely incompatible with the concept Euzkadi, as explained as late as 1973 by the censor of a Basque book:

> It is the opinion of this reader that it is important to promote, stimulate and support all those works in which the old and glorious and healthy word EUSKAL ERRIA appears; a word still used today by the authentic and noble Basque people. This is an infallible criterion.
>
> Note: The difference between saying GORA EUZKADI and GORA EUSKAL ERRIA is the following:
> GORA EUSKAL ERRIA: Long live Spain and Vasconia.
> GORA EUZKADI: Long live Vasconia and out with Spain. (Torrealdai 1999, 89).

Obviously, Basque nationalists were aware of the clear political undercurrent of the terminology used by the regime, which represented an almost definitive argument for the defenders of the concept of Euzkadi during the long internal controversy. Francoism, "our greatest enemy today, outlaws its name, prohibits its use, imprisons and pursues those who speak it; it would like to see it exiled or better still deceased altogether." If this conceptual persecution was understandable, what the author of this article found inacceptable was the fact that some nationalists closed ranks with the regime by also opting for the concept of Euskal Herria, words that remained "inappropriate terms that may serve to satisfy the vanity of a few, but that irritate and wound the feelings of patriots" (Atxuri 1949).

The split within Basque nationalism that occurred with the foundation of ETA (Basque acronym for Basque Country and Freedom) in 1959 did not initially change anything in the design of the terminological trenches (Clark 1984; Jáuregui 1985; Mees 2003; Elorza et al. 2006). ETA assumed the concept Euzkadi without reservation, initially with "z," as the very name of the organization already indicates: Euzkadi 'ta Askatasuna. Nevertheless, although the foundational manifesto of the organization would acknowledge the Basque government as "the depository of the faith and will of our people," integrating the new organization "into the trajectory and principles arising from it" (Pablo, Mees, and Rodríguez Ranz 2001, 236), the first attempts to move closer to Arana's terminology would soon appear precisely in order to disassociate themselves from traditional nationalism and from its government. This was a government that, in accordance with the autonomy statute of 1936, only included Araba, Gipuzkoa, and Bizkaia, but not Navarre or Iparralde: "Territorially, Euzkadi 'is made up of the historical regions of Alava, Gipuzkoa, Laburdi, Navarra, Bizcaia and Zuberoa' (the 'Principles'). From this, according to ETA, it can be concluded that the Basque government of Paris is not the government of Euzkadi (see Statute of October 6, 1936, article 1, of title 1). Euzkadi is intangibly all of these things" (*Documentos Y* 1979, 503).

From this point onward, ETA and the political organizations around it followed these semantic norms, preferring to use the word Euzkadi as a political reference to the Basque Country in its entirety, yet without entering into the classic debate about the suitability of one concept over another. In fact, in the documents in which the term Euskal Herria appears, both terms are used synonymously. If, in this way, Euskal Herria survived in the discourse of the so-called Basque nationalist left-wing, it was basically due to the influence of one of its leaders and the cofounder of ETA, José Luis Álvarez Enparantza (known by the pseudonym Txillardegi) who represented a current within the movement that defined the Basque nation through the category of language, thereby clearly breaking with the biological concept of nation propagated by Arana. And in 1966, Txillardegi made it clear that the existence of a national language is what "makes Euskal Herria": "*Zerk egin du Euskal Herria? Zerk eman dio bere izakera berezia? Zerk egiten du gure naziotasuna? Zerk bizi gaitu? Zerk bereizten gaitu? Zerk ematen digu gure euskal arima? EUSKARAK EZ BESTERIK*" (Txillardegi 1978, 432). ("What has made up Euskal Herria? What has given it its special character? What has made our national character? What makes us live? What makes us different? What gives us our Basque soul? The Basque language and nothing else").

However, not even Txillardegi was always consistent with this choice of terminology, given that on some occasions he continued to speak and write about Euskadi (but always with an "s"). Thus, in an article titled "Nafarroa da Euskadi" (Navarre is Euskadi"), he argued that "the project of Euskadi is not and never will be anything less than a project to revive the old Navarre" (*Punto y Hora de Euskal Herria*, April 26, 1979).

The preference for the term Euskadi, linked to a parallel, lax, and confused use of the concept Euskal Herria, was also reflected after the end of the Franco era in the body of the statute of autonomy of the Basque Country of 1979 (known popularly as the Statute of Gernika), whose article 1 states that: "The Basque land or Euskal Herria . . . is constituted as an autonomous community within the Spanish state under the name *Euskadi* or the *Basque Country*." Among the Basque democrats of the period, critical voices against this formula were few and far between, although some carried particular weight. One of these was articulated already in the previous debate about the text by Euskaltzaindia, warning of the alleged intention to eliminate the name of Euskal Herria (*Euskera* 24, no. 1, 1979, 115–17). Despite this critical warning, and after the more or less balanced proposals in the 1936 statutory text, from 1979 it was evident that Arana had won the battle. The recuperation and development of Basque autonomy in the new Spanish democracy was closely linked to the concept of Euskadi as a political and administrative definition of the three provinces that were already included in the statute of 1936. At the same time, Euskal Herria continued to be used as a more cultural concept that, by referring to the seven Basque territories, contradicted, to a certain extent, the concept of Euskadi.

As is well known, the option offered by the moderate nationalism of the EAJ-PNV—investing heavily in a fight to recover the autonomy that had been abolished in 1937 as a gradual strategy aimed at a later unification in the long-term of all Basque territories—would set the party against ETA and the Basque nationalist left-wing in the years following the passing of the Statute of Gernika. In spite of this, it is surprising to find that during those initial years of democracy, and at the height of the bloodiest offensive by ETA in its entire history, this opposition would still not cross over to the semantic field because the Basque nationalist left continued to speak of and vindicate the rights of Euskadi in almost all their written texts and proclamations. Thus, for example, the Basque nationalist left "Alternativa KAS" (Kas Alternative, 1976) demanded in point 5 the "recognition of the national sovereignty of Euskadi" (Agiñako et al. 1999, 28). And the term Euskal Herria did not appear in the foundation manifesto of Herri Batasuna (Popular Unity, HB), the political coalition representing the Basque nationalist left, in April 1978. The iconography displayed in public spaces followed the same terminological guidelines arguing, for example, that "*Ipar Euskadi eta hego Euskadi bat dira*" ("Euskadi North and Euskadi South are one") or demanding Basque political refugees' rights to "live in Euskadi." The official slogan for the electoral campaign of 1986 was "*Euskadi aurrera!*" ("Forward Euskadi!") and when, in November of that year, Juan Carlos Yoldi, the ETA prisoner elected member of the Basque parliament, delivered his speech in the chamber, he addressed himself "to the sectors eagerly seeking peace and the freedom of Euskadi" (ibid. 181). Everyone understood, therefore, that Euskadi, in the same way that it had been for Sabino Arana, was also a comprehensive term for the entirety of the Basque territories, including Navarre and Iparralde.

This language remained unaltered until the end of the 1980s and early 1990s. In the official slogans of the *Aberri Eguna* (Day of the Basque Country) organized by HB during the 1980s, the word Euskadi appeared often, while Euskal Herria did not appear at all. However, a change took place in 1990, a year in which the concept of Euskal Herria appeared for the first time in the official motto (*"Autodeterminazioa Euskal Herri berrian"*: "Self-determination in the new Euskal Herria"). The same change then occurred in HB official election slogans. In 1989, the HB slogan during elections to the European parliament continued to be that of *"Herri Batasuna, Euskadiren alternatiba"* ("Herri Batasuna, the alternative party of Euskadi"), yet in the Basque autonomous elections of 1990, this changed to "Euskal Herri Berria" ("The new Euskal Herria"). From this point onward, gradually, and with very few exceptions, the word Euskadi disappeared from the manifestos and from the iconography deployed by ETA and the nationalist left.

This terminological change was no accident and was due to different factors. On the one hand, as indicated already, there were influential people within the Basque nationalist left-wing who had been defending the concept of a nation based on linguistic criteria for some time and who, as a result, felt much closer to Euskal Herria than to Euskadi. In the 1990s, Txillardegi clarified his posture on this subject, abandoning the last vestiges of his more flexible terminological option of previous years even though, clearly, as cofounder of ETA he had to reconcile this option with a justification of the word Euskadi in the name of the terrorist organization, which, according to Txillardegi had been conceived as the name for the future independent and united Basque state (Txillardegi 1997, 287).

There was another important argument for the terminological change appears in this citation. The consolidation of Basque autonomy and of its institutions, led by democratic Basque nationalism, had also brought with it the consolidation of the word Euskadi that, in the context of the autonomous *Realpolitik,* was losing a significant part of its utopian connotations and practically becoming a synonym of the Comunidad Autónoma del País Vasco-Euskal Autonomia Erkidegoa (the Autonomous Community of the Basque Country, CAPV-EAE), accepted not only by the Socialist Party of Euskadi (PSE by its Spanish acronym), but also by the Basque branch of the conservative People's Party (PP by its Spanish acronym), whose official name in Basque (although not often used) is Euskadiko Alderdi Popularra. This consolidation could not be stopped either by ETA's bloody offensive throughout the 1980s (with more than four hundred people killed in the attacks), nor through coup d'etat attempts in Spain such as that of the Guardia Civil (Civil Guard) Lieutenant Colonel Antonio Tejero in 1981. Moreover, in the face of the terrorist violence, and in defense of self-governance, the Ajuria Enea Agreement (1988) had brought together all the Basque democratic parties from which the nationalist left-wing— unwilling and/or incapable of separating itself from the armed group—had become more isolated than ever before. In this context of increasing confrontation with the autonomous system and with the EAJ-PNV as the dominant party, ETA and its political wing HB opted not to continue using a term that had been devalued and that was closely linked to the etymological heritage of the party that, in the opinion of ETA, had now closed ranks with the other pro-Spanish parties. Thus, the rejection of Euskadi was, to a certain extent, also a rejection of the EAJ-PNV. Euskal Herria aimed to symbolize the alternative political project of the Basque nationalist left with its vocation for hegemony, not just limited to the three provinces, but rather aiming to achieve full sovereignty for all Basque territories.

Some authors argue that this terminological change accelerated when Mikel Albisu (known by the pseudonym Mikel Antza) became leader of ETA after the break up of the previous leadership by the French police in Bidarte (Bidart), Lapurdi, in March 1992. Florencio Domínguez mentions the fact that in the twenty-four statements disseminated by ETA during 1991 and the first quarter of 1992, Euskadi appears twenty-one times, while Euskal Herria appears eighteen times. Therafter, in the seven statements drawn up between April and December 1992, Euskal Herria appears seventy-seven times, while Euskadi does not appear at all (*El Correo*, June 22, 2010). Furthermore, in the 1990s this conceptual change was also easier for another reason, and that was because the obstacle presented by the Francoist right-wing that embraced Euskal Herria in merely cultural and regional terms had ceased to exist. With this, the terminological site was free once again.

This semantic maneuver of the nationalist left also generated a kind of echo in terms of the democratic nationalism of the EAJ-PNV, who gradually abandoned their defense of orthodoxy in order to glimpse beyond the terrain of the conceptual game that had been marked by HB and its successors. Although it is difficult to find unequivocal documentary proof to validate this hypothesis, the data available indicates that the discovery and use of the concept Euskal Herria by the *jeltzales* accelerated to the extent to which the party became submerged in a process of radicalization that was accompanied by an increasingly critical reading of the statute of autonomy that, according to the Gipuzkoa leader Joseba Egibar, had been nothing other than a *charte octroyée*, a kind of constitution granted "from above" (in this case, by the Spanish government. In the first political conference approved by the party ten years after the Assembly of Iruñea-Pamplona in 1977, the only time that the concept Euskal Herria was mentioned is in a reference to article 1 of the Statute of Gernika. The rest of the text only talks about Euzkadi, with "z," still in keeping with Arana's spelling. This tendency was maintained in the political conference of 1992 in which Euskal Herria did not appear, but the name Euzkadi is cited fourteen times. In 1995, meanwhile, Euzkadi won by a landslide (63:2).

During the following years, marked by a rapprochement with the nationalist left-wing and the signing of the Lizarra-Garazi Pact in September 1998, a substantial change took place within the EAJ-PNV. The Word Eus(z)kadi did not appear in the text of the Lizarra Pact and reference was always made to Euskal Herria. In the political conference approved in January 2000, Euskal Herria now beat Euzkadi by 31:28. In the document titled "Reconocimiento del ser para decidir. Concreción de la Ponencia Política de EAJ-PNV" (Recognition of the human being's right to decide." Specifying Report of the Political Conference of EAJ-PNV"), approved by the third general assembly of the party, Euskal Herria was mentioned fifteen times and Euzkadi five, with both concepts being treated synonymously ("Euzkadi-Euskal Herria"). In the 2004 conference, the previous line was maintained (Euskal Herria mentioned thirty-eight times, and Euzkadi thirty-three). Thereafter, however, the Lizarra agreement broke down and peace efforts promoted by Spanish prime minister José Luis Rodríguez Zapatero also came to halt following an ETA car-bomb at Madrid's Barajas airport in December 2006. The EAJ-PNV— under the leadership of the new president Iñigo Urkullu—now found itself in a phase of recapitulation and revival of the old essence of pragmatism and moderation, and its terminological practice also took a new turn. Is it a mere coincidence that in the conference of 2007 the word Euzkadi regained its lost ground (fifty-two mentions), while Euskal Herria appeared only once and only in relation to language? (www.eaj-pnv.eu/esp/salaprensa.asp).

In any event, it was clear that the semantic offensive of the Basque nationalist left-wing had injected new life into the old controversy about the naming of the Basque Country. However, on this occasion, the impact of terrorism and political polarization would complicate this debate even further, given the significant amount of political exploitation and emotional baggage involved. With the concept of Euskal Herria appearing as something highly linked to nationalist left-wing discourse, the historical meaning of the concept was practically forgotten, to such an extent that many of those who continued to use it—even though they rejected Batasuna (the successor party to HB) and ETA's ideas and ways of going about things—found it necessary to justify this use. This was the case, for example, of the pacifist movement Gesto por la Paz de Euskal Herria (Gesture for peace in Euskal Herria) (*Bakehitzak* 40, 2000). But there were also movements in the opposite direction. In 2008, more than 160 current and former Basque soccer players signed a statement in Basque refusing to play the traditional friendly Christmas match played by the Basque team, under the name of "Team Euskadi." In 2007, the Basque Soccer Federation had given in to the pressure, authorizing the match to be played that year under the name "Euskal Herriko Selekzioa" (Team Euskal Herria). When attempts were made the following year to recover the historical name, the soccer players put their feet down, arguing that "the institutions have emptied the term Euskadi of all content" (*"mamiz hustu dute"*) and that the "Basque nation" that they were supposed to represent, made up of the seven territories, "is called Euskal Herria" (www.eitb.com/deportes/futbol/detalle/31915/comunicado). There was no match in 2008 or in 2009. In 2010, a compromise was reached with the name "Euskal Selekzioa" (Team Basque), and the match was played again. Their aversion toward representing the colors of Euskadi does not, however, seem to have abated the eagerness of some of the players to accumulate prestige and money, since they did not see, nor continue to see, any problem in terms of identity or terminology when representing the colors of the Spanish national team when called upon to do so. As Pello Salaburu puts it, "They have not even complained that it is called the 'team of the Spanish State.'" (*El Diario Vasco*, Feb. 26, 2010).

The controversy also spilled over into the world of education when in 2004 the delegate of the Spanish central government in the Basque Country, Carlos Urquijo of the PP, demanded that all the textbooks that included the term Euskal Herria be withdrawn, threatening legal initiatives if the Department of Education of the Basque government, led by a minister of Basque Solidarity (EA by its Basque acronym) at the time, ignored this request (*El Correo*, March 11, 2004). After several years of debate, the intervention of the courts, and a report from Euskaltzaindia confirming "the correctness, accuracy, and appropriateness of the name Euskal Herria to refer to the group of seven provinces or territories; a name that is not assimilable to nor equivalent to any political and administrative realities" (Euskaltzaindia 2004, 1), Isabel Celáa, the new Socialist minister for Education tried to resolve the lawsuit with the approval of a new basic education curriculum. According to Celáa, this new regulation aimed to eliminate the "ideological baggage" and the "indoctrination" that, in her opinion, weighed down the previous text due in large measure to the unsuitable usage of the term Euskal Herria. The new term was not removed from this regulation, but its use was linked to "a linguistic and cultural concept and not to a territorial or political and administrative entity as up to now" (*El Correo*, April 20, 2010). At the same time, the foral government of Navarre adopted a much more categorical measure, stating that "textbooks that include Navarre in Euskal Herria will be prohibited next year," and that the schools who continued to use this prohibited school material would be sanctioned (*ABC*, June 17, 2010).

Basque Politics and the Basque language in the Twenty-First Century

As is clear from the above exposition, the debate about the name (names) of the Basque Country continues unabated after more than a century. Apparently, nothing has changed since Humboldt noted the division of the "unfortunate Basque nation" and the impossibility of finding a name that was acceptable to all. As in the early nineteenth century, and contrary to the predictions of the German scholar and politician, the Basque language continues to be the most significant defining element of the autochonous culture. And the seven Basque territories that Axular already named in the seventeenth century also continue to exist and are attached to different state entities. In short, Euskal Herria continues to exist as an ethnic and cultural concept, a concept that encapsulates the different Basque political and administrative realities of Euskadi (the CAPV-EAE), of the Foral Community of Navarre and the Département of Pyrénées-Atlantiques, which takes in the three French-Basque territories.

Nevertheless, this initial impression of total stagnation does not correspond to the reality of a much more dynamic and ever-changing historical process. This is not the place to analyze in detail all the transformations produced in the Basque Country over the last centuries, but it is worth paying particular attention to one of the most important consequences of these transformations that affects the relations between linguistic and cultural reality on the one hand, and the political and administrative reality on the other. Very briefly, since the recovery of Basque autonomy in 1979, and thanks to the deployment of self-government throughout the following years, for the first time in history–if we ignore the brief interval from 1936 to 1937—Euskadi has been put at the service of Euskal Herria, which is to say that culture has benefited from politics. This is the case above all in the CAPV-EAE in which, according to the statistical data of 2006, 71 percent of the total population of Euskal Herria live (Foral Community of Navarre: 20 percent, Northern Basque Country 9 percent) (Basque government, *IV Encuesta Sociolingüística* 2008, 199). The extensive powers of self-governance, above all in the field of education, have proven to be an efficient tool not only in halting the secular process of decline and suffering of the Basque language, whose disappearance had been predicted by scholars such as Humboldt, but actually for having reversed trends in the younger age groups of the population. In the CAPV-EAE, Basque is the co-official language alongside Spanish. In Navarre, it is only co-official in one of the three linguistic zones regulated by the foral law on Basque (1986) and in France the Basque language is not officially recognized. It is worth pausing for a moment to consider, from a historical perspective, the power of a process whose only possible goal seemed to be the disappearance of the Basque language. According to the data collected by Louis-Lucien Bonaparte and later updated by Ladislao Velasco, toward the end of the 1870s, the province of Gipuzkoa was almost completely Basque-speaking, Bizkaia was more than 80 percent Basque-speaking, Iparralde 65 percent, Navarre 20 percent, and Araba 10 percent (Bonaparte 1883; Velasco and Fernández de la Fuente 1983, 474–90). In 1970, after the first wave of industrialization and immigration from other areas of Spain in Bizkaia and Gipuzkoa, and in the middle of a second wave that also affected the two provinces of Araba and Navarre from the 1960s on, the situation had already changed drastically, above all in the two territories that had been most significantly industrialized and most affected by the massive influx of non-Basque immigrants: in Bizkaia, only 16 percent of the population now spoke and understood Basque, and in Gipuzkoa less than half of the population (44 percent) considered themselves *euskaldun*, Basque-speakers (Núñez 1977, 26–28). Clearly this data is not exact and should be interpreted with care, but, even so, it reflects a clear downward trend.

Turning to the situation in 2006, representing nearly thirty years of political autonomy in the CAPV-EAE and the Foral Community of Navarre, in the former the statistics reflect a slow but constant increase in the bilingual population of each one of the three territories.

Table 1.1. Evolution of the percentage of bilinguals in the EAE-CAPV, 1991–2006 (%)

Bilinguals	1991	1996	2001	2006
Araba	7	11.4	13.4	14.2
Bizkaia	16.5	20.9	22.4	23
Gipuzkoa	43.7	46	48	49.1
EAE-CAPV	**24.1**	**27.7**	**29.4**	**30.1**

Source: *IV Encuesta*, 19.

Although in Navarre the decline has been stopped, the recovery of the language is much slower.

Table 1.2. Evolution of percentage of bilinguals in Navarre, 1991–2006 (%)

	1991	1996	2001	2006
Bilinguals	9.5	9.6	10.3	11.1

Fuente: *IV Encuesta*, 142.

In Iparralde, by contrast, where so far claims for the creation of its own political administrative entity (a single Basque département) have been rejected by the different central governments, Basque continues to decline.

Table 1.3. Evolution of the percentage of bilinguals in Iparralde. 1996–2006 (%)

	1996	2001	2006
Bilinguals	26.4	24.8	22.5

Source: *IV Encuesta*, 78.

A glimpse at the linguistic competences by age groups in the CAPV-EAE suggests that the increase in the bilingual population in Euskadi is due, above all, to the Basquisation of the new generations in the school system. In 2006, almost 60 percent of young people between sixteen and twenty-four years old are actively bilingual.

Table 1.4. Linguistic competence by age groups, EAE-CAPV, 2006 (%)

	Population 16 years of age of greater		
Age groups	Bilingual	Passive bilingual	Monolingual Basque speakers
>65	25.0	9.0	66.0
50–64	21.3	13.2	65.6
35–49	25.7	22.0	52.3
25–34	37.3	26.0	36.7
16–24	57.5	24.9	17.6
Total	30.1	18.3	51.5

Source: *IV Encuesta*, 21.

If the school system is fundamental for Basquisation, the possibility of also continuing education in Basque at university therefore represents a decisive step in a society that is attempting to establish the conditions for moving toward real bilingualism. In this sense, the Universidad del País Vasco / Euskal Herriko Unibertsitatea (University of the Basque Country, UPV/EHU) has played a decisive role. In the relatively few years of its still short lifespan since it was founded in 1980, it has provided the economic and human resources needed so that, in 2011, around three quarters of all obligatory credits were also offered in Basque. It has also made a commitment in its *Plan Director de Euskara* (Master Plan for Basque, 2007), to ensure that all new degrees to be introduced within the framework of the European Higher Education and Research Area will also be offered in the language. Basque society appears to be showing its thanks for this measure with a growing demand: the number of students who decide to enroll in a Basque group is increasing year on year. In the 2009–2010 academic year, this percentage reached 46 percent among students enrolling for the first time at the UPV/EHU (Pablo and Rubio 2006; *UPV/EHU en cifras* www.ehu.es/p200-shstatct/es/contenidos/estadistica/universidad_cifras_2009_2010/es_cif_2010/universidad_cifras.html).

Clearly, neither the efforts of the Basque public university nor the achievements of the educational system in the CAPV-EAE would have been possible without the strong support of institutions and, above all, the Basque government. The fact that, since the restoration of Basque autonomy up to the year 2009, the Basque government was led by a Basque nationalist of the EAJ-PNV—in 2009, and after negotiating an agreement with the PP, the Socialist Patxi López attained the *lehendakaritza* (presidency)—reflects the strength of Basque nationalism in the CAPV-EAE. By contrast, in Navarre, Basque nationalism continues to be a minority yet influential force, and in the French Basque Country it is scarcely noticeable among the crushing domination of the main blocs of the state right and the state left. Nevertheless, and despite the strength of Basque nationalism in Euskadi, it is important to qualify two points with regard to linguistic policy. First of all it is important to note a point that is confirmed by all the surveys: the concern for the language and its promotion reaches far beyond nationalist sectors in Basque society. In second place, this has meant that a good part of the legislation that has regulated linguistic policies, such as, for example, the law on the normalization of the use of the Basque language (1982), has been the result of a consensus also shared by the institutional representatives of the second largest political tradition in Euskadi: Basque socialism; whether while in opposition, or from the coalition governments led by José Antonio Ardanza of the EAJ-PNV (between 1986 and 1998). Fernando Buesa, the Socialist minister for education killed by ETA in 2000, initiated the Basque public education act and the law on teaching bodies in 1993, which enabled many *Ikastolas* (schools that teach entirely in Basque) to join the public network or to join the network of state-subsidized private schools.

The pursuit and development of this kind of consensus has been the basis upon which a significant part of linguistic policy in Euskadi has been built. This is a policy that, without doubt, in general terms and from a historical perspective, has been successful and beneficial for the Basque language and culture, even though it is now faced with new challenges such as that of extending the everyday use of the language. This problem will also need to be tackled pragmatically, and with willingness to compromise, because in a society as diverse and heterogeneous as that of the Basque Country, no single recipe will suffice with a subject as sensitive as that of language. Linguistic policy must continue to be an interconnected subject with supporters in the two main political blocs: Basque nationalists and non-nationalists (or Spanish nationalists). All the electoral processes offer reasonably accurate portrayals of these similar sized blocs, often with advantages for the Basque nationalists in the autonomous elections, and for the non-nationalist bloc in the general elections, as shown in figure 1.1 (Mees 2009, 168).

Figure. 1.1. Evolution of voting by blocks

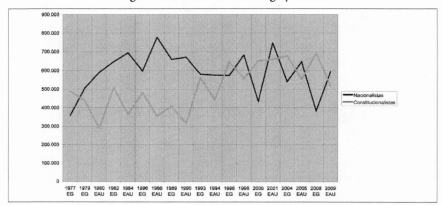

Source: Eustat, election result archive, www9euskadi.net/q93TodoWar/q93desplegar; El Diario Vasco, 3 March 2009. Abbreviations: EG = general elections; EAU = autonomous elections; JJGG = provincial government elections.

Nationalists: EAJ-PNV, EA, Euskadiko Ezkerra (EE) hasta 1990; Herri Batasuna / Euskal Herritarrok (in 2005 PCTV-EHAK: Partido Comunista de los Territorios Vascos—Euskal Herrialdeetako Alderdi Komunista); Aralar. In 2009, the voided votes are added. Their total is calculated after subtracting the 4,035 voided votes of the 2005 elections from the 100,924 votes counted in 2009. In these elections the nationalist left was declared illegal, which led to the voided votes.

Constitutionalists: Unión del Centro Democrático (UCD), PSE-PSOE, AP/PP, Unidad Alavesa (UA), Centro Democrático Social (CDS), Partido Comunista de España / Izquierda Unida-Ezker Batua (PCE/IU-EB).

The permanent cessation of terrorist activity announced by ETA on October 20, 2011, if it is confirmed , may pave the way toward the consecution of the interconnected consensus that is vital for the daily construction of the Basque nation in all fields. In this new, hypothetical scenario, it would not be out of place to think that in the not too distant future a name may be found for this small country without a name and/or with too many names, that will be recognized by all.

2

The Legal System of a Bilingual Society

ALBERTO LÓPEZ BASAGUREN,
the University of the Basque Country (UPV/EHU)

The proclamation of the constitution of 1978 in Spain created a profound transformation to the basis upon which Spain and its political system was conceived. One of the most significant elements of this transformation lies in the recognition of Spain as a diverse reality, both linguistically and culturally. The preamble to the constitution clearly manifests the will to: "Protect all Spaniards and the peoples of Spain in the exercise of . . . their cultures and traditions, languages and institutions." This mandate was reflected in the establishment of a system of official languages attributed to the languages spoken in Spain's autonomous communities (ACs), which together with Spanish, were given the statuses of the official languages in their respective territories.

The constitutional pronouncement was destined to have momentous consequences. Legal development during more than thirty years of the new political regime (a long time in Spain's tragic constitutional history) has led to profound transformations in political and social reality, ensuring the full dignity and recognition of regional languages. This has resulted in a striking growth in the knowledge of these languages by the inhabitants of the territories in which they are spoken and significantly strengthen its institutional and social use.

At the time, there was a major constituent consensus about the appropriateness and significance of recognizing the official status of languages other than Spanish that proposed a symmetric status, parity, and equity, in the territories alongside Spanish as the official state language. This is the path followed by the statutes of autonomy (1979), notably in the Basque Country and in Catalonia.

* Research Team Grant IT509/10 of the Directorate General on Science Policy of the Basque government. Research Project on "Models for recognising linguistic diversity: between coercion and freedom of language" granted by the Spanish Ministry of Education and Science (ref. SEJ2007-67178).

In recent times, however, the consensus appears to have ended. Legislation in the Autonomous Community of Catalonia concerning the Catalan language, especially in the language policy act of 1998 (Act 1/1998 of Jan 7), which replaced the linguistic normalization act of 1983 (Act 7/1983 of April 18), has been oriented toward establishing a preferential use of Catalan (and its exclusive use as the language of instruction), which breaks with the idea of symmetry between the statuses of both official languages. This resolution was reaffirmed in the reform of the autonomy statute of Catalonia (2006) that subsequently raised constitutional problems—given that it relegated the Spanish language—before Spain's Constitutional Court (CCR [Constitutional Court Ruling] 31/2010, of June 28).

The Basque Country has not followed this route. There was just one attempt to propose a similar measure by the Department of Education during the eighth legislature (2005–2009), which had no practical effect. By contrast, the development of the debate known as Euskara XXI (the basis for a language policy in the early twenty-first century) was driven by the Department of Culture within the Basque Language Advisory Board. This effort was steered toward reaffirming and strengthening the basis of consensus found in the statute of autonomy and the basic law on normalization of the use of Basque (Act 10/1982 of Nov 24) and attempted to accommodate contemporary circumstances, problems, and challenges facing Basque society during the twenty-five years of this language policy. The effort avoided embarking on the path that gave preference to the Basque language as the "territorial" language (Basque government 2009b).

The Constitutional Basis of Multilingualism in Spain

Multilingualism in Spain is recognized in the Spanish constitution, yet it is only partially regulated. Article 3 of the constitution establishes two basic elements that are essential to a multilingual system. First, the declaration of Spanish as the official state language (paragraph 1), and, secondly, the claim that, "the other languages spoken in Spain are also official in the respective autonomous communities" (paragraph 2). These two factors set the limits within which a system of multilingualism could develop in Spain (Solozabal Echavarria, 1999). Some of the problems that have arisen in recent times lie precisely in an inadequate interpretation of the meaning of each of these two elements (López Basaguren, 2007).

Spanish as the Official State Language and the Duty to Know It

The first basic element of the constitutional system of multilingualism is the declaration of Spanish as the official state language. This provision materializes and is linked in the constitution to the right to use and the duty to know

Spanish. The statement that Spanish is the official state language has important consequences. The constitution undisputedly establishes a territorial (rather than institutional) principle in determining the official state language. This means that Spanish is not only the official language of the central institutions of the state, but also the official language throughout its territory. This also includes the ACs and therefore affects all their institutions (CCR 82/1986).

This element is important because it highlights that the Spanish system departs radically from the norm in multilingual federal systems. In these systems, the *principle of territoriality of languages* prevails, which means that in each region or area its own language is official. In these areas, federal institutions are multilingual although this is not the case for the regions as a whole that, apart from some exceptional cases,[1] typically have only one official language. Multilingualism at the federal level is often the result of the addition of many different monolingual territories.

The option within the Spanish constitution for a system in which Spanish is the official language in every institutional setting is based on the sociolinguistic reality of Spain, which is radically different from that of federal systems to which reference has been made. Territorial monolinguistic systems are characterized by a large linguistic homogeneity in each territory, where most people only know the local language and in which no common language is spoken by the whole population of the federation.[2] In Spain, however, in areas with an individual native language, there are large groups (sometimes the majority) whose language is Spanish and, to a greater or lesser extent (sometimes the vast majority) do not know the regional language; and Spanish is spoken by everyone across the board. Under these conditions, it seemed logical to establish Spanish as the general official language, including in the territories with their own language. Any other option did not fit this reality. A different question altogether is whether the official languages of the ACs should have some sort of "federal" status ahead of the institutions and apparatuses of the central state, rather than being strictly limited to the territory of the respective AC.

The constitution links the provision of Spanish as the official state language to the right to use and the duty to know Spanish. This statement means,

---

1. Only in exceptional situations does official bilingualism exist: in Switzerland, in the cities of Biel/ Bienne, Fribourg (in practice although not legally), and in the very special trilingual case of the canton of Graubünden; in Brussels, Belgium; and in New Brunswick, Canada. There are also equally exceptional situations that recognize minority language rights, as in Quebec, Canada (with respect to the Anglophone minority) and Ontario (with respect to Francophone minority). This occurs also in Belgian municipalities with "language facilities" on the outskirts of Brussels.

2. Therefore, determining the official language can be reached at the municipal level even when there is linguistic diversity in a territory, as in Switzerland's bilingual and trilingual cantons. It is worth noting that this situation has raised some of the major political conflicts in contemporary Belgium.

primarily, that all Spanish people have the right to use the Spanish language in any part of the country and before any authority. The duty to know Spanish has been a source of considerable debate and some confusion in the jurisprudence of Spain's Constitutional Court (CC). These difficulties have focused on determining the legal significance of establishing that duty, and problems have arisen as to whether it was possible to establish a similar duty (of knowledge) for the individual languages of the ACs.

The CC ruled that the duty to know Spanish is a presumption that all Spaniards are familiar with the language, and that such a presumption cannot be assumed among the individual languages of the ACs (CCR 82/1986 and CCR 84/1986). Therefore, it rejected the possibility early on (CCR 84/1986) that the ACs could establish a similar duty to know the language of the respective AC. The CC considered that such a duty is not inherent in the official regional languages to the extent that the constitution does not enforce it and establishes this duty only in respect to Spanish.

With this argument it would appear that the CC believes that the constitution's silence on the question of the duty to know the ACs' different languages opposite to the duty to know Spanish, must be interpreted as a constitutional refusal to accept the capacity to establish a similar duty of knowledge of the regional language as a part of its legal status. Under these conditions, one cannot attribute such a meaning to the constitutional silence on the matter. The constitution is limited to regulating the legal status of Spanish as the official state language, whatever the status of the other official languages is, so that constitutional decisions regarding Spanish have no bearing whatsoever constitutionally upon any of the other official languages (López Basaguren 1988, 2007).

Secondly, one must consider the legal significance of the duty to know an official language. In a situation of official monolingualism, the duty to know the official language is a condition inherent to that legal status, and results in the presumption that everyone already knows the language in question. Thus, no citizen can legitimately claim ignorance against its use by the public authorities and thus it guarantees the full validity of acts performed by using official language. Yet, this is not an irrefutable presumption; it is a presumption *juris tantum* (a legal but refutable presumption) that gives rise to certain situations, such as those affecting inalienable constitutional rights (CCR 74/1987, on the fundamental right to legal counsel for a detainee).

Furthermore, in a situation of official bilingualism the consequences arising from the duty to know Spanish are conditioned by the right of citizens to use any of the official languages (CCR 82/1986, third legal basis). This means that public authorities cannot exclusively use Spanish when the legal status of the regional language entails the right its use. The inadmissibility of the claim of ignorance of Spanish, which derives from the duty to know it, is somewhat negated in territories with a second official language and an enshrined citizen's right to use it. In truth, nor would establishing a duty to know a regional language allow the authorities to use it exclusively, because it would violate the right of citizens to use Spanish as the official language.

What is the legal significance, therefore, of imposing a duty to know an official language in a situation of official bilingualism? It involves mainly the ability of the government to impose compulsory learning of the official language in the educational system. Thus, the duty to know Spanish, as established in the constitution, require its compulsory learning in the educational system for all students as well as the citizen's right to use it.

In the Spanish constitutional system, nothing prevents imposing the duty to know a regional language when regulating its legal status as an official language, with identical effects as those resulting from the duty to know Spanish. The duty to know the official regional language permits educational authorities to require the compulsory learning of the official regional language for all students. This is precisely what has occurred in practice, until now, even in the absence of an express legal claim establishing the existence of a similar duty. All the ACs have imposed the obligatory learning of their respective regional languages in official compulsory education, and even in their use as a teaching language, either partially or completely.

In any case, the question of the ability to establish a duty to know the official regional language has been substantially resolved in a case ruling. The 2006 Catalan statute established the duty and right of all citizens of Catalonia to learn Catalan, as parallel to the right and duty to know Spanish (section 6.2). In addition, the CC validated its constitutionality (CCR 31/2010), rectifying the position taken in 1986. Nevertheless, there remains a degree of interpretative uncertainty.[3]

This effect of the duty to know the official languages is significant, because it breaks with the ruling of linguistic separatism that prevails in virtually all multilingual federal systems in which the territorial language is imposed (territorial monolingualism systems) or in those in which citizens have an absolute linguistic choice (official bilingualism systems).

---

3. The CC considered that the nature of the duty to know Catalan is different from the duty to know Spanish, that it would not constitute a "general duty for all citizens of Catalonia" but rather an "individual and reasonably necessary duty to know Catalan," an obligatory fulfillment that, "has its own specific place in the field of education . . . and in that of the special binding relationships that link the Catalonian administration with its civil servants, [who are] obliged to satisfy the right of linguistic choice recognized in Section 33.1 SA of Catalonia" (CCR 31/2010, Legal Basis14, Letter b).

Native Languages as Official Languages of Autonomous Communities: Their Regulation in the Statutes of Autonomy

In asserting that Spanish is the official state language, the constitution states that, "the other Spanish languages are also official in the respective autonomous communities in accordance with their statutes." The constitution, therefore, primarily provides that regional languages have an official nature. The official status of such languages has a geographically limited character, confined to the territory of the respective AC. However, compared to Spanish, this official status is *territorial*. In other words, it is binding in all public authorities based in the AC in question, including all apparatuses of central state administration in each territory (CCR 82/1986).

The constitution requires that regional languages have official status, but does not specify their characteristics, in contrast to what it does with Spanish. This is due to a conscious and explicit constitutional option attributed to the SA of each AC and the recognition of the legal status of each regional language. By linking the official nature of a particular regional language to its institutionalization as an AC, the constitution requires the existence of a significant regional consciousness as a basis for legal recognition of that status. Above all, the purpose is to keep regional languages in the hands of the community in which they are based, although the SAs are not an exclusive product of the unilateral will of the respective communities. This feature shows a noteworthy deference of the constitution toward the AC in which the language is spoken (Prieto de Pedro 1996).

The fact that the SAs reserve the right to determine the characteristics of the legal status of regional languages as official languages means that the constitution leaves the legal question of multilingualism partially open. The SAs implement the regulations of the constitution, yet they have a limited role in determining the characteristics of the legal status of the regional language as the official language in the territory of the ACs. Thus, among other powers, the SA may determine whether the official status of the language in question should apply to the entire territory of the AC (or just part of it, when the distinctive language is rooted only in designated zones), and also the right to use the language or its compulsory incorporation in the educational system.

The SAs, therefore, had a very important area of provision, although most opted for a comparable system. All ACs opted to regulate the legal status of their official regional language in a symmetrical way to the status of Spanish as the official language in the same territory with its official status being extended to the whole territory of the AC. Only Navarre (in order to establish linguistic zoning) and Valencia (that did so in a more reduced way) are the exception. This resulted in a loss of perspective with respect to the scope of the SA.

Finally, it should be noted that article 3.2 of the constitution limits the intervention of the SAs in determining the legal status of the individual languages of the ACs. This means that under no circumstance can the SAs encumber or impinge on the system of Spanish as the official state language. This statement may seem superfluous, yet the boundaries have been pushed in attempting to establish a preferential nature for the regional language, notably in 2006 in Catalonia. In this instance, in order to establish a preferential nature for the regional language (Catalan) it was necessary to alter the characteristics of the legal status of Spanish as the official language and to regulate the characteristics of the legal status of the regional language in the SA. This is what has essentially, within the linguistic field, been declared unconstitutional by the CC (CCR 31/2010; López Basaguren 2011).

The system of official bilingualism in the ACs should be composed of two different elements: Spanish as derived from the constitution (whose usage is governed by state law); and, as regards the regional language that derived from the SA of the corresponding AC (whose development is legislated by the AC). These are complementary, but independent, elements that together make up the legal system of official bilingualism in each AC with an official regional language. These elements also set limits, respectively. In other words, each prevents excluding or limiting (within citizens' rights) the full use of "the other" official language.

The Legal System of a Bilingual Society in the Basque Country

The passing of the SA of the Basque Country in 1979 was necessary in order to determine the legal status of the Basque language (Euskera or Euskara) as the official language of the Comunidad Autónoma del País Vasco-Euskal Autonomia Erkidegoa (CAPV-EAE), together with Spanish. This was very important, given the particular features surrounding the Basque language at that time (and that still surround it, despite the great changes fashioned in more than thirty years). When the SA was passed, Euskara was a minority language in Basque society. Its knowledge and use were geographically unevenly distributed, and it had been lost for some time or even since time immemorial in a substantial part of the overall teritory. Euskara remained a language restricted to certain functional realms within which its use was restricted and traditionally excluded, among other areas, from institutional life. For the most part it was linked to the family environment and rural society.

Moreover, political representation in Basque society lacked an apparent majority by any political sector when drafting the statute. Thus, in a climate that still benefited from the political consensus that had given birth to the Spanish constitution, it was essential to build a broad consensus in drafting the laws across all parliamentary political forces. The language issue initially seemed more slippery yet it was possible to reach an agreement. For all of the above reasons, the regulation contained in Article 6 of the SA—which contains the bylaws concerning the status of the Basque language as an official language—is fascinating not only because of its legal status, but also because of the components of the political consensus it took to reach a decision on such a delicate topic. The bylaws contained in the statute are relatively brief. Thus, it is necessary to analyze further legislative developments and examine whether these developments have maintained or weakened this consensus.

In implementing the provisions in the SA, the Basque language law was passed (Act 10/1982 of Nov 24, basic normalization of Euskara). It remains essential in the regulation of the legal system of bilingualism in the CAPV-EAE. The Basque parliament has also passed other laws that significantly affect the development of the legal system of bilingualism. The two laws with most impact were: the law on the Basque civil service (Act 6/1989 of July 6), which regulates the recruitment, career-track, and organization of public employees; and the public education law (Act 1/1993 Feb 19), which governs the educational system and its organization. Both laws have accompanied major developmental regulations relating to language issues.

The Basque Language as an Official Language: Full Legal Status and a Restorative Character: Sociolinguistic Diversity in the Basque Country

In analyzing the legal status of the Basque language as an official language of the CAPV-EAE one should first mention the establishment of a generalized system of official bilingualism. In accordance with Article 6.1 of the SA, the Basque language is official language throughout the territory of the CAPV-EAE, without any territorial restriction. In light of its traditional territorial distribution and its vastly minority status, this decision has had major consequences, insofar as it has meant—contrary to what occurred in Navarre—a rejection of linguistic or territorial zoning and the delimitation of the Basque language as an official language.

The decision to give official status to the Basque language had a primarily political origin, and was linked to the Basque nationalist ideology, yet it was accepted by virtually the entire political spectrum. In other words, it alluded to protecting minority speakers, it was linked to the (political) idea of Euskara as the language of the Basques (whether they spoke it or not), and it paved the way for the promotion of the language beyond its already existing community of speakers—with the intention of converting it into the mainstream social language.

This decision also had other grounds and favored the reduced spatial dimension of the CAPV-EAE. The internal mobility of the population has led to a significant segment of traditional speakers into territories in which the Basque language was barely spoken, a phenomenon especially important in large urban areas. Although Basque-speakers are still the slim minority in these areas, they represent a very important group of great significance in terms of the linguistic community.

Article 6.1 of the SA states that all inhabitants of the CAPV-EAE—anywhere in its territory—have the right to know and use the Basque language. The right to use the Basque language has no limitations or restrictions, so the official status of the Basque language is symmetrical to the status of Spanish as the official state language. Thus, the Basque Country possesses a system in which both are official languages simultaneously, with identical characteristics (Cobreros Mendazona 1989).

This characterization of the legal status of the Basque language is restorative in light of the SA. In other words, the second paragraph of Article 6 states that the institutions of the CAPV-EAE must "ensure the use of both official languages, regulating their official capacity, and shall grant and regulate the measures and means to ensure their knowledge . . . taking into account the sociolinguistic diversity of the Basque Country." Apart from some systematic errors (the institutions of the CAPV-EAE do not have the power to regulate the official character of Spanish), this section is of vital importance in the balance that allowed such a broad consensus on the language issue. With it, the drafters of SA highlighted the awareness that there was a mismatch between the ambitious legal status of the Basque language as an official language and poor sociolinguistic reality of the CAPV-EAE as regards Euskara (along with the need to temper the "willfulness" that this decision stressed).

Consequently, the SA situated the foundation of a legal regime based on the Basque language in its development and practice; in a delicate balance between the right to use and learn the Basque language anywhere in the territory of the CAPV-EAE and the need to take into account its minority status in many areas of the territory (López Basaguren 1988). This practice required a language policy attenuating the requirements arising from such a minority status.

The legislative development concerning the statutory regulation of the system of official languages has significantly marginalized the practical development that was cautiously introduced into the SA. It is of great significance that in the 1982 law on Euskara the reference concerning the need to take into account the sociolinguistic situation of the Basque Country disappeared (except in regard to education) focusing exclusively on ensuring the right to use the Basque language in any part of the Basque Country without encumbrance whatsoever.

The practical effects of the SA's requirement have been limited to the field of public administration, which must take into account the number of

Basque-speakers in a geographical area in order to determine the percentage of public employees that possesses the required knowledge of the Basque language (decree 86/1997 of April 15, which concerns the process of normalizing Euskara in public administrations, Articles 11 and 12). Yet, these calculations incorporate several elements of distortion. On the one hand, they have set reference territorial units (the province) that are considered equally despite having large internal imbalances from a sociolinguistic point of view. Within these units are identified speakers who claim to know the Basque language, although a very high percentage have learned the language at school and come from Spanish-speaking families in territories where the Basque language is nonexistent or there is a negligible presence of traditional speakers. Moreover, most of these individuals lack basic communication skills and hardly ever use Basque in their interactions with public bodies. On the other hand, the law added a clause that labeled them "quasi-Basque-speakers," in which formulations gave them an impact of half a point, given their limited knowledge of the language makes them unable to use the Basque language effectively in daily public life.

The major problems encountered in the development of the language policy, which is increasingly challenged in some of its effects and future impact, comes from the marginalization of the delicate balance that was established in the SA. This balance was replaced by a "willfulness" that only can thrive in authoritarian and extremely ideological contexts.

Freedom of Language: The Duty to Know and the Right to Use Official Languages

The legal system of official languages in the CAPV-EAE is based on the principle of freedom of choice and language available to every citizen. The SA incorporates this principle by providing that all citizens have the right to know and use any of the official languages. This right carries with it the corresponding duty of public authorities to use the official language a citizen chooses.

The Spanish constitution states that Spanish is the official state language and links this condition both to the right of all citizens to use it and the duty to know it. The SA states, with respect to the Basque language, the right of all citizens to know and use it. In the SA, however, there is no express duty to know the Basque language. Does this mean that the legal status of the Basque language is not fully symmetrical to that of Spanish? This alleged lack of symmetry must be discarded (López Basaguren 1988, 2007).

The resolution of the SA for a status of the Basque language in which all citizens have the right to use it nullifies the effects, within the territory of the Basque Country, of the duty to know Spanish; or rather, it prevents public authorities from favoring Spanish. Thus, it is impossible to claim ignorance because of the existence of a duty to know. This flies in the face of the citizens' right to use the official language of their choice. The right of use has an "active" side, which is realized when an individual citizen manifestly or implicitly expresses his or her option. Their language choice also has a "passive" side, which requires public authorities to use both official languages simultaneously when the citizen has not been given their express language choice, or when public authorities guide citizens in any general or indeterminate manner. This is the requirement set forth in all systems with several official languages and in all the legal systems of the ACs with an official regional language. One exception to this was the change of perspective adopted by the SA of Catalonia in 2006, which eliminated requiring the use of both official languages and established the preferential use of Catalan.

When there are two official languages simultaneously in the same territory, the right to use either of them becomes the axis of the legal system of official languages and impedes the ability of choice to public authorities. In conclusion, the absolute right to use any official language by any citizen characterizes the legal system of the Basque Country. This requires public authorities to use the official language chosen by the citizen, or by default, both official languages simultaneously.

Freedom of language that citizens hold was successfully developed (although technically deficiently) in the law on Euskara (section 5.2), which breaks down the different areas for exercising the right to use any of the official languages. These are areas that are detailed thus: (1) the right to communicate in the official language of one's choice with the administration and with any organization based in the CAPV-EAE; (2) the right to receive an education in both official languages; (3) the right to receive publications, radio programming, and television and other media; (4) the right to develop professional, labor, political, and trade unions, and (5) the right to speak in any official language at any meeting.

This principle has had an especially momentous development in education. The law on Euskara (section 15) establishes the right to receive instruction, "in both Basque and Spanish at all educational levels" and (section 16) stipulates that the educational system shall respect the right of linguistic choice (paragraph 1), so that students will study in the official language of their choice. One limit is imposed: the compulsory learning of the official language that has not been chosen as language of instruction. In regard to Spanish, this imposition is fully legitimate in the system of official languages in the constitution but, in regard to the compulsory study of the official regional language, the choice depends on the SA. Paragraph 2, article 16, reemphasizes this principle by linking the exercise of the freedom of language to the sociolinguistic reality of the Basque Country, adapting the former to the latter. It states that the government will regulate "linguistic models" in each school by taking into account "the will of the parents or guardians and the sociolinguistic reality in the area."[4] This sentiment is reiterated in the public school act (article 21). However, the balance between the two criteria had a purely temporary function, to the extent that it was possible to ascertain the parent's desired language model for their children's education.

Certainly, it is very difficult (politically) not to meet the demand of parents. Over the past thirty years, the problem in the Basque Country is the belief that linguistic, personal, and social circumstances are not obstacles to the widespread extension of Basque language teaching. Nor do these circumstances limit the quality of that education. This conviction is the basis of the overwhelming preference for models with the Basque language as the language of instruction (in whole or in part) by people for whom the Basque language is not their native tongue (in areas that speak mainly Spanish). The problems that surround this issue are taboo in Basque society; nonetheless, the proper functioning of these models is highly dubious in the manner purported.

Promoting Knowledge and Use of the Basque Language

Finally, a third element noteworthy in the system of official languages of the CAPV-EAE (without which it would not be possible to understand the development of the language policy of the past thirty years) is the promotion of awareness and use of the Basque language: or the lynchpin of the language policy.

The regulation of the official languages of the CAPV-EAE does not exclusively limit its guarantee of the right to use the language by those who already speak it, or its traditional speakers, one might say. Rather, it reflects the desire to cultivate the Basque language so that knowledge of the language will expand beyond those who learn it in familial and territorial areas in which it is traditionally spoken. It also cultivates the social use of language, not only by the addition of new speakers, but also by the correct functional use in fields in which it was not traditionally used.

This process requires tremendous effort. This is not only quantitative but, in many cases, the very special qualitative effort of the very communities themselves. In some areas, the aim was ambitious and sometimes excessive. Thus, the results are quite varied. Some communities have been able to obtain strikingly successful results in respect to linguistic quality, suitability, and development in fields that were unknown to the traditional speakers themselves. Specifically, the dramatic literary development, both in its cre-

---

4. The regulation of linguistic models in teaching is contained in decree 138/1983 of July 11, which regulates the use of the official languages in secondary education.

ative aspect and in literary translation, that has occurred over the years perhaps helps explain this aforementioned proficiency. Public authorities have devoted substantial resources to promote this kind of development.

Politicians, however, have obsessively paid attention to the quantitative increase of speakers. Education was destined to play a role in this. The problem appears to have been a blind confidence in the effect of introducing the Basque language into education. It was assumed that anyone who learned the language would necessarily become an effective and regular speaker. Yet schools cannot always work miracles. This is even less the case when facing such a task with a high number of teachers who are "neo-speakers." Nonetheless, these practices have significantly increased the number of people who know (for better or worse) the Basque language. The problem is that most have not become genuine speakers, yet the parameter of the language policy acts as if they were. A distortion was created (for example, in access to public service) and frustration caused (for example, in the field of education). If continued, these practices will lead to failure of the policy of expanding the Basque language and cause growing opposition to the aims pursued and the means used to pursue to them. The cultivation of language in society is not easily changed, no matter how much "willfulness" contributes to the scheme.

The Basque Language in Navarre

The system of official languages in Navarre has distanced itself from the CAPV-EAE system with one essential act: the territorial extension of the official character of the Basque language (López Basaguren 1988; Arzoz Santisteban 2006). The improvement law (organic law 13/1982 of August 10, improvement of the *foral* system of Navarre) provides, firstly, that Spanish is the official language of Navarre (paragraph 1 of article 9); adding that, "Basque will also have the status of an official language in the Basque-speaking zones of Navarre." Finally, the organic law indicates that a Navarrese *foral* law "will establish these zones, will regulate the official use of Basque and, within the framework of general state legislation, establish the teaching of this language (paragraph 2, article 9).

Therefore, Navarre opted for the territorial limitation of the official character of the Basque language in a policy that was related mainly to the protection of traditional speakers of the language in the territory in which it has long been spoken. Although this policy was radically criticized (though for strictly political reasons and especially by Basque nationalist sympathizers), it was on par with the long-established observation that protects minority languages in Europe; a protection that is linked to the traditional territories where speakers live (European Charter for Regional or Minority Languages, ECRML; López Basaguren 2010).

In order to carry out the provisions of the improvement law, the Navarrese law on Basque was passed (act 18/1986 of December 15). The act aims to protect the right of citizens to know and use the Basque language by guarding its revival and ensuring its use and its teaching. This shall be done, "in accordance with the principles of volition, gradualness, and deference in relation to sociolinguistic reality of Navarre" (article 1.2). In this sense, the law distinguishes between the standing of the Basque language as the language of Navarre (on a par with Spanish), which entitles all citizens to use it and know it as the official language. Spanish is then used generally, and the Basque language is used officially only in the traditional Basque-speaking areas.

The Navarrese law on Basque determines the areas in which the Basque language is official. Yet it does so in a more flexible form than what would have emerged as a consequence of the law of improvement. It establishes three separate areas that together form the "Basque-speaking zone," the "non-Basque-speaking zone," and the "mixed zone." The territorial limits of the Basque-speaking zone is flexible and it includes some municipalities that do not have traditional speakers. Furthermore, the creation and definition of the "mixed zone" is commendable because it shows flexibility in terms of the protection of the Basque language in Navarre. It covers a wide territorial area, which is heavily populated, including the capital, Iruñea-Pamplona, and its primary urban areas. In these municipalities, the traditional community of speakers (in which there ever were any) is long gone. However, a significant number of Basque-speakers have moved back to urban areas of the Iruñea-Pamplona as a result of internal migration. Although this is not their traditional territory and they represent a very small percentage of the population, they are significant as a group of Basque-language speakers.

The flexibility involved in the creation of the mixed zone has had a greater significance given its effects on territorial language rights, which manifests an expansion of the language rights of Basque-speakers beyond its established area (in tandem with an expansion of the Basque-speaking community itself). This is manifest to the extent that certain tools—especially in teaching—are utilized for expanding the population that command the Basque language and who live among people from families who do not speak the language (especially in areas where there is not a traditional community of speakers). The regime of linguistic rights in the Basque-speaking zone is absolute and revolves on the right to use any official language. Thus, it is the same as that seen in the CAPV-EAE, and does not require further discussion.[5]

---

5. The right to use the Basque language by inhabitants of the Basque-speaking zone is independent of where public bodies may be located. This is what led to the High Court of Justice of Navarre, and then subsequently Spain's Supreme Court, to outlaw article 15 of decree 29/2003 of February 10, on the

In the mixed zone, citizens are also entitled to use the Basque language in government, so the legal status of the Basque language in this area is equal to any corresponding official language. Even in the non-Basque-speaking zone, the right to address public authorities in the Basque language is recognized. Although in this zone, the administration may require a translation, or use the translation service of the government of Navarre, as they deem appropriate. This contextualizes the distinction between the right to use the Basque language that belongs to all citizens of Navarre and the territorial limitation of their official functions.

The most significant element in the system of official languages of Navarre is in the field of education. The law on Basque initially states the universal right of all citizens to receive an education in Spanish and Basque, yet it differentiates how this right can be exercised in each of the language areas. In the Basque-speaking zone, it recognizes the right to study in the official language which is chosen freely, yet it is mandatory to study the other official language to ensure mastery of both official languages by the end of the mandatory non-university education period. In the mixed zone the law states that the Basque language should be incorporated into teaching "gradually, progressively, and adequately in the creation of schools in which Basque-language instruction can be provided for those who request it." The law also stipulates the teaching of Basque in non-university levels of education to students who desire it, so that, "at the end of their schooling they obtain a sufficient level of knowledge of that language" (article 25). Finally, in the non-Basque-speaking zone the law stipulates the encouragement of the study of the Basque language in the educational system, funded by public authorities (in whole or in part), "with the intention of promotion and development" of the language "according to the demand" (article 26).

According to a current report by the Committee of Experts of the ECRML at the Council of Europe, this has resulted in almost all pupils in compulsory education in the Basque-speaking zone to undertake studies entirely in Basque in preschool, primary, and secondary education, or, to a lesser degree in the bilingual model. Almost 30 percent of students in compulsory education in the mixed zone study in Basque (whether in the full or in the bilingual model) and a high number of students in the non-Basque-speaking zone study Basque as a subject.

---

use of the Basque language in public proceedings and government administration. This decree stated that the public bodies and proceedings located in the mixed zone (including when they address citizens within the Basque-speaking zone) should be conducted in Spanish, "unless the parties expressly request the use of the Basque language, in which case they may be made bilingually" (See the rulings of the High Court of Justice of Navarre, 29.10.2004, 16.12.2004, 9.12.2004, and the Supreme Court ruling of 19.05.2009, which confirmed the rulings of the High Court of Justice of Navarre).

Consequently, from the perspective of the legal protection of the speakers of Basque in Navarre, the legal regulation seems appropriate enough given its sociolinguistic distribution. Nevertheless, one cannot disregard the extra effort involved in protecting Basque-speakers and the language's incorporation into an educational system outside the traditional settlement area of the speech community. Problems arise in the practical implementation of some legal precepts.

The Basque Language in the French Basque Country

The legal status of the Basque language in the French Basque Country is radically different from what has been depicted thus far. The French Basque Country lacks political autonomy, thus all legislation is made for the whole French Republic.

The French Constitution states that French is the language of the Republic (article 2.1), and only in 2008 did a reform enter timidly into the constitution with a reference made to other languages stating that, "regional languages belong to the patrimony of France" (article 75-1).

France has had a particularly extremist attitude regarding language and, generally, its relationship with internal minorities. Upon ratifying the International Covenant on Civil and Political Rights (1966), France entered a reservation to article 27 that denied the existence of its national, ethnic, linguistic, and religious minorities. France has ratified neither the Framework Convention for the Protection of National Minorities (1995) nor the Council of Europe's ECRML (1992).

The French Constitutional Council has played a leading role in this case, contradicting an actual ruling that ratified the ECRML (decision 99-412 DC of June 15, 1999). It argued that considering the allocation of specific rights to "groups" of speakers of regional or minority languages "violates the constitutional principles of indivisibility of the Republic, of equality before the law, and unity of the French people" and is contrary to the constitutional writ that declares French the language of the Republic. In France, therefore, there is no other official language other than French. Moreover, it is the only language that can be used before public officials and in administrative proceedings.

In the field of education, the norms regulating the use of French (law 94-665 of August 4, 1994, also known as the Toubon Law) stipulates that French is the language of instruction. And article 75-1 of the French Constitution provides no right to teach regional languages in the educational system.[6]

---

6. The Constitutional Council has ruled on this matter in decision no. 2011-130 QPC of May 20, 2011.

Teaching, however, has enjoyed a relatively high degree of flexibility. For example, the statutes of autonomy in Corsica and French Polynesia provide for the instruction of the respective languages in the educational system. The Constitutional Council has considered this compatible with the Constitution (decision no. 91-290 DC, 1991 of May 9, on Corsica, and decision no. 96-373 DC, of April 9, 1996 on French Polynesia, respectively). However, according to the Constitutional Council the use of regional languages is constitutional, "in so far as they are not legally binding and that . . . they do not intend to eliminate the rights and obligations applicable to those students enrolled in schools and to all users of schools" to receive education in French.

In general, the French education code encourages the optional teaching of regional languages and cultures as part of pupil's basic educational formation (article L 121-1) according to the various regional educational milieus. This occurs by way of agreement between the state and local authorities in which these languages are spoken and upon consultation of the Higher Council of Education (article L 312-10).[7] Language instruction is always voluntary, with the exception of the Corsican language in nursery and primary schools, which is taught on a compulsory basis (article L 312-11-1 of the education code, incorporated by law no. 2002-92 of January 22, 2002).

The inclusion of regional languages in direct instruction has been very difficult. A ministerial decree from the Department of Education on July 31, 2001, allowed certified centers of regional languages (according to the decree 2001-733 of July 31, 2001), in either of two educational settings ("regional language" schools or "regional languages" sections in schools) in order to develop a regional language education. This decree allowed two methods: the "immersion" method (instruction principally in the regional language) and the "equal time" method (half the instruction in French and half in the regional language). These methods require learning two languages (in addition to French), plus the fact that French is the language of exams, public service entrance examinations, theses, and dissertations, with only justified exceptions (article L 121-3 of the education code).

The Council of State annulled the two methods (decision no. 238653 of November 29, 2002). It believed that the "immersion" method exceeded "the needs of regional language learning" and might possibly lead to "abolishing the requirement to use French as the language of instruction" under the education code. The "equal time" method was, moreover, ruled invalid due to its failure to establish, "rules on the distribution of different disciplines among French education and in the teaching of the regional language, as it

---

7. This has allowed the expansion of education in the Basque language in French Basque schools. See the educational plan on the website of the Public Bureau of the Basque Language: www.mintzaira. fr/fr/oplb.html (last accessed May 7, 2012).

does not ensure that at least part of the teachings of these disciplines is done in French." Consequently, it reiterates the same destructive practices found in the "immersion" method.

Before the decision of the Council of State, the ministerial decree had already been modified by order of the minister of education on February 25, 2002 (which significantly limited the foregoing provisions) and also by the order of the minister of education on April 19, 2002 (which amended the regulation of the "immersion" method), thereby ensuring the instruction of French in schools.

In response to the decision of the Council of State, the minister of education issued a new decree on May 12, 2003 concerning the issue of "equal time" in the instruction of bilingual education and regional languages. This decree delimits the precise time distribution for each language and provides that no subject can be taught exclusively in a regional language, except when learning the language itself.

3

Basque and Romance Languages: Languages with Different Structures

IGONE ZABALA and ITZIAR SAN MARTIN,
the University of the Basque Country (UPV/EHU)

Linguists remain unable to find a clear phylogenetic relationship between Basque and the rest of the world's languages, so that it appears as an isolated branch on the genealogical tree of those language families. Nevertheless, this apparent genetic isolation should not be confused with physical isolation, since from both a synchronic and a diachronic perspective, Basque has always been in contact with other languages, on which it has left its mark and from which it has received countless contributions. Thus, Basque's phonetic and phonological system is not too distinct from that of the Romance languages with which it is in contact. This similarity appears to be, at least in part, the consequence of contact with Latin and subsequently with French and Spanish, and more specifically, as a result of numerous lexical borrowings taken from those languages (Trask 1998).[1] Nevertheless, together with the lexicon taken from other languages, Basque has a rich and clearly differentiated lexical patrimony of its own, and at the same time, it has maintained essentially intact a morphosyntactic system very different from that of the Romance languages with which it is in contact and with which it contrasts significantly from a typological perspective. This contrast in the degree to which Romance languages have been assimilated, between lexical and phonological levels on the one hand and the morphosyntactic level on the other, is not surprising from a linguistic perspective because it is well known that the superficial levels of a language (the lexical and phonological levels) are the most susceptible to linguistic change.

---

1. Estimates are that around half of the words used in everyday Basque are loans from Latin and from the Romance languages. However, from today's perspective, one might speculate that the way in which Basque has been able to enrich its original lexicon with new resources might be one of the keys to understand the surprising survival of this minority and minorized language.

In this chapter, we will briefly survey some of the most characteristic typological traits of Basque in contrast to the equivalent traits of the two Romance languages with which it is in close contact. The first section will address ergativity. This might be considered Basque's most exotic trait, if we take into account the fact that ergativity is not found in the Romance languages currently in contact with Basque nor indeed in any other European language (except for Georgian and some Caucasian languages). The second section will focus on the head parameter, which clearly differentiates Basque and the Romance languages, because the former is a head-final language, while the latter are head-initial. The third and final section will examine some syntactic traits that manifest some similarities and certain differences in degree between the Romance languages and Basque: verbal agreement and the pro-drop parameter, on the one hand, and word order, on the other.

Ergativity in Basque: An Island Amid the European Accusative Languages

One of the characteristics common to all the dialects of Basque that contrasts most strongly with the typology of the Romance languages is its ergative-absolutive case-marking system. In Basque, as in other ergative languages, the subject of a transitive predicate receives ergative case, which is the morphologically marked case (*-k*) (1a), while the subject of an intransitive predicate shows the same case as the object of a transitive predicate, the absolutive case (1b). In accusative languages, such as the Romance languages, in contrast, the subject of any kind of predicate is always in the nominative case (2a, 3a) and is thereby differentiated from the objects of transitive predicates, which are in the accusative case, morphologically marked in some contexts via a preposition (2a). It should be noted that in Basque, transitive verbs select the auxiliary *edun* "to have" (1a), while intransitive verbs, in contrast, are conjugated with the auxiliary *izan* "to be." We find the same contrast in the selection of the auxiliary in French (3a-b), but not in Spanish (2a-b).[2]

 (1) a. Jonek Miren ekarri du etxera.   [Basque]

     Jon-ERG Miren(ABS) bring have(PRES.3sg.A-3sg.E) house-DET-to

     "Jon has brought Miren home."

---

2. One should point out that not all intransitive verbs in Basque have the same syntactic behavior. Specifically, the so-called unergative verbs (*irakin* "to boil," *lan egin* "to work," *telefonatu* "to phone") behave like transitives (Levin 1983, Laka 1993a) and assign the ergative case to the subject, in addition to selecting the auxiliary *edun* "to have." In Romance languages such as French and Italian, we also find a different selection of the auxiliary in the intransitive verbs classified as unaccusative, such as *venir* "to come," and unergative, such as *téléphoner* "to phone" (Burzio 1986).

    b. Jon etxera etorri da.

       Jon(ABS) home-DET-to come be(PRES.3sg.A)

       "Jon has come home."

(2) a. Juan ha traído a María a casa.   [Spanish]

       Juan(NOM) has brought to María(ACC) to house

       "Juan has brought María home."

    b. Juan ha venido a casa.

       Juan(NOM) has come to home

       "Juan has come home."

(3) a. Jean a amené Marie chez lui.   [French]

       Jean(NOM) has brought Marie(ACC) house his

       "Jean has brought Marie home."

    b. Jean est venu à la maison.

       Jean(NOM) is come to DET home

       "Jean has come home."

Beyond the assignment of case to the arguments, the marking of finite verbs for person and number agreement in Basque reflects an ergative-absolutive system: the morphemes corresponding to the subjects of unaccusative verbs (4a) have the same form (*n-* for first-person singular) and the same distribution (initial) as those corresponding to the objects of transitive verbs (4d) and are different from the subjects of transitive verbs (4b-c-d): *-t* and *-zu*, respectively, for first-person and second-person singular.[3]

(4) a. Ni etorri naiz.

       I(ABS) come be(PRES.1sg.A)

       "I have come."

    b. Nik liburua ekarri dut.

       I-ERG book-the(ABS) bring have(PRES.3sg.A-1sg.E)

       "I have brought the book."

    c. Zuk liburua ekarri duzu.

       you-ERG book-the(ABS) bring have(PRES.3sg.A-2sg.E)

       "You have brought the book."

    d. Zuk ni ekarri nauzu.

       you-ERG I(ABS) bring have(PRES.1sg.A-2sg.E)

       "You have brought me."

---

3. There are exceptions to these rules in auxiliaries corresponding to the past tense and the potential mode, a phenomenon known as ergative displacement (Laka 1993b).

Finally, it must be emphasized that in the case of Basque, ergativity is solely morphological and not syntactic. In languages with ergative syntax, the syntactic behavior of the arguments reflects their morphological marking, so that arguments in ergative case behave differently from arguments marked with the absolute case in some syntactic contexts. In contrast, in Basque there is syntactic asymmetry between subjects and objects, independent of their morphological marking (ergative or absolutive), as is common in languages with accusative syntax.[4]

According to typologists, only 10 to 20 percent of the world's languages are ergative, and all of them are languages that, at least at present, are not in contact with Basque and are geographically dispersed: the Caucasian languages (such as Georgian), the Eskimo-Aleut languages, the Mayan languages, and some Australian aboriginal languages. Consequently, considering the pressure of the languages with which it has been and is in contact, especially the Romance languages, it is surprising that Basque has not given way in this morphological aspect and has maintained this highly characteristic trait intact.

Basque and the Romance Languages: Mirror Structures Derived from Opposite Values for the Head Parameter

Basque and the Romance languages select opposite values for the head parameter, a basic parameter of Universal Grammar that completely determines the structure of a language. The Romance languages are head-initial, while Basque is a head-final language, with the consequence that a majority of the structures (compound words, phrases, and sentences) of the two kinds of languages are mirror images of one another. It does not appear that close linguistic contact with the neighboring Romance languages (Spanish and French) has had a decisive influence on this fundamental parameter of any language's grammar. We will begin by describing the most frequent processes of affixation and the formation of compound words in Basque and will compare them with those of the surrounding Romance languages. Next, we will discuss the contrast between Basque postpositions and Romance prepositions. Third, we will describe the structure of Basque noun phrases and determiner phrases and will compare their most prominent characteristics with those of the Romance languages. To conclude this section, we will very briefly describe the structure of periphrastic verbal forms. By way of summary, we can say that most com-

---

4. In Basque, there are asymmetries in the syntactic behavior of subjects and objects, independent of their case marking, as reflected in the following phenomena: in the interpretation of the subjects of non-finite subordinate clauses acting as complements of control verbs such as *ahaztu* "to forget," in the distribution of reflexives, and, in northern dialects, in the genetivization of the objects of nonfinite clauses.

pound words in Basque are head-final, that Basque has postpositions and not prepositions, and that in this language the functional categories that head the different types of phrases and sentences (determiners, aspectual morphemes and auxiliaries that accompany the verb, and subordinators) are located to the right of the lexical heads. In addition, because Basque is an agglutinative language, most of its flexive elements are affixes that join to one another and to the lexical roots, giving rise to compound words. This example illustrates the differences among the three languages mentioned.

(5) a. Oliba-olioa erosiko duela esan du.   [Basque]
   olive-oil-DET buy-FUT Aux-COMP say Aux

   b. Ha dicho que comprará el aceite de oliva.   [Spanish]
   has said that buy-FUT DET oil of olive

   c. Il a dit qu'il achètera l'huile d'olive.   [French]
   he has said that-he buy-FUT DET-oil of-olive
   "He has said that he will buy the olive oil."

Lexical Morphology

Basque clearly manifests a head-final lexical morphology that differs in numerous aspects from that of the Romance languages. On the one hand, Basque has a large number of suffixes and very few prefixes (around seventy-five derivational suffixes compared to only two productive prefixes), while the Romance languages make use of many prefixes.[5] On the other hand, as expected for a head-final language, the formal and semantic head of a derived word is always the element at the right in Basque, so that prefixes always behave as modifiers.

(6) a. $[[eder]_A\text{-}\textbf{tasun}]_N$
   beautiful-NOMINAL SUFFIX
   "beauty"

   b. $[des\ [\textbf{egin}]_V]_V$
   PREFIX-do
   "undo"

---

5. The process of modernization, indispensable in order to adapt to all the communicative contexts in which Basque has been immersed in recent decades, has required an enrichment and massive adaptation of the lexicon, and the lack of prefixes has been mentioned as a deficiency on more than a few occasions. Nevertheless, from a typological perspective, it seems that among the languages of the world, there is a clear preference for suffixation over prefixation and infixation. This preference has been related to an easier processing of the words (Hawkins and Gilligan 1988).

In the Romance languages, suffixes are typically heads of their derived words. However, prefixes sometimes behave as semantic heads of their derivatives and sometimes as modifiers (Gràcia and Azkarate 2000).

(7) a. $[\text{sobre}[\textbf{carga}]_N]_N$ [Spanish]
         $[\text{sur}[\textbf{charge}]_N]_N$ [French]
         "overload"

      b. $[\textbf{sub}[\text{suelo}]_N]_N$ [Spanish]
         $[\textbf{sous}\text{-}[\text{sol}]_N]_N$ [French]
         "underground"

The Basque equivalents of prefixed words in the Romance languages are in many cases compound words with a locative noun (*aurre* "front," *atze* "behind," *arte* "between/among," and so on). If we compare prefixed words in Spanish with their Basque equivalents, we can easily see the regularity of the Basque constructions, which are always head-final (8a, b), in contrast to the asymmetries of the Romance languages (7a-b).

(8) a. $[\text{gain}_N[\textbf{zama}]_N]_N$
         over-**load**
         "overload"

      b. $[\text{lur}_N[\textbf{azpi}]_N]_N$ [Basque]
         ground-**under**
         "underground"

Other derived words that contrast with the Basque equivalents are the so-called parasynthetic derivatives in which a prefix and a suffix are involved simultaneously (9a). If we analyze these structures, it is easy to see that a "noun-suffix" derivative does not exist in this language (*#carcelar*, *#prisonner*). Basque does not have a rule for forming derivatives by parasynthesis, but it is interesting to observe the contrast between structures (9a-b), since in some cases, the Basque equivalent of a Romance parasynthetic derivative is a derivative that joins two suffixes, which once again shows the robustness of the head-final trait in Basque morphology.

(9) a. *encarcelar*   [Spanish]
         emprisonner   [French]
         in-prison-VERBAL SUFFIX
         "to imprison"

      b. $[[[\text{espetxe}]_N\text{-}ra]_P\text{-}tu]_V$ [Basque]
         prison-to-VERBAL SUFFIX
         "to imprison"

Compound formation processes are extraordinarily diverse in Basque, and some rules are highly productive, such as those that give rise to different kinds of root compounds. Basque root compounds are always head-final. Observe that the examples in (10a,b) have opposite meanings and, on the other hand, that the semantics and the grammatical category of the compound word are those of the head, which is located at the right:

(10) a. azukre-**kanabera**
  sugar-cane
  "sugar cane"

  b. kanabera-**azukre**
  cane-sugar
  "cane sugar"

(11) a. egon**gela**
  to stay-room
  "living room"

  b. uler**terraz**
  to understand-easy
  "easy to understand"

In some cases, one might think that we are faced with compounds of similar structure in Basque and the Romance languages, but the semantics and the grammatical category of these similar words immediately reveal that the underlying structures differ. For example, the compounds in (12) appear to have a [V+N] structure. In the Basque word, however, the head is the noun (12a), while in the Romance word (12b) the semantic head is the verb, which is located at the left. Nevertheless, the verb is not the structural head, since the compound is nominal:

(12) a. idaz**makina**   [Basque]
  to write-machine
  "typewriter"

  b. **lava**platos   [Spanish]
  lave-vaisselle   [French]
  washes-dishes
  "dishwasher"

In the Romance languages, improper compounds, in which the elements are joined by means of a preposition (13a), are much more frequent than root compounds (*ferrocarril* "railway," *bocacalle* "entrance to a street"). In Basque, however, improper compounds are much less abundant. Moreover, there is a clear contrast with the Romance languages in the order of their components (13a-b):

(13) a. **ama** *de* casa   [Spanish]
       maîtresse de maison   [French]
       lady of house
       "housewife"

     b. etxe*ko*andre   [Basque]
       house-*of*-lady
       "housewife"

Prepositions versus Postpositions

Basque uses postpositions instead of prepositions, unlike Romance languages. Put another way, as expected from a head-final language, Basque is a post-positional language. In addition, due to Basque's agglutinative character, its simple postpositions are suffixes (14a), while the prepositions of the Romance languages are more independent (14b).

(14) a. mendira   [Basque]
       mountain-DET-to
       "to the mountain"

     b. al monte   [Spanish]
       à la montagne   [French]
       to DET mountain
       "to the mountain"

One of the characteristics usually highlighted when describing the nominal morphology of Basque is the syncretism of the agglutination between the article, which is also a suffix (*-a/ak*), and the postpositions, because it is not always easy to differentiate the morphemes corresponding to those elements (14a): *-a* + *-ra* → *-ra*. Due to this syncretism, grammars often refer to the paradigms that result from the agglutination of nominal flexion morphemes as "declension." However, as Juan Carlos Moreno Cabrera (2007–2008) argues, syncretism also exists in the spoken Romance languages (14b), but is minimized in written texts due to spelling rules. Even so, in some cases syncretism is systematic and is maintained in written texts: *a* + *el* → *al*. Finally, independent postpositions also exist in Basque, which head postpositional Romance complexes mirror their equivalents (15a-b).

(15) a. etxe*tik* **kanpo**
       house-from outside
       "outside the house"

b. **fuera** *de* casa
   outside of house
   "outside the house"

Structure of the Noun Phrase and Determiner Phrase

One of the characteristics of Basque that calls the attention of Romance speakers is the number of words that end in *-a* or *-ak*, even in contexts in which the words appear in isolation, as in the signposting of cities or buildings. This phenomenon is not due to there being more words that end in the letter *-a* in Basque than in other languages: the suffixes *-a* and *-ak* are the singular and plural article, respectively, and occupy the final position in the noun phrase. The perception of the abundance of endings of this kind is increased by the fact that in Basque, the majority of noun phrases, including those with a non-specific reading, require a determiner. As a result, many noun phrases (mass nouns and any noun in the plural) are ambiguous between a specific and a non-specific reading (Laka 1993a):

(16) a. Liburua ekarri du.
       book-DET.sg.(ABS) bring Aux
       "He has brought the book."

   b. Ardoa ekarri du.
      wine- DET.sg.(ABS) bring Aux
      (i) "He has brought some wine."
      (ii) "He has brought the wine."

   c. Liburuak ekarri ditu.
      book- DET.pl.(ABS) bring Aux
      (i) "He has brought some books."
      (ii) "He has brought the books."

This need for an article has been linked to the lack of inflection for number in Basque nouns and the consequent need to specify number by means of a determiner (Laka 1996; Artiagoitia 2002). In the case of Spanish, the presence or absence of a determiner is linked to a specific (17a) or nonspecific (17b) reading of the noun phrase, respectively. In the case of French, a specific reading is obtained, as in Spanish, by means of the article (18a), but the nonspecific reading maintains the singular or plural article, although amalgamated with the preposition *de*, which assigns partitive case to the noun phrase (18b).

(17) a. Ha traído **el** vino / **los** libros.
       has brought DET.sg. wine / DET.pl. books
       "He has brought the wine / the books."

b. Ha traído vino / libros.
   has brought wine / books
   "He has brought some wine / some books."

(18) a. Il a emporté **le** vin / **les** livres.
   he has brought DET.sg. wine / DET.pl. books
   "He has brought the wine / the books."

b. Il a emporté **du** vin / **des** livres.
   he has brought PART-DET.sg. wine/ PART-DET.pl. books
   "He has brought some wine / some books."

Basque also has a partitive suffix (*-ik*) that always gives rise to a nonspecific reading, but this suffix is only acceptable in polarity contexts such as negative (19a-b), interrogative, or conditional sentences. The partitive suffix has
also been considered a type of determiner (Laffite 1944; 1979, Laka 1993a).

(19) a. *Ardorik ekarri du.
   wine-PART bring Aux
   "He has brought some wine."

b. Ez du ardorik ekarri.
   NEG Aux wine-PART bring
   "He has not brought any wine."

Demonstratives, unlike articles, are independent words both in Basque
and in the Romance languages and they always give rise to specific readings. In
addition to the different selection of values for the head parameter in Basque
and the Romance languages, the internal agreement in gender and number
within the noun phrase in the Romance languages is worth highlighting (21),
in contrast to its complete absence in Basque (20). It must be emphasized that
in Basque, nouns can be morphologically marked for number, but not for
gender, with the exception of a few nouns referring to human beings taken
from the Romance languages (*aktore/aktoresa* "*actor/actriz,*" corresponding
to English "actor/actress"). Nevertheless, determiners are not marked for
gender, so that gender agreement is always absent.

(20) a. aktore beltz **hauek**
   actor.(m.) black these
   "these black actors"

b. aktoresa beltz **hauek**   [Basque]
   actress (f.) black these
   "these black actresses"

(21) a. **estos** actores negros

   these(m.pl.) actor.(m.pl.) black.(m.pl.)

   "these black actors"

   b. **estas** actrices negras   [Spanish]

   these (f.pl.) actress(f.pl.) black (f.pl.)

   "these black actresses"

In Basque, the determiner is always located at the end of the noun phrase, in accordance with the predictions of the DP hypothesis (Abney 1987) for a head-final language. According to this hypothesis, the determiner is the head of the noun's functional projection, in the same way that the inflection constitutes the head of the verb's functional projection. Nevertheless, not all modifiers of a noun occupy a prenominal position because most adjectives are located to the right of the noun and are ungrammatical if located to the left (22b). This is not surprising, since adjectives are considered adjuncts, and adjuncts are frequently situated to the right of the head in head-final languages.[6] The exceptions are adjectives derived using the suffixes -*ar*, -*dun*, and -*zko* and some gentilic loan words such as *frantses* "French," which may appear either before or after the noun (23).

(22) a. etxe zuria

   house white-DET

   "the white house"

   b. *zuri etxea.

   white house-DET

(23) a. bilbotar mutila

   Bilbao-from boy-DET

   "the boy from Bilbao"

   b. mutil bilbotarra

   boy Bilbao-from-DET

   "the boy from Bilbao"

In the Romance languages, qualifying adjectives usually appear in post-nominal position (24a), but a prenominal position is also possible when they function as epithets (24b).

---

6. The order [N+Adj.] attested both in Basque and in the Romance languages, seems to be much more extended among the languages of the world than the order [Adj.+N], found in English, for example (Dressler 2005).

(24) a. las casas blancas   [Spanish]
        les maisons blanches [French]
        DET(pl) house-pl. white(fem.pl)
        "the white houses"

     b. las blancas casas [Spanish]
        les blanches maisons   [French]
        DET(pl) white(fem.pl).house-pl.
        "the white houses"

Adnominal modifiers, which carry a genitive or locative genitive postposition (*-ren* or *-ko*), are placed to the left of the noun (25). In all cases, the determiner is always located at the end of the entire phrase. The order of adnominals when each modifies the contiguous noun is the mirror image of the equivalent phrase in the Romance languages.[7]

(25) a. [[[Bilboko] lagunaren] etxea]   [Basque]
        Bilbao-GEN.LOC. friend-DET-GEN. house-DET
        "the house of the friend from Bilbao"

     b. [la casa [del amigo [de Bilbao]]]   [Spanish]
        [la maison [de l'ami [de Bilbao]]]   [French]
        DET house of DET-friend of Bilbao
        "the house of the friend from Bilbao"

Verb Structure

Basque has a small number of verbs with synthetic forms for the progressive aspect, but the majority of verbal forms are periphrastic. The first element of the periphrastic forms joins the lexical root of the verb and an aspectual suffix, and the second element is an auxiliary that joins the morphemes of person, tense, and mood. The aspectual morphemes and the auxiliary constitute the inflection that heads any sentence, and its position to the right of the verb is to be expected in a head-final language. In subordinate clauses, the subordinator that joins the subordinate clause to the main clause is in most cases a suffix that is joined to the verb and located to the right of the inflection (26a). The structure in the Romance languages is the mirror image of that in Basque, with the inflection to the left of the verb and the subordinator to the left of the inflection (26b), just as would be expected in a head-initial language.

---

7. However, when several adnominals modify the head noun of the entire phrase, there is a syntactic hierarchy among the modifiers and the resulting phrase does not match its mirror image in the Romance languages (Zabala 1996): thematic adnominals (subject, object, and so on), which always carry the postposition *-ren*, are located further from the noun than adnominals with the locative postposition *–ko*, which usually have adverbial value.

(26) a. etorri dela   [Basque]
         come-PERF. Aux-3s.A-COMP.
         "that he has come"

     b. que ha venido   [Spanish]
         COMP Aux(3s.N) come
         "that he has come"

Some Syntactic Characteristics of Basque and the Romance Languages: Similarities and Differences

In this section, we will focus on two fundamental aspects of syntax that are considered highly important in linguistic typology. We will make a brief comparative survey of verbal agreement and the possibility of dropping the arguments of the sentence, and we will put forward several considerations about word order in the sentence. In doing so, we will see that Basque manifests extreme values for these parameters compared to the Romance languages, because it shows verbal agreement for the ergative, absolutive, and dative arguments, and in addition, can drop-these three arguments when the pragmatic context allows it. At the same time, in informal-contexts, the verb can also show agreement with the interlocutor (addressee). As far as word order in the sentence is concerned, Basque is much freer than the Romance languages with which it is in contact.

Verbal Agreement and the Pro-drop Parameter

One of Basque's most prominent characteristics is the richness of its verbal agreement, because the verb agrees with the ergative, absolutive, and dative arguments, whether these are nominal (27a) or clausal (27b). Although it may appear that this system is unlike that of the Romance languages (27c-d), it must be emphasized that they are not in fact that different. The clitics of the Romance languages, even if they are independent morphemes, can be considered markers of agreement, so that there is a certain degree of redundancy in both Basque and the Romance languages: the person, number, and case markers are reflected both on the arguments and on the auxiliary or the clitics that accompany that auxiliary.

(27) a. Nik zuri loreak ekarri dizkizut.
         I-ERG you-DAT flower-DET.pl.(ABS) bring Aux(3pl.A-2sg.D-1sg.E)
         "I have brought some flowers to you."

     b. [Mirenek niri loreak ekartzeak] biziki poztu nau.
         Miren-ERG I-DAT flower-DET.pl.(ABS) bring-NOMIN-ERG extremely gladden Aux(1sg.A-3sg.E)
         "That Miren has brought me flowers has gladdened me a lot."

    c. Yo a ti te he traído flores.

        I(NOM) to you(DAT) you(DAT) Aux(1.sg-N) brought flower-pl.(ACC)

        "I have brought some flowers to you."

    d. [El que Miren me haya traído flores] me ha alegrado mucho.

        the that Miren(NOM) I(DAT) Aux(3.sg-N) brought flower-pl.(ACC)

        I(ACC) Aux(3.sg.N) gladden much

        "That Miren has brought me flowers has gladdened me a lot."

In fact, the system is not that redundant, because the arguments are frequently dropped when the pragmatic context allows it, and in these cases, they are reflected only on the verb. In this context, interesting phenomena arise that are attributable to contact between Basque and Spanish. On the one hand, Basque speakers tend to silence the clitics equivalent to the arguments when using Spanish. On the other, Spanish speakers who are in contact with Basque tend to use the clitics even in cases when the arguments are explicit. For some authors, such as Bernard Comrie (2008), this fact might reflect a change in the nature of the clitics, which might begin to resemble the dependent morphological markers of agreement in Basque.

The phenomenon known as "Person-Case Constraint" or "me-lui constraint" supports this possibility of equating the clitics of the Romance languages with the agreement markers in Basque. In fact, in Basque (28a), as in Romance languages such as Spanish and French (28c), as well as in Georgian, Warlpiri, and Arabic, in finite sentences that contain subject, direct-object, and indirect-object arguments, the direct object is restricted to the third person (Laka 1993b). However, this restriction does not apply in non-finite sentences (28b), which indicates that it is a phenomenon associated with verbal agreement.

  (28) a. *Zuk Mikeli ni aurkeztuko naiozu.   [Basque]

        you-ERG Mikel-DAT I(ABS) introduce-FUT Aux (1sg.A-3sg.D-2sg.E)

        "You will introduce me to Mikel."

    b. [Zuk ni Mikeli aurkeztea] ideia ona litzateke.

        you-ERG I(ABS)Mikel-DAT introduce- NOMIN -DET(ABS) idea good

        should be

        "It would be a good idea for you to introduce me to Mikel"

    c. *Agnès me lui présentera.   [French]

        *Agnès me le presentará.   [Spanish]

        Agnès I(ACC) he(DAT) present.FUT.3sg

        "Agnès will introduce me to him."

Although the agreement between the Basque auxiliary and the arguments of the sentence can be equated to some extent with that of Romance verbs, Basque verbs have a peculiarity that is highly unusual from a typological perspective. We are referring to what are known as allocutive forms, used in informal pragmatic contexts.[8] In allocutive verbal forms, the verb shows gender agreement with the addressee: -na- for a female (29a) and -a- for a male (29b).

(29) a. Nik Mireni loreak eman zizkionat.

I-ERG Miren-DAT flower-DET.pl.(ABS) give Aux(3pl.A-3sg.D-3sg. Alok.fem-1sg.E)

"I have given the flowers to Miren (addressee is female)."

b. Nik Mireni loreak eman zizkioat.

I-ERG Miren-DAT flower-DET.pl.(ABS) give Aux(3pl.A-3sg.D-3sg. Alok.masc-1sg.E)

"I have given the flowers to Miren (addressee is male)."

To conclude this section, we will mention the pro-drop phenomenon or the possibility of silencing the arguments of the sentence. Basque allows the silencing of all the arguments (ergative, absolutive, and dative) (30a), while Spanish only allows the silencing of the subject (30b), and French does not allow the silencing of any of the sentence arguments (30c). Consequently, these three languages exemplify a continuum in their values for the pro-drop parameter.

(30) a. Ekarri dizkizut.

bring Aux (3pl.A-2sg.D-1sg.E)

"I have brought to you (some objects known by the context)."

b. Te los he traído.

2sg.(DAT) 3pl.(ACC) have(1sg.N) bring

"I have brought to you (some objects known by the context)."

c. Je te les ai emporté.

I(NOM) 2sg.(DAT) 3pl.(ACC) have(1sg.N) bring

"I have brought to you (some objects known by the context)."

Word Order in the Sentence

In agreement with their values for the head parameter, the basic structure for the verb phrase in Basque is OV, while in the Romance languages it is

---

8. From a typological perspective, this phenomenon is not very common although similar systems do exist in other languages that mark honorifics or beneficiaries (Ortiz de Urbina 1989; Oyarçabal 1993).

VO. One does not always find this basic structure, nor is it even the most frequently found structure within any given corpus because, as we will see in this section, Basque is a free word order language and the basic structure can appear altered in many pragmatic contexts. Nevertheless, that the basic order is OV is clearly reflected in lexicalized verbal expressions (*min hartu* "to hurt oneself," *min eman* "to hurt," *hitz egin* "to speak," and so on):

(31) a. Min hartu du.   [Basque]
          hurt take Aux
          "He was hurt."

     b. Se ha hecho daño.   [Spanish]
          he has do hurt
          "He was hurt."

It is usually assumed that, according to Joseph H. Greenberg's typological criteria (1963), Basque is an SOV language (de Rijk 1969). In other words, the neutral order of sentence elements in Basque is SOV, while the Romance languages are SVO languages. Consequently, in the basic order of the sentence, the subject would be expected to occupy the initial position both in Basque and in the Romance languages. However, the coincidence in the position of the subject does not contradict the prediction of the head parameter, because the subject is located in the specifier of the Inflection, and the most common case is for specifiers to be located to the left of the head. On the other hand, one should remember that the orders in which the subject is located to the left of the object constitute 95.77 percent of the sample studied by Greenberg (1963), and that in the same work the SOV and SVO orders appear in 44.78 percent and 41.79 percent, respectively, of the languages studied. It thus appears that, as far as this typological trait—the basic order of the elements of a sentence—is concerned, Basque and the Romance languages manifest the values of Universal Grammar found in the majority of languages. Nevertheless, it must be stressed that from a syntactic perspective, this order considered neutral becomes entirely blurred, because Basque is a free word order language and has greater liberty to order the elements of a sentence than we find in the Romance languages. This freedom is coherent with the richness of its flexive morphology, which marks the semantics and the syntactic function of each of the arguments and adjuncts almost without ambiguity, so that the position of the elements within the sentence does not determine their syntactic function.

Basque's free word order is assumed in almost all grammars, and Jean Ithurry (1920; 1979) already mentioned in his grammar of the Lapurdian dialect that a four-element sentence like the one in (32) allows twenty-four perfectly grammatical orders. However, although the semantics and function of the elements in the sentence do not change when their order is altered, the twenty-four possible orders mentioned are not equivalents pragmatically. The order of (32a), with the verb at the end and the arguments ordered according to their syntactic hierarchy (ergative-dative-absolute) is usually considered neutral in syntactic studies and it is argued that it would be the expected response to a question such as *Zer gertatu da*? "What happened?" (Laka 1996). The sentences in (32b) and (32c), for their part, would correspond to different presuppositions: in (32b), *sagarra haurrari* "the apple to the child" would be the known information or the point of departure for the predication (Topic), and *aitak* "the father" would be the element providing new information or the element that is to be contrasted: in short, the Focus. In (32c), on the other hand, *aitak sagarra* "the father the apple" would be the Topic, and *haurrari* "to the child" would be the Focus.

(32) a. Aitak haurrari sagarra eman dio.

father-the-ERG child-the-DAT apple-the(ABS) given Aux(3sg.A-3sg.D-3sg.E)

"The father has given the apple to the child."

b. Sagarra haurrari aitak eman dio.

apple-the(ABS) child-the-DAT father-the-ERG given Aux(3sg.A-3sg.D-3sg.E)

"It is the father who has given the apple to the child."

c. Aitak sagarra haurrari eman dio.

father-the-ERG apple-the(ABS) child-the-DAT given Aux(3sg.A-3sg.D-3sg.E)

"It is the child that the father has given the apple to."

It should be noted that among the twenty-four possible orders of the example in (32), the verb does not necessarily have to appear at the end (33a,b). Sebero Altube (1929) defended (although this affirmation has been debated) that the Focus of the sentence (also called *galdegaia*) always has to be located to the left of the verb in Basque (33a), and that if the verb appears at the beginning or after a pause, what is being focalized is the affirmation of the utterance (33b).

(33) a. Aitak eman dio sagarra haurrari.

father-the-ERG given Aux(3sg.A-3sg.D-3sg.E) apple-the(ABS) child-the-DAT

"It is the father who has given the apple to the child."

b. Eman dio sagarra haurrari aitak.

given Aux(3sg.A-3sg.D-3sg.E) apple-the(ABS) child-the-DAT father-the-ERG

"Yes, the father has given the apple to the child."

The neutral order, which would be typologically identified as SOV, would be expected when all the information is new, at the beginning of a narrative, for example. However, the study of oral and written usage makes clear that even in contexts in which all the information is new, such as at the beginning of a narrative, Basque speakers have numerous options for organizing the elements of a sentence in accordance with their communicative intentions. Clear evidence of this can be found at the beginning of the parable of the prodigal son, which has been translated into many different ways by different writers using different dialects (34). The SOV order of (33a) would be the one expected in this "neutral" context, but language use shows us that the freedom of word order in Basque is joined with a much greater pragmatic flexibility than is normally supposed by some grammars and style manuals, which are influenced to a great extent by Altube's restrictive ideas (Hidalgo 1994). The speaker will assign different prosody to each of these sentences, in accordance with the informational structures possible in the pragmatic context in question (in this case, the beginning of a narrative).

(34) a. Gizon batek bi seme zituen. Gizon batek / BI SEME zituen
   man a-ERG two son(ABS) had
   "A man had two sons."

b. Gizon batek zituen bi seme. Gizon batek zituen / BI SEME
   man a-ERG had two son(ABS)
   "A man had two sons."

c. Bi seme zituen gizon batek. BI SEME zituen gizon batek
   two son(ABS) had man a-ERG
   "A man had two sons."

As can be seen, a rising intonation is assigned in all cases to the object (*bi seme* "two sons"), and when this element occupies a preverbal position, it forms a single phonological phrase with the verb, while when the element with rising intonation is postverbal it appears preceded by a marked pause. Bittor Hidalgo (1994) conducted an exhaustive and quantitative study of the written tradition of the different dialects of Basque and clearly found that, as in (34b), the focus appears in a postverbal position in many other cases. Despite the fact that all the options in (34) frequently appear in literature and in the spoken language, in the early twentieth century, Altube (1929) maintained that orders of the type found in (34b) are a consequence of interference from the Romance languages and that in Basque's own order, the Focus always has to occupy a preverbal position, and that the verb tends to occupy the final position in the sentence. According to Altube's model, then, a sentence like (34b) would only be correct in Basque if it was answering the question *Nork zituen bi seme*? "Who had two sons?" and the order that would maintain the essence of the language in this neutral context would be (34a), with the verb at the end. If we compare the examples in (34) with their equivalents in a Romance language, such as Spanish, we find that the only word order that is undoubtable in Spanish is precisely the equivalent of (34b): *Un hombre tenía dos hijos.* This leads us to believe that the rules on word order formulated by Altube are more restrictive than the language's own grammar and correspond more to an eagerness to mark a distinction from the Romance languages than to a descriptive grammar based on actual use.

It must be stressed that Altube's rules found great success among the authors of twentieth-century written texts in the southern dialects and in the early phases of the implementation of unified or standard Basque, to the point of being respected in most cases in formal registers. Nevertheless, as literary production in Basque has grown and the language has gained new areas of use in media, public administration, and academic spheres, Altube's restrictions have been observed to reduce a text's communicative effectiveness and have been questioned, both in practical style manuals (Zubimendi and Esnal 1993), where strategies for making texts more comprehensible are proposed, and in descriptive research (Hidalgo 1994). In fact, Altube himself acknowledged that both in written texts and in spoken language, when the Focus is a long element, and especially with discursive verbs such as the verbs of saying (*esan* "to say" or *erantzun* "to answer"), there is a tendency to move the verb forward. Even so, he characterized orders of this kind as interferences from the Romance languages and maintained that (35a) is the correct order in Basque, and (35b) is a case of interference.

(35) a. Bihar lan asko daukala eta bulegoan geratuko dela esan dit amak.
   tomorrow work much has-that and office-the-in stay-FUT. Aux -that say Aux mother-ERG
   "Mom told me that she will have a lot of work tomorrow and that she will stay in the office."

   b. Amak esan dit bihar lan asko daukala eta bulegoan geratuko dela.
   mother-ERG say Aux tomorrow work much has-that and office-the-in stay -FUT Aux -that
   "Mom told me that she will have a lot of work tomorrow and that she will stay in the office."

It is sufficient to compare the examples in (35) with their Spanish equivalents to realize that Altube considered as a form of interference what is precisely the only option possible in Spanish: *Mi madre me ha dicho que mañana tiene mucho trabajo y que se quedará en la oficina.* This leads us to think that, once again, his stylistic proposal condemns an option that is possible within the grammar of Basque, in order to distinguish further from the syntax of the Romance languages. In the 1990s, Basque recovered in its formal written and oral texts options like that of (35b), which are nowadays not only accepted but even recommended in style manuals as strategies to facilitate sentence processing.

The ease of effective processing of syntactic chains is a universal capacity that interacts with the grammar of a language and, according to John A. Hawkins (1994), the difficulty of processing different types of sequences can be measured. Hawkins (1994, 57) maintains that "words and constituents occur in the orders they do so that syntactic grouping and their immediate constituents (ICs) can be recognized (and produced) as rapidly and efficiently as possible in language performance." The existence of orders like that of (35b) and speakers' preference for them are explained precisely by this principle. In (35a), we are unable to identify all the constituents of the sentence until we process the last word in the sequence, but in (35b) we need only arrive at the fourth word in order to construct a mental map of the entire structure. The existence of sentences like (35b) can be explained by universal principles of language processing, without the need to resort to interference from the Romance languages. Correspondingly, we find that a sequence such as *Amak [bihar lan asko daukala eta bulegoan geratuko dela] esan dit*, in which the subordinate clause is inserted between the subject (*amak* "mom") and the verb (*esan dit* "said to me"), despite the fact that it corresponds to SOV order and although it would in principle be grammatical in Basque, has a very low level of acceptability among speakers. Hawkins (1994, 7–9) relates this restriction, which is very frequent among all languages, to the processing difficulty of center-embedded clauses.[9]

Basque also uses other strategies that can be explained by the principles described by Hawkins (1994), such as, for example, the use of preposed particles that anticipate information about the subordinator, which is joined to the verb of a subordinate clause as an affix and often habitually appears at the end of the subordinate clause (36). Preposed particles of this kind are also classified by Altube (1929) as contaminations from the Romance languages, but they are treated today, both in style manuals (Zubimendi and Esnal 1993) and in theoretical studies (Ortiz de Urbina 1998), as strategies that can facilitate the processing of sentence constituents and increase communication effectiveness. Redundant elements of this kind, since they are copies of the subordinator, are not indispensable in order to obtain grammatical sentences

---

9. Center-embedded clauses are considered grammatical in Japanese but not in Persian. In Basque they are considered grammatical but are not very acceptable stylistically.

from the point of view of Basque syntax, but in specific pragmatic contexts, they can contribute to a text's comprehensibility:

(36) Amak esan dit **ezen** bihar lan asko daukala eta bulegoan geratuko dela.
      mother-ERG say Aux **that** tomorrow work a lot has-**that** and office
      stay-FUT Aux-that
      "Mom told me that she will have a lot of work tomorrow and that
      she will stay in the office."

Unlike Basque, which can modify the informational structure of an utterance by resorting solely to a change in the order of the constituents, the Romance languages need to resort to periphrasis in order to emphasize different elements. In Spanish, for example, utterances such as (37a) are perceived as neutral and periphrastic constructions such as those in (37b) are used in order to emphasize a particular element.

(37) a. El padre le ha dado la manzana al niño.
         the father 3sg-DAT has given the apple to-the child
         "The father gave the apple to the child."

     b. Ha sido el padre quien ha dado la manzana al niño.
         has been the father who has given the apple to-the child
         "It was the father who gave the apple to the child."

In Basque, periphrastic constructions similar to those of (37b) (*Aita izan da haurrari sagarra eman diona*) are frequently used, but other kinds of mechanisms for emphasizing focalized elements also exist. The eastern dialects, for example, bring the auxiliary forward in order to form a phonic group with the *wh-* words or with the focalized element (38b, 39b).

(38) a. Nor erori da? [Standard Basque]
         who fall Aux?
         "Who fell?"

     b. Nor da erori? [Eastern dialects]
         who Aux fall
         "Who fell?"

(39) a. Mikel erori da. [Standard Basque]
         Mikel fall Aux
         "Mikel fell." or "It was Mikel who fell."

     b. Mikel da erori. [Eastern dialects]
         Mikel Aux fall
         "It was Mikel who fell."

In the western dialects, on the other hand, and quite extensively today in unified Basque, the verb *egin* "to do" is used to focalize the action of the verb, in a similar way to English *do*-support (40).

(40)   Autotik irten eta erori egin da.
         car-from get out and fall do Aux
         "He got out of the car and he fell."

In conclusion, we can state that Basque is a free word order language, so that the sentence's informational structure (theme-rheme) determines the order of elements in an utterance to a much greater extent than those elements' syntactic function. It is the richness of the language's flexive morphology, which endows each element with a high degree of semantic transparence, that facilitates this freedom of order.

4

A Small Country, a Small Language, Many Dialects and Accents

Jesus Mari Makazaga,
the University of the Basque Country (UPV/EHU)

The Basque Country is actually quite small (only about 20,900 square kilometers or 8,000 square miles with little more than 3 million inhabitants) and the Basque language is equally small with regard to the number of people who speak it (1,234,000 or less than half of the population).[1] Yet despite this, it has a wide variety of dialects, subdialects, and local forms of speech.

Proof of that variety is seen, for example, in the large number of names that the Basque language is known by among its speakers: *euskera, euzkera, euskala, eskuara, eskuera, eskara, eskera, eskoara, euskiera, auskera, uskara, üskara, oskara, uskera, uskaa, uska,* and so on. This is a sign of the Basque language's limited homogeneity throughout the Basque Country, as discussed in chapter 5. Koldo Mitxelena[2] (1987, 37) refers to the diversity of the Basque language thus:

> We all know, those abroad as well as those at home, since it is widely disclosed news, that the Basque language is not uniform. "Uniform" does not exactly mean that it is not "one," assuming that it makes sense to preach this about a language: it means that it has not had a variation that serves, in its standard capacity, as a point of reference for certain uses of the language. On the contrary, it has been, and is divided into differentiated dialects and

---

1. According to an Eustat (Basque Statistics Institute) survey done in 2006, there were 775,000 fluent speakers and 459,000 people that understood the language but had difficulty expressing themselves well in it. Furthermore, in the Basque diaspora, more than one hundred thousand people preserved or regained Euskara thanks to the Euskal Etxeak (Basque social clubs throughout the world, especially in the Americas).

2. The name of Koldo Mitxelena, a Basque linguist, also appears spelled as "Luis" and as "Michelena," depending on the Basque or Spanish spelling used.

speech, some literary and some not. Historically, in the Basque Country,[3] in the territory where Euskara was spoken, the sociolinguistic and political situation did not favor establishing a standard, uniform version of the language, and instead led to dialectal and subdialectal diversity.

In the first place there was political-administrative fragmentation: historically as well as currently, the Basque Country has depended upon different administrations that in turn have had different linguistic policies. Currently, the Basque-speaking community is broken into two large regions and divided by two states (France and Spain); the Spanish state-dependent area is in turn divided into two autonomous communities: the Comunidad Autónoma del País Vasco-Euskal Autonomia Erkidegoa (CAPV-EAE, the Autonomous Community of the Basque Country) and the Comunidad Foral de Navarra-Nafarroako Foru Komunitatea (Foral Community of Navarre, CFN-NFK).

Moreover, the Basque language did not enjoy official status in any public administration for centuries. It was, then, a language that had historically remained outside the realms of both public administration and education, and a language that had been orally passed on from generation to generation for centuries. One should also bear in mind geographical factors. In other words, much of the Basque Country is mountainous, which led to a degree of isolation between neighboring municipalities and counties.

All of this contributed to a situation, as noted, that favored dialectal diversity and greater separation between the dialects. This separation was clear, for example, between the continental (in France) and peninsular (in Spain) dialects of Euskara. And these dialectal and subdialectal differences were easily preserved then throughout the centuries.

That was the situation until virtually the end of the twentieth century, when several important developments resulted in a decline in the distinctive nature of the dialects of Euskara throughout the Basque Country as a whole, and especially among the younger generations: The end of the Franco regime in Spain in 1975; the implementation and development of a unified language (Euskara Batua, Standard or Unified Basque) from the late 1960s on;[4] an improvement in the sociolinguistic status of Euskara from the 1980s on through official recognition and development of the language in environments in which it had been prohibited until this time, such as public administration, education, and culture;[5] and the pressure of other languages spoken in the Basque Country (mainly Spanish and French).

---

3. For the concept of what defines the "Basque Country," see chapter 1.
4. On this, see chapter 5.
5. Environments, incidentally, where Euskara Batua had been imposed. See chapter 7.

References to Dialects in Basque Literature

Since the beginning of written Basque literature, much has been made of the diversity of dialects, subdialects, and local forms of speech in Euskara and, because of this, the difficulty in writing the language. Indeed, writers, grammarians, and dialectologists that have studied Euskara have all spoken often of this in their works.

Bernard Etxepare,[6] the author of the first book published in the Basque language, the *Linguae Vasconum Primitiae* (1545), remarks in the work that, of the many different varieties of the language, that of the area of Garazi (Pays de Cize) in Lower Navarre deserved the honor of having elevated Euskara to the literary level ([1545] 1995, 230 [in English]). Another Navarrese writer, the Protestant pastor Joanes Leizarraga, explains in the introduction to his translation of the New Testament ([1571] 1979) that he had to overcome the difficulties of Euskara's dialectal diversity when creating an intelligible variation for all readers. In the end he created a unified variation that his readers could understand, fundamentally from the continental Basque provinces of Lapurdi, Lower Navarre, and Zuberoa: "The existing diversity in the way of speaking in the Basque Country is well-known because it varies almost from house to house" (quoted in Zuazo 2010, 50).

In his seventeenth-century book *Gero* (Later), Pedro de Axular from Lapurdi notes the impossibility of using expressions that would be intelligible to all Basques. In his opinion, it was the Basque-speaking territory's political division that led to this linguistic diversity: "I know that I cannot cover all ways of speaking, because they are numerous and diverse in the Basque Country: in Navarre, Lower Navarre, Zuberoa, Lapurdi, Bizkaia, Gipuzkoa, Araba, and many other places. Not all Basques have the same laws and customs, or the same language, since they belong to different kingdoms" (quoted in Zuazo 2010, 50).

Arnaut Oihenart (1657), a Zuberoan historian, also comments on Basque dialects in his seventeenth-century work. He links the dialects to ancient tribes and identifies four of them: that of the Aquitanians, spoken in Iparralde (the northern Basque Country); that of the Vascones, from Navarre; that of the Varduli, from Gipuzkoa and Araba; and that of the Caristii from Bizkaia. Below I will address to what extent the dialects can be linked with these ancient tribes as well as how far they can be differentiated along the lines of different ecclesiastical dioceses.

---

6. The name Bernard Etxepare may appear, according to the citation, as Bernardum Dechepare, Bernard Detchepare, Bernart Etxepare, or Beñat Etxepare.

In the eighteenth century, Joannes d'Etcheverry,[7] a writer and doctor from Sara (Sare) in Lapurdi, observed that a Basque speaker from Lower Navarre or Zuberoa could not understand another from Bizkaia or Araba, nor could a Basque-speaker from Otsagabia (Ochagavía) or the Erronkari-Roncal Valley (both in Navarre) communicate with another from Baztan (Navarre) or Lapurdi: "Given that the Basques belong to different kingdoms, it is no wonder that speech variations are observed. Some regions maintain a relationship with one of these kingdoms and other regions with another kingdom, and the result of these different relationships is that each one borrows from two distinct foreign languages, and that is the origin of the divergences, which will ultimately cause the permanent extinction of the language" (quoted in Zuazo 2010, 51).

In short, the first writers of Basque literature addressed the topic of dialectial variation in some detail. Fundamentally, the Basque territory's administrative division and the influx of Spanish and French (in the peninsular and continental Basque Country respectively) were the two reasons that justified, according to these authors, the Basque language's dialectal and subdialectal diversity. The lack of a common and accepted code by all persisted until well into the twentieth century. Finally, as explained in chapter 5 of this book, a unification process began in 1968 that ultimately enjoyed remarkable success.

Works on Basque Dialectology

Following the sixteenth- and seventeenth-century texts mentioned above, the first works to formally study and classify the dialects of Euskara were published in the eighteenth century. Establishing the boundaries and the classification of a language's variations is not an easy task because, on one hand, dialects (and languages as a whole) are dynamic and discontinuous realities that change over time, and on the other, the various linguistic phenomena that define and distinguish one dialect from another differ in both their form and extent. Dialectologists analyze these phenomena and, by defining their scope, establish such internal divisions within a language; divisions that are liable to change throughout the history of the language in question.

One might say that the precursor of Basque dialectology was the eighteenth-century writer, Father Manuel Larramendi. In his book on Basque grammar, *El imposible vencido, El arte de la lengua bascongada* (The Impossible Overcome, The Art of the Basque Language, 1729), he speaks of only three dialects: Gipuzkoan, Bizkaian, and Navarrese or Lapurdian (he hardly made

---

7. Joanes Etxeberri, termed "de Sara" (of Sara), is also cited in the literature as Joannes d'Etcehverry.

a distinction between these last two). Later, in his *Diccionario trilingüe castellano, bascuence y latín* (Trilingual Spanish, Basque, and Latin Dictionary, 1745) and above all in his *Corografía de Guipúzcoa* (Geography of Gipuzkoa, 1756; 1969), he expanded that classification and ended up with five dialects: Zuberoan, Lapurdian, Navarrese, Gipuzkoan, and Bizkaian.

In the second half of the nineteenth century, a figure emerged that would be a beacon of Basque dialectology during the following century, Prince Louis Lucien Bonaparte (1863). He was the first person to more or less systematically study the dialects of Euskara, primarily relying on auxiliary verb forms. He made five trips to the Basque Country to collect data and to study the different Euskara dialects firsthand. With the help of several collaborators, from whom he requested translations of biblical texts (easily comparable texts) and from catechisms, he collected a lot of material,[8] which he later published in London through the press that he had in his own home.

Bonaparte proposed four different divisions of Basque dialects. The fourth classification (1869) was practically followed to the present day and became a reference point for subsequent scholars. He summarized this classification in *Le Verbe Basque en Tableaux* (The Basque verb in tables, 1869) and drew up his linguistic map—*Carte des Sept Provinces Basques* (Map of the seven Basque provinces, 1863)—accordingly, on which he meticulously charted the boundaries of the dialects, subdialects, and even variations within these. Both the map and his study of Basque verbs were considered benchmarks in Basque dialectology during the following century. In the fourth and last division, he distinguished the following eight dialects (along with twenty-five subdialects and fifty local variations): Bizkaian, Gipuzkoan, Nothern High Navarrese, Southern High Navarrese, Lapurdian, Zuberoan, Eastern Low Navarrese, and Western Low Navarrese. He encompassed the eight dialects in three large groups: the group formed only by Bizkaian; the group formed by Gipuzkoan, Lapurdian, Northern High Navarrese, and Southern High Navarrese; and the group formed by Zuberoan, Eastern Low Navarrese, and Western Low Navarrese.

Bonaparte was followed by a number of individuals who also studied the dialectical variations of Euskara. These included scholars from both the Basque Country and abroad. Among them, one might mention Julien Vinson, Willem J. Van Eys, Arturo Campión, Pierre Broussain, Jean Bourciez, Dámaso Inza, Georges Lacombe, and so on. Among those that followed Bonaparte, however, one figure stands out: Resurrección María de Azkue,

---

8. At that time the Basque language was already very scarce in all the territory where it had been commonly spoken (as may be seen on the map). In Araba, it was only spoken in the area around Aramaio and in some border areas of the province with Bizkaia and Gipuzkoa; in Navarre it was no longer spoken south of Tafalla.

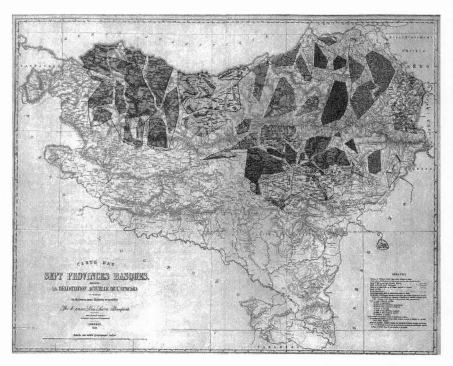

Figure 4.1. Carte des Sept Provinces Basques (1863; Map of the seven Basque provinces)

the first president of Euskaltzaindia (the Royal Academy of the Basque Language). While it was true that he possessed less dialectological rigor than that of Bonaparte (Camino 2009, 506) as a tireless compiler of linguistic data, Azkue nevertheless made important contributions to Basque dialectology. He kept the basics of Bonaparte's classification, although he proposed some modifications: he considered Roncalese to be a separate dialect, for example, and he placed the two High Navarrese dialects into one group and the Low Navarrese dialects in another. Consequently, according to Azkue's scheme, the number of dialects was reduced to seven.

Under the tutelage of Euskaltzaindia and shortly after the academy was established in 1919, Azkue led a team that created a threefold phonetic, morphologic, and lexicographic questionnaire titled *Erizkizundi Irukoitza*. A large team of researchers subsequently traveled the length and breadth of Euskal Herria (the Basque Country) carrying out a project that was intended, according to Luis Villasante (quoted in Echaide 1984, 9), "to provide a reliable data bank for making decisions on a common or unified literary language." Between 1922 and 1925, the pollsters asked fifty-two questions on phonetics, sixty-nine on morphology, and sixty-eight on lexicon, in 260 towns in both the peninsular and continental Basque Country.

It would not be until decades later, after the bleak years of the Franco regime came to an end in the mid-1970s, that more research on Basque dialectology was published. One of the first significant studies to be published in the contemporary era was the *Euskalerriko Atlas Etnolinguistikoa* (Ethnolinguistic atlas of the Basque Country, 1983), sponsored by the Aranzadi Society (a Basque scientific association) through its Ethnology Department. Despite the fact that some of the pollsters involved in the survey lacked linguistic training, it still offered a wealth of information not only of ethnological interest, but also of linguistic and dialectological importance.

In terms of individual works, Pedro Irizar's well-founded and detailed studies dealing with Basque auxiliary verb morphology from different dialects are worth mentioning (also spelled Yrizar, 1981, 1991a, 1991b, 1992a, 1992b, 1992c, 1997, 1999a, 1999b, 2002a, 2002b, 2002c, and 2008). In recent years, there has been a proliferation of studies on Basque dialects by (among others) Gotzon Aurrekoetxea (1992 [with Videgain], 1995), Xarles Videgain (1991, 1992 [with Aurrekoetxea]), Iñaki Camino (1997, 2003, 2004, 2009), Iñaki Gaminde (1999, 2007), Jose Ignacio Hualde (1997, 2002), Orreaga Ibarra (1995), Rosa Miren Pagola (1991), Pello Salaburu (1984, 2005), Txillardegi (1978, 1984), and Koldo Zuazo (2003, 2006, 2007, 2008, 2010).

Mention should also be made—for its size and scope—of Euskaltzaindia's *Euskal Herri Hizkeren Atlasa* (Atlas of Basque forms of speech) project, a study of local Basque dialects under the academic responsibility of Adolfo Arejita and the technical direction of academics Gotzon Aurrekoetxea and Xarles Videgain. This work began in 1983, following the conclusion of the third Euskaltzaindia forum on dialectology held in Markina (Bizkaia). The atlas covers the fields of phonology, morphology, syntax, and lexicon, and is based on a questionnaire of 2,762 questions and 145 respondents. The first three published volumes of the illustrated atlas concerned lexical matters (Aurrekoetxea 1986).

After more than a century without any significant modification of Bonaparte's original classification of Basque dialects, in 1997, Koldo Zuazo, a professor at the Universidad del País Vasco/Euskal Herriko Unibertsitatea (University of the Basque Country, UPV/EHU), began work on updating and renaming the categories. Among other changes, he groups Lapurdian and Low Navarrese into a single dialect and grants Eastern Navarrese the status of an independent dialect. He also changes the name of the Bizkaian dialect to Western, that of the Gipuzkoan dialect to Central, and that of High Navarrese to Navarrese. Accordingly, his classification is as follows: Western, Central, Navarrese, Navarrese-Lapurdian, Eastern Navarrese, and Zuberoan.

Furthermore, he recognizes several mixed zones that serve as transitions between the adjoining dialects or subdialects; in other words, they are zones in which both dialects (or subdialects) were spoken equally, and in which there has been a gradual shift from one dialect (or subdialect) to a neighboring one. To give a few examples, he considers the area formed by the municipalities of Elgoibar, Mendaro, and Mutriku within the Debabarrena (Lower Deba) region of Gipuzkoa to be a Western and Central dialect mixed zone; and the Irun, Hondarribia, and Lapurdian coast zone to form a mix of the Central, Navarrese, and Navarrese-Lapurdian dialects.

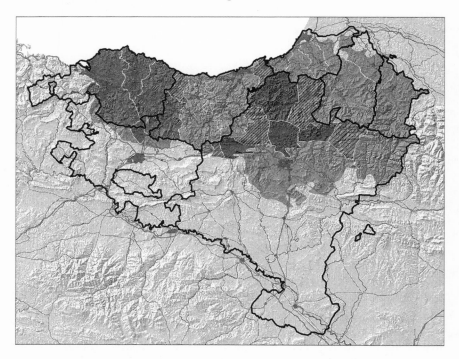

Figure 4.2. Modern map of Basque language dialects, according to Koldo Zuazo

Current Basque Language Dialects

Taking Zuazo's more modern and commonly accepted classification as a reference point, we will take a cursory journey (from west to east) through the different Basque dialects and their most significant features.

Western Dialect

Traditionally called *Bizkaiera* (Bizkaian), Zuazo now terms this *Mendebaleko euskara* (Western Euskara) because the dialect's boundaries do not coincide exactly with those of Bizkaia. Thanks to documents and toponyms from that time, we know that the Western dialect was spoken during the Early Middle Ages throughout Bizkaia and Araba, as well as in La Rioja Alta (the upper part of La Rioja province) and the eastern part of the province of Burgos. Today, however, these boundaries have been pushed back and, apart from in Bizkaia itself, the Bizkaian dialect is spoken in the Debagoiena (Upper Deba) region of Gipuzkoa and in the northern part of the Araba in the municipalities of Aramaio and Legutio (Legutiano). In addition, the variation of Euskara that was spoken in Araba historically also belonged to the Bizkaian dialect.

Zuazo now recognizes two subvarieties within the Western dialect: the eastern subvariety that includes the Euskara spoken in the regions of Uribe-Kosta, Mungialdea (the Mungia area), the Txorierri and the Nervion Valleys, as well as in the municipalities of Zeberio, Arratia, and Orozko; and the western subvariety spoken in the regions of Lea-Artibai and Durangaldea (the Durango area) in Bizkaia, Aramaio in Araba, the Debagoiena region of Gipuzkoa, and the municipalities of Mallabia, Ermua, Eibar, and Soraluze in the Debabarrena region, also in Gipuzkoa. Zuazo points out, moreover, that there are intermediate variations between the two subvarieties in the forms of Euskara spoken in the Busturialdea region (Bizkaia), and the municipalities of Otxandio (Bizkaia) and Legutio (Araba) variants; and, as previously mentioned, between the Western and Central dialects (in Elgoibar, Mendaro, and Mutriku, in Gipuzkoa).

The Western dialect possesses a distinctive personality and has rather differentiated features from the rest of the dialects. As regards its phonology, these distinctive features are: the evolution -a + a > -ea (neska + a > neskea "girl"); the use of the vowel u in alternations (uri/hiri "city," urun/irin "flour," ule/ile "hair," urten/erten/irten "to leave"); sibilant neutralization (s, z > s; tz, ts >tz); palatalization -itz- > -tx- ([h]aritz >aretx "oak," gaitz > gatx "difficult") and -iz- > -x- ([h]aize > axe "wind,", goizean > goxean "in the morning," el[e]iza > elexa "church"; and dissimilation barri "new," txarri "pig" (as opposed to berri, txerri).

In the nominal morphology there is a distinctive suffix: -gaz sing. and -kaz pl. in the sociative case (laguna[ga]z "with a friend" and lagunakaz/ lagunekaz "with friends"), the suffix -iño (erlaziñoa "relation" or "relationship," estaziñoa "station," konfesiñoa "confession") vs. -io (Central: konfesioa), -ione (Eastern: konfesionea); the use of the verbal suffix -tzen in certain expressions (the Eastern: afalten goiaz vs. the Central: afaltzera goaz "we are going to have dinner"); the conservation of ancient ablative forms (kalerik kale "from street to street," etxerik etxe "from house to house"); different forms of demonstratives (Eastern: onek vs. Central: hauek "these (ones)"; Eastern: orrek vs. Central: horiek "those (ones)").

In verbal morphology, there is a distinct use of the stem *eutsi* in the tripersonal auxiliary verb (Eastern: *ekarri deutsat* vs. Central: *ekarri diot* "I have brought to him/her (some object known by the context)"; the stem *egin* in place of *ezan*[9] in potential and imperative subjunctive verb forms, the Eastern: *egin daigun* vs. Central: *egin dezagun* "let's do it," Eastern: *egin neike* vs. Central: *egin nezake* "I could do it"; differentiated verb forms in the Nor-Nori verbs: *jat(a), jak/n, jako, jaku* (with different pronunciation: [y-], [dx-], [x]); transitive bipersonal verb forms in -*o*- (Eastern: egin *dot* vs. Central: *egin det, egin dut* "I have done it").

Regarding lexicon, just as in Zuberoan (the dialect that is the furthest removed from all others in Euskara), the Western dialect has many of its own words and lexical variants. These include: *gura izan* "to want," *berba* "word," *ei* "it is said that," *ederto* "nicely" or "fine," *bariku* "Friday," *ortu* "vegetable garden," *sama* "neck," *oratu* "to seize," *olgeta* "play," *gitxi* "little," *gatzatu* "curds," *pernil* "ham," *okela* "meat," *odoloste* "blood sausage," *jaramon* "attention," *lei* "ice," *madari* "pear," *mihin* "tongue," *lapiko* "cauldron" or "cooking pot," *edur* "snow," *artazi* "scissors," and *lantzean behin* "once in a while."

There are documents containing research on the Bizkaian dialect that date back to the sixteenth century. One early study, *Refranes y sentencias del Bascuence* (Basque proverbs and sayings, 1596) by Esteban Garibai, a historian from Arrasate-Mondragón (Gipuzkoa), is a collection of proverbs, ballads, and poetic songs. In 2004, a late sixteenth-century manuscript written in the Western dialect—considered to be the first purely literary work in the Basque language—by Joan Perez de Lazarraga was discovered. In general, Bizkaian was not used as a literary dialect until the nineteenth century, mainly thanks to the works of Juan Antonio Mogel and Pedro Antonio Añibarro.

As noted, the Western dialect is one with a marked personality, with many distinctive features compared to other dialects, due in part to its geographically marginal character and also in part to external language factors such as what Mitxelena terms "hyper-Bizkaian". Mitxelena coined this term to define a movement of certain writers between the late nineteenth and early twentieth centuries who were Bizkaian dialect purists, meaning that during this time they sought to artificially accentuate the distinctive features of their dialect with respect to the features of all other dialects of Euskara:[10]

For years, perhaps since the end of the past [nineteenth] century, the deliberate effort to confuse Bizkaian with what I call . . . hyper-Bizkaian has

---

9. The asterisk indicates that this verb form, which is an auxiliary and part of the infinitive, is reconstructed from personal verb forms that are used.

10. Juan Mateo Zabala is cited as the forerunner of this movement with his book on grammar *Verbo regular del dialecto vizcaíno* (The regular verb in the Bizkaian dialect), published in 1848.

wrought havoc by simply applying the following rule: something is the Bizkaian language if and only if it appears there and not in all other variations of
the language (from which one continues to assume, however, that Bizkaian is
a dialect); if this always desirable, extreme perfection is not achieved, something is Bizkaian as long as it has less joint participants, or in other words, as
long as it is not common Basque (Mitxelena 1987, 43).

Those writers sought to avoid Bizkaian forms common to other dialects,
on the basis that they were foreign or contaminated by the Gipuzkoan dialect.
Thus, recent, more analogical verb forms seemed more fitting of Bizkaian to
them: for example, the auxiliary verb *dauz* instead of *ditu(z)*, the most common and widely used form in this dialect. Despite not being very widespread
throughout the dialect, distinctive forms were promoted at the expense of
more widely used and traditional forms common to other dialects.

It goes without saying that this type of movement, which delved into
dialectal differences, artificially hindered communication between speakers
of the different dialects of Euskara. In the case of Bizkaian, the result was that
people began to conceive this as a language (thereby imagining two Basque
languages: Bizkaian and the rest) rather than as dialect, part of many dialects
with different origins (Zuazo 2010, 83-87).

Central Dialect

Traditionally called *Gipuzkera* (Gipuzkoan), Zuazo now terms it *Erdialdeko
euskara* (Central Euskara), due to its central geographical location in the
Basque Country and because the dialect's boundaries do not exactly match
those of Gipuzkoa: as already stated regarding the Western dialect, Bizkaian
was spoken in the western area of Gipuzkoa (in the Debagoiena region and
in the municipalities of Soraluze and Eibar in the Debabarrena region); furthermore, the dialects in the easternmost area of Gipuzkoa (in the municipalities of Irun and Hondarribia) are not considered purely central; elsewhere,
the Gipuzkoan or Central variation is spoken in part of the Sakana Valley in
Navarre. Zuazo distinguishes four subvarieties within the Central dialect: the
Beterri subvariety (in central and northeastern areas of Gipuzkoa); that of the
Goierri (in the southeastern part of Gipuzkoa); the Urola subvariety (in the
northwestern part of Gipuzkoa); and the Gipuzkoan of Navarre (in the north-
western part of Navarre).

The Central dialect has been very important in the development of
the Basque language. Since it is the variety used in the central part of the
Basque-speaking territory, it is the most easily understood dialect by the
greatest number of Basque-speakers; furthermore, it has a rich literary tradition dating from the eighteenth century. All of this, combined with the fact
that the Central dialect has enjoyed great prestige among Basques since then,

has resulted in it becoming, along with some features of the Lapurdian and Navarrese dialects, the foundation of Unified or Standard Basque (Euskara Batua, see chapter 5).

The Central dialect does not have many distinctive features that make it particularly different from the rest. Being at the center of the Basque Country, as noted, many of its linguistic innovations have been extended to the dialects around it. In other words, it has not preserved the same number of archaisms that are common to Euskara's more marginal dialects.

In phonology, a key feature is the epenthetic consonant in speech from the dialect's northern area (*buruba* "head," *ogidda/ogidxa/ogija/ogixa* "bread"); double vowel simplification (*zaharra > zarra*, "old"); frequent palatalization of certain consonants (*aditu > a(d)ittu* "expert," *egina > e(g)iña* "done," *ilargi > illargi*, "moon"); lack of aspiration (the voiceless *h*); and the velar pronunciation *j*- ([x]), mainly characteristic of this dialect (*jan* "to eat," *jarri* "to put," *jakin* "to know").

The absolutive and ergative plural are not distinguished from one another in morphology (it is marked by -*ak* in both cases: *mutilak etorri dira* "the boys have come"/*mutilak ekarri du(t)e* "the boys have brought it"; the bipersonal transitive verb forms in -*e*- (Central: *egin det* vs. Western: *egin dot*, Navarrese: *egin dut* "I have done it"); the use of the particle *al* in questions (*egingo al dezu?* "Will you do it?"); the evolution in certain verb forms -*ai*- > -*a*- (*etorri zait > zat* "it/he/she has come to me," *etorri zaizu > za(t)zu* "it/he/she has come to you"); and another of the dialect's characteristics is the infix -*txi*- for some allocutive verb forms (*eman nion > nitxon* "I gave him/her (some object known by the context)"; *nau > natxiok* "me" (nor-nork form); *nago > natxiok* "I am"; *nabil > natxabillek* "I'm walking").

Regarding the lexicon, the following is a sample of some terms used in this dialect:[11] *arkakuso* "flea" (*kukuso* "flea"), *babarrun* (*indaba* "bean"), *bailara* (*ibarra* "valley"), *mami* (*gatzatu, gaztanbera* "curds"), *triku* (*kirikino* "hedgehog"), *hots egin* (*deitu* "to call"), *korrika* (*lasterka* "running"), *aitona* (vs. *aitita* "grandfather"), *amona* (vs. *amama, amatxi* "grandmother"), *behatz* (*hatz* "finger"), *esnatu* (*iratzarri* "to wake up"), *faborez* (*mesedez* "please"), *mingain* (*mihi* "tongue"), and *urruti* (*urrun* "far").

Navarrese Dialect

Nafarra (Navarrese), the name that Zuazo gave this variant, is spoken in the northern part of Navarre. It was traditionally called *Goi-nafarrera* (the High Navarrese dialect). It is a dialect that has been in a continuous decline in the south during the last few centuries, but is still currently spoken in the regions

---

11. That is not to say that they are necessarily exclusive of it.

of Bortziriak (Cinco Villas, the Five Towns), Malerreka (Alto Bidasoa, the High Bidasoa), and the Sakana Valley, and in the municipalities of Oronoz-Mugairi, Bertizarana (Bértiz-Arana), Goizueta, Beintza-Labaien (Beinza-Labayen), Saldias, Ultzama (Ulzama), Lantz (Lanz), Anue, Atetz (Atez), Odieta, Esteribar, Erroibar (the Erro Valley), and Auritz (Burguete).

Zuazo subdivides the Navarrese dialect into the following: the Western subdivision (the Sakana Valley, Bortziriak, Malerreka, and Bertizarana); the Central subdivision (Ultzama, Lantz, Atetz, Anue, and Odieta); and the Eastern subdivision (Esteribar and Erroibar). Along with these subvarieties, three mixed varieties are recognized: that of the Burunda Valley (a mix of the Western, Central, and Navarrese dialects), the Baztan Valley (a mix of the Navarrese and Navarrese-Lapurdian dialects), and the Aezkoa Valley (a mix of the Navarrese, Navarrese-Lapurdian, and Eastern Navarrese). Iruñea-Pamplona lies at the heart of the Navarrese dialect because it is the geographical point from which most influence has historically been exerted on the different areas in which Navarrese is spoken.

Today, evidence suggests that the Navarrese subdialects in the Pyrenean area, neighbors of the Navarrese-Lapurdian dialect, share less and less traits with those dialects. Common characteristics in the different forms of speech within these the two dialects are diminishing from one side of the political or state border to the other. This is the case with the Baztan Valley variant for example, which increasingly shares more traits with the Navarrese dialect and less with Navarrese-Lapurdian dialect.

One of the most distinctive features of the Navarrese dialect is the marked accent, which goes on the penultimate syllable; and related to the marked accent, there is also a phenomenon characteristic of the Navarrese dialect: the apheresis (*ekarri* > *karri* "to bring," *eman* > *man* "to give," *ezagutu* > *zautu* "to know") and syncope (*abere* > *abre* "animal," *dutelakoz* > *dutelkoz* "because they have"). Mention should be made of the *-on* ending in some loan words from Spanish (*frontona* from *frontón* "pelota court," *abiona* from *avión* "plane," *kamiona* from *camión* "truck" vs. *frontoia, abioia, kamioia* in the rest of the dialects); the pluralizer of tripersonal verb forms was usually *-it-* (*ditio* vs. Central: *dizkio, ditit* vs. Central: *dizkit*); and the stem *-ki-* in the bipersonal intransitive verb forms (*zakidan* vs. Central: *zitzaidan*).

Regarding lexicon, some of the dialect's characteristic words are (Central dialect variants in parentheses unless otherwise stated): *banabar* (*indaba* in the Western dialect, "bean"), *beratz* (*bigun* "soft"), *goatze* (*ohe* "bed"), *listua* (*tua* "saliva"), *ostots* (*trumoi* "thunder"), *sor* (*gor* "deaf"), *ugalde* (*ibai* "river"), *garagarzaro* (*ekain* "June"), and *garil* (*uztail* "July").

Navarrese-Lapurdian Dialect

In those that had traditionally been considered two to three dialects (Lapurdian and Low Navarrese, with the latter divided into Western and Eastern by Bonaparte), Zuazo really does not see sufficient reason to make such a distinction and so he thinks of them as only one dialect, which he terms Navarrese-Lapurdian (*nafar-lapurtarra*).

Three subvarieties are currently acknowledged within the Navarrese-Lapurdian dialect: the Western subvariety, in the regions of Ahetze, Senpere (Saint-Pée-sur-Nivelle), Ainhoa, and Sara (Sare) in Lapurdi, and the Navarrese districts of Zugarramurdi and Urdazubi (Urdax); the Central subvariety, in eastern Lapurdi and in Lower Navarre, the cantons of Baigorri (Saint-Étienne-de-Baïgorry) and Lekuine (Bonloc); and the Eastern subvariety, in Arberoa (Arberoue), Oztibarre (Ostabarret), and Garazi in Lower Navarre, and Luzaide (Valcarlos) in Navarre. The language spoken in the Lapurdian coastal zone (*kostatarra*) is recognized as a mix between Navarrese-Lapurdian, Central, and Navarrese. Similarly, the form of speech in Amikuze (Pays de Mixe), in northern Lower Navarre and bordering Zuberoa, bridges the Navarrese-Lapurdian and Zuberoan dialects.

In the sixteenth century, Joannes Leizarraga (1571; 1979) used a type of lingua franca for his New Testament translation into Euskara so that all of his readers could understand it. He took the Lapurdian dialect's morphology as the basis and combined it with Low-Navarrese and Zuberoan elements. However, that venture did not find much support or following. From the seventeenth century on, writers influenced by the authors like Pedro de Axular and Joannes Etxeberri de Ziburu (see under Etcheverry 1712; 1976) found a way to develop Basque literature using the speech of the Lapurdi coast. Thus, classic Lapurdian was streamlined and became a model for writers on both sides of the border.

In the wake of a decline in the economy of Lapurdi after the French Revolution, many young people left the province and this in turn caused the Navarrese-Lapurdian dialect to lose specific importance within the Basque language as a whole. And in the mid twentieth century, Pierre Lafitte published his *Gammaire Basque (navarro-labourdin littéraire)* (Basque grammar (Literary Navarrese-Lapurdian) 1944; 1979), offering a grammar of the dialect.

As in the case of the Central dialect, the Navarrese-Lapurdian dialect does not have many distinctive features: one could cite the lack of palatalization of some consonants (*in, il,* and *it* are pronounced without palatalization); the appearance of the palatal consonant *x-* (similar to the initial consonant of "she" in English) at the start of a word as opposed to what is often *tx-* (as in the initial consonant of "chair" in English) in the Central dialect (*in* for example *xingar* "bacon," *xapela* "beret," *ximista* "lightning," *xirula* "flute," *xoko* "corner," and *xori* "bird"); the endings *-oin* (for example, *arrazoin* "reason," *kartoin* "cardboard," *meloin* "melon," *patroin* "pattern" or "skipper") as opposed to *-oi* in the Cntral dialect, and, in some loanwords from French, *-aia* (*bisaia* from *visage* "countenance" or "face," *domaia* from *dommage* "shame" or "pity," *salbaia* from *sauvage* "wild," and so on); the use of the pronouns *nehor, nehori,* and *nehun* "someone/anyone" (Central: *inor, inori,* and *inon*); and the verbal allocutive construction called zuketa and xuketa (neuter, *nik ekarri dut* "I have brought it"; the allocutive zuketa, *nik ekarri dizut* "I have brought it"; the familiar and intimate allocutive xuketa mostly used among and to address women, *nik ekarri dixut* "I have brought it"; and the familiar, intimate common allocutive, *nik ekarri diat/dinat* "I have brought it (male/female addressee)").

As regards the lexicon, some terms used in this dialect include (Central dialect variants in parenthesis): *auzapez* (*alkate* "mayor"), *fitsik ez* (*ezer ez* "nothing"), *gako* (*giltza* "key"), *guri* (*bigun* "soft"), *sehi* (*zerbitzari* "server"), and *xingar* (*urdai* "bacon").

Zuberoan Dialect

This dialect is the most easterly variant of Euskara. It is spoken in almost all of Zuberoa and in the municipality of Eskiula (Esquiule), which belongs administratively to the neighboring province of Bearn. Native speakers call it *xiberotarra* or *Xiberoko eüskara*.

According to Zuazo, the dialect is divided into two subdialects: the subvariety from Pettarra (Lower Zuberoa or Barhoue or Basse Soule), to the north; and that of Basaburua (Upper Soule or Soule Subiran or Haute-Soule), to the south. The Euskara of Amikuze (in the north-western zone of the Zuberoan dialect) is thought to be a transitional variation between the Zuberoan and Navarrese-Lapurdian dialects.

Given its location in the north-eastern part of the Basque Country, it shows Occitan influences (above all in phonology and lexicon). To give just one example, this most characteristic feature of the Zuberoan dialect, the phoneme /ü/, originates from Occitan. On the other hand, due to its geographical and administrative remoteness (administratively, Zuberoa is first connected to Bearn rather than Lower Navarre and Lapurdi), it is, along with the Western dialect, the most linguistically removed dialect from the Basque language's central area and from Euskara Batua, in phonology as well as in morphology and lexicon. In turn, it is the dialect closest to Roncalese, which belongs to the Eastern Navarrese dialect. Indeed, Bonaparte himself considered it to be a single dialect.

With regard to the Zuberoan dialect's distinctive features, aside from the aforementioned phoneme /ü/, the following are worth noting: the evolution *au > ai: gaiza* (*gauza* "thing"), *gai* (*gau* "night"); *u > ü; o > u: uhuñ* (*ohoi* "thief"), *hun* (*on* "good"), *nur* (*nor* "who"), *nuiz* (*noiz* "when"); *i - ü > ü - ü: düzü, nündüzün, ükhüzi* (*ikuzi* "to wash/clean"), *üthüri* (*iturri* "source"); the maintenance of the nasal vowels: *āhāl, āmā, āhāri, mīhī*; the preservation of voiced sibilant consonants as well; a stronger aspiration than that of Navarrese-Lapurdian (*bethi, aiphátü, ikhúsi, belhar, lanhú*); and voiceless occlusives imposed in this context: *n, l + p, t: -entako, sükhalte* (*sukalde* "kitchen"), *etxalte* (*etxalde* "farm"), *igante* (*igande* "Sunday"). It also has a strongly marked stress (usually on the penultimate syllable: *bezaláko*).

The following features stand out in morphology (nominal and verbal): the extremely common use of the prefix *arra-: arramaiatz* (*ekaina* "June"), *arraseme/arralhaba* ("grandson/granddaughter," *biloba* "grandchild"); the feminine prefix *-sa: alhargüntsa* (*andre alarguna* "widow"); the suffix *-er* for the dative plural; the variable *-kilan* for the sociative suffix; the suffixes *-ra/-rat* for proper nouns and *-ala* or *-alat* for common nouns (*Altzükürat* "to Altzükü"/*herrialat* "to the village"); the verbal allocutive construction called *zuka* or *zuketa*; and the use of the verb stem **eradun* in tripersonal structures, which has resulted in *ei: deit* (*dit*), *deitade* (*didate*), *deizüt* (*dizut*). Finally, some examples of the Zuberoan lexicon include: *agitü* ("to happen"), *borthü* ("mountain pass"), *ekhi* ("sun"), *elki* ("to go out"), *hunki* ("good" or "well"), *lili* ("flower"), *manex* (Lapurdian/Lower Navarrese), *ürhentü* ("to finish"), and *üsü* ("often").

Incidentally, the word *manex* is thought to be derogatory when used to refer to neighbors that do not speak Zuberoan. The dialectal rivalry between Zuberoans and Navarrese-Lapurdians is well known. In his eighteenth-century work *Corografía de Guipúzcoa*, Larramendi denounces the following (1756; 1969, 314): "The Zuberoan dialect, especially in the spoken sense, is very masculine and strong; and that is why the Lapurdians accuse it of being rough; they retaliate by describing Lapurdian as effeminate and fussy, and there are always some dialects whispering about the others with little discretion." Even today, it is not unusual to hear derogatory comments among speakers of either dialect.

Eastern Navarrese Dialect

This is the Euskara spoken in the Zaraitzu-Salazar and Erronkari-Roncal Valleys in north-eastern Navarre, although in the latter case, no native speaker of the dialect exists today. They are quite distinct from the rest of the Basque dialects.

Bonaparte was unclear about the classification of this dialect: in his first classification he linked it to the Zuberoan dialect, but gradually changed his opinion and finally put it in with the Eastern Low Navarrese dialect. After seeing the many features that they share, Zuazo encompasses the two variations into the Eastern Navarrese dialect, while still recognizing that they share many characteristics with Zuberoan and Navarrese.

With regard to the distinctive phonological features of Eastern Navarrese, one should mention the Roncalese endings -d/-r in first person verb forms (vs. Central: -t): dur ('dut'), dakid ('dakid'); and the Roncalese evolution i > x (anaia > anaxe "brother," leiho > lexo "window," leizar > lexar "ashtree," oihal > oxal "cloth"; in morphology, the suffix -en stands out for its use in all types of verbs in the future tenses (itzuliren "will return", hasiren "will begin," and so on), the Salazarese innovation -a + a > -ara (uskara + a > uskarara), the Roncalese ending -tan vs. Central: -t(z)en (xan → xatan in Roncalese, jan → jaten in the Central dialect "to eat" → "eating," manatu → manatan, "to order" → "ordering" in Roncalese).

As far as the lexicon is concerned, we should highlight the following words (compared with their most frequently used equivalents in other dialects): abendu (azaro "November"), azken abendu (abendu "December"), añai (zekale "rye"), besatxurro (ukondo "elbow"), bizar (kokots "chin"), eltxano (eltze "pot"), emaro (emeki, poliki "slowly"), kuxela (lehengusu "male cousin"), and ler (pinu "pine"). There are also different terms for the same concepts in both areas: aitaborze and amaborze (aitona and amona "grandfather" and "grandmother"), bellitu (iratzarri "to wake up"), kalles ("Roncalese") are from the Zaraitzu-Salazar Valley; and amaño (hurbil "close"), antxume (oinutsik "barefoot"), bordaltu (ezkondu "to marry"), eguatxa (ibaia "river"), elerran (mintzatu "to speak"), erkin (irten "to go out"), lotu (itzali "to put out"), and ñotto (txiki "small") are from the Erronkari-Roncal Valley.

The When and Why of Dialectal Division

As noted previously, in the first written mention made of Basque dialects, the seventeenth-century Zuberoan historian Arnaut Oihenart linked the distribution of these dialects to the distribution of the ancient tribes that inhabited the Basque Country. He differentiated between four dialects: that of the Aquitanians, spoken in Iparralde; that of the Vascones, spoken in Navarre; that of the Varduli in Gipuzkoa and Araba; and that of the Caristii in Bizkaia.

In addition to that possibly ancient relationship between tribal distribution and that of the dialects, in the twentieth century the theory was advanced of a possible link between the distribution of ecclesiastical dioceses and that of the dialects (Caro Baroja 1943). Some scholars upheld that the boundaries of the ecclesiastical dioceses were related to the boundaries of the ancient

tribes, and that the modern dialects were a reflection of that distribution. This
led to the idea that the Basque dialects were indeed ancient.

Some present-day dialectologists, however, are skeptical about the relationship between the tribes, the dioceses, and the dialects. Although some
of the boundaries of the dioceses do coincide with those of the dialects—for
example, in the neighboring area between the Western and the Central dialects in the Debabarrena region—in other more eastern zones of the Basque
language there are no connections at all. According to Zuazo in his study on
the origin of Basque dialects (2007):

> In Iparralde . . . we accept that there are at least two dialects: Zuberoan and
> Navarrese-Lapurdian. Well, the provinces in Iparralde are divided into three
> dioceses and it would appear that they were occupied by one single tribe.
> Nor does the "tribes-dioceses-dialects" relationship fit Gipuzkoa or Navarre
> either. Ecclesiastically, the greater part of those two provinces was framed in
> a single diocese, that of Iruña [Pamplona]. However, they were populated
> by two different tribes, the Vascones and the Varduli, and from the linguis-
> tic perspective, they spoke two principal dialects, and we should not for-
> get the peculiar speech from the Navarrese valleys of Zaraitzu-Salazar and
> Erronkari-Roncal.

He concludes his argument against these possible connections in this way: "It
should also not be forgotten that the ecclesiastical dioceses caused the disappearance of the Basque tribes later on, and because of that, it would be pure
chance if those same boundaries were replicated after several centuries had
passed" (2007).

As regards the ages of the dialects, which is also related to their origin
and distribution, Mitxelena (1987, 50) defends the thesis that they cannot be
very old, mainly for two reasons: On the one hand, because of the large number of characteristics they all share (which would be rather improbable if they
were so ancient); and on the other, because of the high number of innovations common to all the dialects, a fact that would be difficult to explain if the
dialectal division was so ancient. To give an example, the abundant number
of words that came from Latin followed a similar evolution in all the dialects.
Based on these reasons, among others, Mitxelena argues that Basque dialectal
fragmentation probably occurred after the eleventh century.

Zuazo (2007) believes that a third argument should be added to Mitxelena's thesis: "The only truly divergent dialects are the lateral ones, in other
words, the Zuberoan, Roncalese, Salazarese, and the Western [dialects]. The
differences are slight and not very important in the central dialects, which
would not be the case if it were a question of the dialects in antiquity." Regarding when and why the dialects split apart, Zuazo (2007) says: "the physiog-
nomy of the current dialects was already visible in the sixteenth century,

at the time when the first written documents appeared. They were formed throughout the Middle Ages, probably alongside how we know the Basque provinces took shape." He goes on to say:

The reordering of the Basque provinces that occurred between the eleventh and twelfth centuries could have affected the subsequent language evolution and it was perhaps then when the first important step was taken in the process of Euskara's dialectalization . . . Another important step was taken, in all probability, between the second half of the eighteenth century and the first half of the twentieth century. The Gipuzkoan literary dialect emerged during the mid-eighteenth century, Bizkaian and Zuberoan took shape in the nineteenth century, and Navarrese-Lapurdian in the twentieth century, which led to a separation between the different dialects. The role of Bonaparte and his collaborators in the nineteenth century was also decisive. His zeal for clearly and distinctly demarcating the borders of dialects, subdialects, and even those dialects that he considered peculiar resulted in these borders deepening even more.

It should be noted that since Euskara Batua was created in 1968, we have been witnessing a convergence of the Basque dialects (and also a gradual loss of the dialects' characteristic features). At the same time, however, there has been a greater distancing between the Euskara of Iparralde and Hegoalde, due to the influence of the two official languages (French and Spanish) that are spoken on each side of the administrative border. Zuazo (2007) adds the following: "the divergent tendency is still alive in Bizkaia as well, mainly favored by those groups that wish to promote a Bizkaian standard in that province."

Studies in Recent Years

Besides the general studies and dialectological atlases mentioned above, numerous monographs have been published on local forms of speech in recent years; the list of local forms of speech that have been studied is long (above all in the peninsular Basque Country), and include studies of Euskara in (among others): the Aezkoa Valley, Antzuola, Aramaio, Areso-Leitza, Azkoitia, the Baztan Valley, Beasain, Bergara, Berriz, Eibar, Elgoibar, Ermua, Goizueta-Aramaio, Hondarribia-Irun, Imoz, Lasarte-Oria, Lezo, Mallabia, Arrasate-Mondragón, Oiartzun, Ordizia, Orio, Otxandio, the Sakana Valley, Ultzama, Urdazubi-Zugarramurdi, Zaldibia, Zarautz, Zestoa, Zumaia, and so on. In addition, the tireless dialectologist Iñaki Gaminde has studied local forms of speech in various (and mainly Bizkaian) municipalities: Abadiño, Bakio, Bermeo, Derio, Gatika, Leioa, Lezama, Mungia, Meñaka, Urduliz, Zaldibar, Zamudio, and so on.

At present, while such monographs on local types of speech are still being published, they are gradually being replaced by other types of studies.

On the one hand, these include dialectological studies that cover wider areas than those of the local dialects alone, once many of these dialects have already been characterized; for example, see the work of Irene Hurtado (2001), Iñaki Camino (2003), Zuazo (2006), Edu Zelaieta (2008), and Amaia Apalauza (2010). On the other, there are studies that incorporate Internet-based new technologies, and have also been helped by the creation of an oral dialectal corpus, for example the EUDIA (Euskara Dialektalaren Ahozko Corpusa, Corpus of Oral Dialectal Basque) and AHOTSAK (Euskal Herriko hizkerak eta ahozko ondarea, Basque Country Dialects and Oral Heritage).[12] Other recent studies include research on Basque dialects from a more sociolinguistic perspective, which tend to agree that the distinct characteristics of the local forms of speech and dialects are increasingly fading among the younger speakers. Among others, one might note the work of the EUDIA research group,[13] led by Gotzon Aurrekoetxea, one of whose objectives has been to study linguistic variation according to extralinguistic factors such as the age and origin of the speakers.

I do not wish to conclude this modest work without mentioning the tremendous efforts of UPV/EHU professor Iñaki Camino in his latest work (2009), an unsurpassable theoretical, methodological, and historical compendium of dialectology in general and of Basque dialectology in particular. It undoubtedly signifies a great step forward in the study of Basque dialectology.

---

12. See their respective websites in the bibliography.

13. One such project is, for example, *Euskararen soziolinguistiko-dialektologikoa* (Sociolinguistic-dialectologic atlas of the Basque language). See EUDIA in the bibliography.

5

The Search for a Common Code

PELLO SALABURU and XABIER ALBERDI,
the University of the Basque Country (UPV/EHU)

The Basque language, unlike other neighboring languages, lacked a common code and a shared writing system until very recently. Writers did not have a clear model or a well-defined writing standard to abide by. In fact, although there had been quite a few previous attempts to develop a minimum standard, above all throughout the twentieth century, the truth was that the first rules accepted on an ongoing basis by the group of authors that wrote in Euskara[1] did not appear until the late 1960s An important fact to remember is that what is known as "Basque literature" (actually theterm refers to any book published in Basque) is not something that has been around for very long, especially compared to other languages. Indeed, apart from a few inscriptions that appeared on funerary steles, in old place name references, in the glosses of San Millán,[2] in route boundary details, in pilgrimage guides, or in fragments of romances, the undeniable fact was that the first book written in the Basque language did not appear until 1454, the year in which Bernat Etxepare[3] published *Linguae Vasconum Primitiae* in Bordeaux. Until then testimonies of the Basque language were rather scarce. One should make mention of the "Iruña-Veleia" fiasco here: in 2006, several specialists

---

1. We will interchangeably use, as is common, both "Euskara" and "Basque language", or simply "Basque" to refer to the language.

2. These were hand-written annotations in the margins or between the lines of the Latin Codex *Aemilianensis 60*, dating from the end of the tenth or beginning of the eleventh century, and preserved in the Monastery of San Millan de la Cogolla in the autonomous community of La Rioja, Spain. During this time, the region formed part of the Kingdom of Pamplona. There were annotations in Latin, in the Riojan variant of Navarro-Aragonese (considered to be the first words written in Spanish), and also five words in Basque.

3. As noted, Bernart Etxepare may appear cited as, depending on the field, *Bernardum Dechepare, Bernard Detchepare, Bernart Etxepare*, or *Beñat Etxepare*. These variations in writing are directly related to the subject addressed in this article.

announced something of a miracle. They had found hundreds of Basque graffiti inscriptions dating from the third century, discovered in that Roman city near what is now Vitoria-Gasteiz, the capital of the Autonomous Community of the Basque Country (Euskadi). In the end, though, everything was reduced in practice to a crude hoax and parts of an otherwise very important Roman site were destroyed.

This delay in providing an elemental instrument to standardize the use of a language such as Basque raised, in turn, other basic problems: a language could hardly survive in the world today if it lacked a shared common writing code; its speakers could hardly write what they would like to if it lacked clear references; it was much more complicated to establish these references if, at the same time, they were speakers of a minority language, surrounded by two thriving and strong languages, like Spanish and French. In fact, the situation was rather complicated: in the most isolated rural areas of the Basque Country, people had historically been monolingual; it was in the cities where Spanish, French, and Gascon, above all in government circles, had a clear and almost exclusive presence, although many people were Basque-speakers. Indeed, bilingualism (with Latin, Spanish, French, or other languages, depending on the areas and centuries) had always been present in cities and towns of some importance in the Basque Country, as specialists like Koldo Mitxelena have observed on repeated occasions.[4]

Those who wished to write in Euskara had, in turn, another added problem: every one of them, depending on their background and their place of residence, had been educated in different languages. The Basque Country extends to both sides of the Pyrenees, from the extreme northeast of the Cantabrian strip between France and Spain. Those who lived in the Iberian Peninsula would have been educated in Spanish and those who lived on the continental side would have done so in French. This would not have been anything unusual if not for the fact that the written French and Spanish codes did not follow the same pattern. In fact, given that the languages' sounds or phonemes did not coincide, both languages had developed a form of writing that did not "fit" between them. To provide a clear example: few words have been so used, on both sides of the border, as *etxe* ("house"), written in the currently used spelling of Euskara. However, the transcription of the consonant "tx" that appears in the middle of the word (similar to the first consonant of the word "chair" in English) posed serious problems because it is a sound that does not have a French equivalent and is written in Spanish as "ch." Thus, a person that lived in the Spanish area, and was familiar with Spanish writing,

---

4. Koldo Mitxelena also appears cited in literature as Luis Michelena, depending on whether the Basque or Spanish spelling is used. He was the greatest specialist in Basque that our language has known. In English translation see, for example, Mitxelena (2008).

would not have any doubt when writing the Basque word, lacking a specific reference code for Euskara. He or she would write, based on the Spanish code, *eche*, and that is how many writers transcribed the word. On the other hand, anyone who was accustomed to French orthography was not be able to use this grapheme because, in this case, the consonant sounded like the consonant in the word "she," rather than that of "chair." It was, therefore, a spelling that gave rise to very different readings. Thus, in order to avoid a French-like reading the writer that lived in France chose to write *etche*. This was how a basic, commonly used word could appear transcribed in two different ways: *eche* in Spain and *etche* in France. This orthographic problem that we have pointed out was only one of the most basic and elemental problems that affected the search for that common writing code so necessary for a language to thrive, or to simply not disappear.

Problems on Different Levels

We began our exposition with a simple and basic example related to orthography.[5] However, the absence of unification posed problems on many other levels: at least in orthography, morphology, lexicon, and toponomastics (the transcription of the proper names of people and places, within the Basque Country as well as outside). There were fewer problems in syntax, as we will see.

Orthography

We will set aside the problems related to toponymy and lexicon for the time being, in the former case because it is not a central issue of any language at all and, on too many occasions, an easy appeal to inventiveness and imagination. That said, it is true that the transcription of foreign names (used in translations of the Bible above all else) gave rise to multiple versions: in the written tradition of Euskara there were close to a dozen variations of the word "Egypt," including *Ejiptu, Ejipto, Egipto, Ijito, Aijito, Aigito,* and *Egypto*. In the latter case, lexicon problems will be addressed more in their orthographic aspect, as we will see immediately. Nor will we refer, except perhaps briefly, to terminology or that specialized lexicon in distinct fields of knowledge (science, technology, and so on).

Writers were faced with clearly orthographic problems like that of the aforementioned case of *etxe* (written like *etche/eche/etxe*): for example, *ethorri/etorri* "to come," *au/hau* "this, that," *ezne/esne* "milk," *esplikazio/explikazio* "explanation," *ruleta/erruleta* "roulette," *barri/berri* "new," and many others that affected hundreds or thousands of terms. Other morphological problems

---

5. Many of the issues addressed in this chapter appeared in Mitxelena (2008).

existed that affected the morphology of the auxiliary verb, for example, as will be seen. And there were many others straddling the line between the two, with limits that were not easy to define.

In truth, there was, symptomatically, a lack of consensus among Basques, even when it came to transcribing the name of the language itself. In the first written testimony that referred to the Basque language, which appeared in the aforementioned book by Etxepare, it was called *Heuskara*. But other forms abounded among the written testimonies in publications throughout history: *euskara, euskera, eskuara, eskara, euskala, eskuera, eskara, eskera, eskoara, euskiera, uskara, oskara, uskera, uskaa, uska,* and even *uxka,* from testimonies that appeared in practically all the local dialects and forms of speech possible.

To take another example of the problems faced by writers in the Basque language, as soon as a loanword from a neighboring language was adopted, problems immediately arose if the word contained any element that clashed in some way with the more "neutral" syllabic and consonantal structure of Basque. So, a foreign word such as *teléfono* ("telephone") did not pose any problem when transcribing it as *telefono* in Basque orthography.[6] But the matter becomes complicated if we speak of terms whose structures move even further away from that neutrality. Take the Spanish term *pañuelo* ("handkerchief" or "headscarf"), for example. With a palatal consonant "ñ" and a diphthong ("ue") in the middle of the word that was not common in Euskara, different authors opted for distinct paths when transcribing this word in Basque: *pañuelo, pañolo, pañelo, painuelu, pañelu,* and even *paiñolo*. In short, this presented a twofold dilemma that went beyond orthography: it was not a matter of choosing between one letter or another (as in *etxe*), but in making a choice about the proper word structure.

Simple orthography posed problems that did not have an easy solution: a commonly used word such as *berri* ("new") was written as *berri* in the central and eastern dialects, but as *barri* in western speech and dialects. In this case, opting for one form or the other created important problems because it was a term widely used by writers and very common in speech. Choosing between *berri* or *barri* meant encountering opposition groups and marking a distance between the spoken and written language, at least in certain zones.

---

6. Of course defenders of "purism" in the language would always try to find or invent some equivalent in Basque rather than use the original loanword. This is precisely what happened with this word, for which *urrutizkina* (literally meaning "the corner far away") was proposed, thus removing it from the much more universal and commonly used term in several languages: *telefono.* In the end, the second term prevailed, as it was more natural. In any case, even the choice of *telefono* (without the written accent mark) as the Basque form was possible only after rejecting *telephono,* the minority-suggested form.

Nominal and Verbal Morphology

The problems grew, however, when the lines of orthography were crossed. Because Euskara is an agglutinative language, with postpositions instead of prepositions (see chapter 3), the article and the postpositions that are added onto the end of a noun or adjective give rise to the appearance of phonological rules that are not identical in all the dialectical variations. The following very simple examples illustrate this: The definite singular article in Basque is *-a*, which is added onto the end of a noun. Thus, the nouns *etxe, kale* "street," *oilo* "hen," and *mendi* "mountain," with the added article formed the noun phrase *etxea, kalea, oiloa* and *mendia,* respectively. But the problem is that those nominal noun phrases are not all pronounced in the same way. Instead, there are diverse variations such as (the stress is marked in order to better observe the differences) *etxéa/etxía/etxíe/étxia, kaléa/kalía/kalíe, oilóa/ollóa/ollúa/óllua* (we have avoided the explanation of how the consonant is written), and *mendía/mendíe/méndie/mendíxa/mendíxe.*

When the article is added to a nominal whose last letter is "a," as in *alaba* ("daughter"), the result of putting the two vowels together is, in most dialects, to leave a single "a", observing the simple phonological rule: a + a > a. Therefore, this would result in *alaba,* without knowing, if not for the context, whether the article is included or not. However, in western dialects the prevailing phonological rule is very different: a + a > ea, with the resultant *alabea,* and with its corresponding variants: *alabia, alabie,* and *alabi.* In short, there are clearly four or more different forms of saying "daughter." We have chosen basic examples, but they give an idea of the complexity that was involved in formulating the bases of a standard model for Basque that would reflect the writing of all the dialects. Nevertheless, this model was very necessary.

In more complex noun phrases, in which postpositions are agglutinated to the nominal noun phrase, not only do these types of differences reappear more strongly, so do still greater ones. For example, the preposition "with" in English is the equivalent of the Basque postposition "-ekin," which lacks autonomy as a separate word. In this way, the phrase "(I live) with the family" is expressed in Basque as *familiarekin (bizi naiz),* in which the noun (*family*) can be distinguished as well as the postposition (*-ekin*), joined together by the consonant "r," a crutch commonly used by Euskara in these contexts. And in which the internal "a" actually reflects the previously mentioned double "a" (incorporating the article): *familia + a + rekin.* However, this postposition is different in more western forms of speech: in these forms, the same concept is not expressed as *familiarekin* but instead as *familiagaz;* in the same way that *alabarekin* "with the daughter" from other dialects is *alabeagaz* in the prevailing version of these forms.

Verbal morphology presents even greater differences, and some of the characteristics of auxiliary verb morphology are explained in chapter 3. Because the auxiliary must agree with three different arguments (the absolutive, ergative, and dative) there are hundreds of different Basque verb forms.[7] If we include the differences in register, the number of forms are even greater: choosing the *hi* form in Basque, the informal form of "you (singular)" and more or less equivalent to the Spanish and French *tu*, instead of the more "educated" *zu* form (that nowadays has become much more common than the former to the extent of virtually eliminating the use of *hi* among many speakers) entails the use of hundreds[8] of its own forms that differ from the neutral register. The problem was that these verb forms differfrom one dialect to the next. So the auxiliary verb corresponding to the phrase "I have given you apples" can also have different variations, exclusively limiting one to the verb: *sagarrak eman dizkizut / derauzkizut / deutsudaz* (apples - to give - aux). As we can see, there were three different forms of the auxiliary verb that all meant the same but differ according to local forms of speech: *dizkizut, derauzkizut*, and *deutsudaz*. There were even more forms, although here we just mention three of the most emblematic.[9]

Luis Lucien Bonaparte[10] made five trips to the Basque Country between 1856 and 1869. As a result he published numerous versions of biblical texts that were translated into dialects and variations of Euskara through his London printing press. In those well-cared-for editions,[11] and in the numerous manuscripts that he left behind after his death, one can clearly see the nature of the differences that we have been speaking about. The final result renders such a large linguistic distance between the speakers that they have difficulties understanding each other, unless they take the trouble to study the language a bit and are able to read and write in Euskara. We conclude this section, therefore, with a final example that is a little more complex: the sentence "Some time ago, Pedro came from Egypt and brought us many chickens and animals" would have had these different versions:

Antxina, Egyptotik etorri ta emon euskuezen Kepak ainbeste ollasko ta aliamalia

---

7. All these forms can be accessed at www.ehu.es/seg/morf/5/16/1 (Last accessed June 19, 2012).

8. See www/euskaltzaindia.net/dok/arauak/Araua_0014.pdf (Last accessed June 19, 2012).

9. The reason for these different verb forms is that, in reality, there are distinct verbs, some of which lack an independent existence. In other words, they only function as auxiliaries of other "main" verbs (those that contribute semantic significance).

10. Louis Lucien Bonaparte (1813–1891), nephew of Napoleon I, a tireless scholar and traveler that contributed to the fields of chemistry, mineralogy, and linguistics in several European countries. The dialectal classification of Euskara that he proposed during his lifetime had remained in force until very recently.

11. Euskaltzaindia republished all of them. See Bonaparte (1991a)

Antzina, Egyptetik ethorri eta eman zerauzkigun Piarresek hainbertze oilasko eta animalia

Actually, there is not a single matching word between those two versions, and these two examples are not exagerrated cases. Other versions that are even less alike could be cited. It is no wonder, then, that those who took the trouble to write the first texts in Euskara explicitly referred to this problem.

The Need for a Standard Model

In fact, writers experienced enormous difficulty in finding a model that was minimally coherent and understandable outside of the local environment in which it had been generated. The need for a standardized text did not appear, then, overnight. On the contrary, it has been a long and drawn out process, as we will see in the following paragraphs. Yet Euskara would have to wait until the late 1960s in order to have an initial embryo.

Some Brief Historical Notes

Joanes Leizarraga published the first known translation of the New Testament into Euskara in 1571. Little is known about his life: in all probability, he was a Catholic priest who, at the urging of Jeanne d'Albret, queen regnant of Navarre from 1555 to 1572, supported the new ideas of Protestantism (Calvinism) and for that reason he translated different texts into Basque, with the objective of spreading Reformation ideas among ordinary people. We know of Leizarraga almost entirely through his texts in translation, Leizarraga is mostly known for his translations, but his work, endorsed by four Protestant ministers, was excellent. Thus he was quite aware of the difficulties he faced and, in his own words: "Everyone knows what difference and diversity there is in Vasconia in the manner of speaking almost from one house to another" (cited in Mitxelena 2008, 236).

Almost a century later, in 1643, Pedro Axular published the book *Guero* (Later),[12] an outstanding work in the history of Basque literature. For a long time he was thought to be the best prose writer in history. In his comments to the reader he indicates that he was aware that he could not respond "to all the different forms of speech in Euskara, because each person speaks in distinct ways and in different forms in Euskal Herria." Thus, he says that some people say *behatzea,* and others *so egitea* to express the notion of a "glance" or "gaze." Some prefer *haserretzea* and others *samurtzea* to say "anger"; some *ilkitzea* and others *jalgitea* to express the idea of "taking out"; in some places

---

12. This book can be read and downloaded for free at klasikoak.armiarma.com/idazlanak/A/AxularGero.htm (Last accessed June 19, 2012).

hauzoa, in others *barridea,* to say "neighborhood," and so on. He is referring to problems regarding a common lexicon, beyond any terminological
questions.

Arnaud Oihenart (1657) saw the need to explain, at the end of his published proverbs, the meaning of terms taken from what he outlined as six
distinct varieties, so that other Basques could understand them. Meanwhile,
doctor and writer Joanes de Etxeberri[13] (1668–1749), labeled "from Sara" so
as not to be confused with his namesake "from Ziburu," pointed out that it
was no wonder that there were so many different variations of the Basque language. As he observed, Basque-speakers lived in different kingdoms in which
other languages were spoken that "contaminated" the Basque language and
acted as yeast, gradually changing Euskara until it would eventually disappear. At the same time, the Jesuit Manuel de Larramendi (1660–1766) published the first Basque grammar, written in Spanish. In the work, he indicates
that "Basque has the Gipuzkoan dialect, that of the Seigniory or Bizkaian, and
Navarrese or Lapurdian, that is commonly the same, although there is quite
a mixture from the all other dialects; and this is also what is happening in
Araba, which participates in all of them, more or less syncopated, and varied"
(1729, 12). In his well-known *Diccionario Trilingüe* (Trilingual dictionary,
1745) Larramendi returned again to the same subject: "in Lower Navarre,
Lapurdi, and Zuberoa there are differences and dialects, especially in verb
endings, and they are listed in the *Arte* ,[14] for example: *darot, deraut, draut,*
etc., and there are other minor differences, which are understood without any
difficulty" (Larramendi 1745, 7). He then indicated many differences among
the distinct languages.

This was the norm that was repeated in one form or another by many
writers, above all by those whose intention it was to reach readers of other
dialects and forms of speech. During the nineteenth and twentieth centuries,
many authors on both sides of the border began, if not to propose common
writing models, then at least to make observations concerning the alphabet
needed to write in Basque. However, they were not very successful.[15] This all
led to much debate that examined the common need and prepared the field
for concrete proposals, although many years would pass before all accepted a
standard model. Meanwhile, use of Basque was losing ground in both France
and Spain, and it disappeared altogether during the nineteenth century in
large areas of Navarre.

---

13. See Joannes Etcheberry "Sarakoa" (1712).

14. Translator's Note: Arte refers to the Art of the Basque Language - another of Larramendi's
works.

15. See the excellent work of Koldo Zuazo (1988).

Bonaparte, as we pointed out, had translations done of many biblical texts into the different Basque dialects and local Basque languages. Given that these were carried out by different translators and from distinct areas, all of them received precise indications on the correct way to write the final transcriptions of the translations. Subsequently, once the text had been accepted after several discussions with the translator, it went on to be published. But Bonaparte encountered a problem: he needed to provide the texts with a certain orthographic unity. So, without any type of prior theoretical discussion, he designed a model himself that, orthographically, was not substantially far removed from the one that would be established among writers one hundred and twenty years later. The decisions that he adopted figured explicitly in some of his publications. Some of the people that collaborated with him, especially those who lived in France, adopted part of those proposals as their own, which notably contributed to the language's unification among French Basque writers. Jean Pierre Duvoisin (1812–1891), for example, completed many translations, including that of the Bible, and also wrote a novel and other texts. He asserted the following in a letter: "Until Prince Louis Lucien Bonaparte came to our lands, each wrote Basque in its own way. . . . This is what the prince occupied himself with, like the great philologist he is. From this the orthography became rational, which authors adopted at once" (cited in Daranatz 1931, 332–33).[16] At the end of the nineteenth century some of these proposals—here we are referring to the orthographic level—were also extended to the peninsular area in Spain and were adopted by Spanish Basque writers. Specialists like José Manterola, Arturo Campión, and Sabino Arana (to name a few) took them as their own, at least in part. Resurrección María de Azkue (1864–1951), one of the founders and the first president of Euskaltzaindia (the Royal Academy of the Basque Language), had already proposed his own model of Basque orthography in 1891. In turn, the principal driving force of Basque nationalism and the founder of the Basque Nationalist Party, Sabino Arana, developed his own opinions on Basque orthography in several writings at the beginning of the twentieth century. Going against that championed by authors like Agustín Cardaberaz (1761), Arana favored use of the grapheme "h," which created a lot of controversy years later, although he seemed skeptical about the possibility of reaching a common model. In his article "Lecciones de ortografía del euskera bizkaino" ("Orthographic lessons from Bizkaian Euskara," 1896), Arana said: "I find it difficult to reach such an agreement of absolute unification" (Arana 1965, 824).[17]

Already by the early years of the twentieth century there had been several disputes between those who agreed with the need to establish a standard

16. Translated from French.
17. This 1896 arcticle is collected in Arana's complete works (1965).

model and those that opposed any type of unification. In many of these disputes, the belief was that the language would be academically manipulated, regardless of how the speakers themselves used it, as if decisions on a common lexicon, morphological patterns, or verbal inflections could could come created "ex novo" from a laboratory and not from the usages of everyday life. The administrative division of the Basque Country into two states, and into several political provinces, did not help in strengthening the position of those who advocated a common model: there were those who wanted to return to the original language and others that wanted to remove all linguistic loanwords from Euskara, even though they had been in place for centuries. There were also those who advocated the use of one of the dialects as a common reference model: Bizkaian, Gipuzkoan, "completed" Gipuzkoan, and so on. The momentum that Basque nationalism gathered in the early twentieth century and the resultant push for Basque cultural societies—particularly Eusko Ikaskuntza (the Basque Studies Society)—contributed to the 1918 founding of Euskaltzaindia, a academy of the Basque language that resembled those that already existed in Spain and France, and in which many of the aforementioned discussions were catalyzed. The academy was intended to be a center that brought all the language's scholars together and its objective, among other things, was to promote research on Euskara and to contribute to literary unification. It should be noted that there was no university at that time in the Basque Country that had a liberal arts faculty. Indeed, it was not until the 1970s that Basque language studies were incorporated as regular study and research subjects in universities.

Toward the 1968 Congress

In 1936, there was an uprising against the government of the Spanish Republic by General Francisco Franco. Following a bloody three-year war, Franco's subsequent dictatorship was characterized by its persecution of (among other things) the use of Euskara. This was more the case in Gipuzkoa and Bizkaia than in Navarre. After attempts by the first Basque autonomous government in the 1930s to create a university in which Basque also had a presence were nipped in the bud by the uprising and civil war, during the Franco years its use in education was of course prohibited. The post-civil war period was a dark time, during which *euskaltzales* (Bascophiles) had to take refuge in their own surroundings for several years. The discussions on linguistic models were, if not set aside, at least reduced to the very minimum.

They were taken up once again in 1946 by Seber Altube, who again proposed writing in the Gipuzkoan dialect ("We must choose the most thriving and used dialect") as the basis for the literary unification of all (Altube 1949, 183). It was not successful for several reasons. Zuazo (1988, 340) points out the following: the Gipuzkoan model was not standardized enough, it was not a unique model; some Gipuzkoan writers did not share Altube's approach; classic literature was not sufficiently valued; and there was no administrative help to boost the model. Federico Krutwig (1921–1928) noted the profound influence that the language would suffer in a society subject to such major changes: rural society was becoming urban and industrial. He observed the need for unification and pushed, along with other militant activists, the use of classic Lapurdian (that used by Axular) as the model that writers should look to. That marked a substantial change with respect to what had been proposed until then because it carried discussion on the model far beyond the Gipuzkoan and Bizkaian references, and prompted the adoption of a model that was not used in popular speech. However, for that same reason it was not practical because it was no longer in widespread use: in short, those who spoke Lapurdian (not the classic version, but the existing and more standard variant) were a minority with regard to the total amount of Basque speakers. Pierre Lafitte (1901–1985) advocated what was termed the Literary Navarrese-Lapurdian model in his well-known grammar (1944). Meanwhile, some people even called for the possibility of employingthe model used among Basque Americans. According to this proposal, having emigrated from different parts of the Basque Country, they had developed in practice and according to areas, models that were more or less unified in order to communicate with each other.

In any case, Krutwig's drive and the proposal, which again took up concerns over the need for a common model, led in in 1964 to a meeting in Baiona (Bayonne, in the French Basque Country). At this meeting, the foundations of what in no time at all came to be known as "unified Euskara" were discussed, and the ill-named Basque "declension" forms were codified.[18] Thereafter, the Gerediaga association organized a meeting in 1968 in Ermua (Bizkaia) at which the Idazleen Alkartea (Basque Writers' Association) discussed and adopted certain proposals. In 1968, too, on the occasion of its fiftieth anniversary Euskaltzaindia convened a general meeting in the Arantzazu Monastery (Gipuzkoa). It was at this meeting that the bases for unifying or standardizing the Basque language were definitively set.

The 1968 Arantzazu Congress and Mitxelena's Proposal

The Basque linguist Koldo Mitxelena, professor of Indo-European Linguistics at the University of Salamanca and the most academically qualified person

---

18. Although nearly all authors and grammars refer to a "declension" in Basque, it is evident that such a declension (in the sense used with Latin, for example) does not exist. Instead, there is a set of postpositions that could be classified into two groups: dependent postpositions, joined to the nominal syntagm (*bideaN*, "IN the road") and independent postpositions (*bidean ZEHAR*, "across the road"). The nominal form (*bide*) that receives the postposition never changes.

in the field of the Basque language, was the person chosen to give the keynote address at the Arantzazu Congress in October 1968, although there were twelve papers in total discussed at the meeting. In fact, in addition to president Manuel Lekuona's opening address, four people were invited to make presentations: Mitxelena ("Orthography"); Luis Villasante ("Word Form"), who was shortly thereafter elected as president of the academy, replacing Lekuona and powering decisive projects in the following years; Ambrosio Zatarain ("New Words"), one of the academics that most strongly opposed the standard model in subsequent years; and Salbador Garmendia ("The Declension"). Euskaltzaindia was at this time formed mostly by men linked to the Church, many of them self-taught, and a few others with more of an academic background. The priest, Manuel Lekuona, was its president.

The truth is that the congress provoked enormous interest among Bascophiles and vivid discussion between those that attended the meetings. In the last few years preceding the meeting, new generations of Basque writers had emerged, educational textbooks for ikastolas had been published, [19] and there was a growing demand for journalists writing in Euskara. The Second Vatican Council ended in 1965 and as a result, the Bible was translated into several Basque dialects. The Basque language world, in general, experienced a profound transformation during those years: in the same year the Arantzazu Congress was held, writer Gabriel Aresti won the Spanish National Prize for Literature for his book written in Euskara; and the following year, Ramon Saizarbitoria published his first novel (see chapter 9). Moreover, in more general terms, *euskaltzales* called attention to the need for studying the language's written tradition. The younger generations, desiring to put what they had learned into practice, and wanting to join the literary trends of the day, felt the need for a unique writing model that could be used without any problems. They demanded the use of Euskara, organized classes, spoke of introducing Basque language studies into the university curriculum, and so on. Clearly, they were creating a paradigm shift that older people were generally rather reluctant to embrace. Those changes were a reflection of a society in turmoil: the influences of May 1968 in France were still very much alive; democratic winds were blowing through Prague and later Portugal; the University of Bilbao was founded in 1968 and later gave rise to the Universidad del País Vasco/Euskal Herriko Uniberstitatea (University of the Basque Country, UPV/EHU) in 1980; and in more general terms, throughout the late 1960s and early 1970s all of Spain was aware that Franco's regime had its days numbered. The Basque language was about to undertake a task of

---

19. Centers for primary and secondary (non-university) education, created by popular and private initiative, which attracted many students and in which all teaching was done in Basque. They grew stronger in the 1960s.

titanic proportions under those conditions: it had to be capable of developing a standard model in a few dozen years, something that other languages had achieved through a continuous and joint effort over hundreds of years.

As the 1968 congress concluded, Lekuona stated that the first steps toward unification had been made (at least on a theoretical level), that the path had been cleared, and that it was now time for everyone to get down to work. It was true. So true, in fact, that in addition to the path, many other things were cleared: Lekuona himself ended up resigning from the presidency because he did not agree with the decisions made and quite a few academics and proposal authors renounced the chosen path and unification model. Intense discussions were held in both Arantzazu and in Basque society as a whole once the congress ended. Although the main ideas in Mitxelena's proposal were almost fully accepted and fervently defended by younger generations, discussions and disagreements among writers remained alive for years.

There were two extralinguistic factors, however, that definitively and effectively contributed to the triumph of the unification model accepted. One of the factors, as we have already pointed out, was generational: more educated and more dynamic younger generations were in favor of the new model and even though doubts were raised over a few issues that were not sufficiently laid out, they began to use it without any problems and to defend it in all the forums. Moreover, the new democratic Spanish Constitution was enacted in 1978; the first Basque autonomous government was formed in 1980; and in 1982 the Basque government passed the law on the standardization and use of Euskara, regulating bilingual teaching models in education. The Basque government, then, clearly believed in a unified language and this was a second key factor leading to its success. The most dynamic generations now wrote in the standard language, in Euskara *Batua*, as the new model began to be called. And young students began to use it in their education.

Mitxelena's Proposal

The keynote address presented by Mitxelena at the Arantzazu Congress was entitled "Orthography."[20] Yet a cursory glance at Mitxelena's text leads one to speculate whether this was actually the title of the address or whether it was something subsequently added on. The topics addressed in his proposal go completely beyond the orthographic field and also delve into the terrain of morphology, lexicon, and even syntax. Mitxelena made a concrete proposal on the characteristics that the common model should have, posing distinct possibilities and promoting the use of some of them. If there was something

---

20. It can be viewed at www.euskaltzaindia.net/dok/euskera/51289.pdf (Last accessed June 19, 2012).

that defined that proposal it was the simplicity and the common sense that it exuded. We will briefly describe some of it below.

Foundations of the Model

The ideal would be, in Mitxelena's opinion, for all Basques to feel comfortable speaking their own dialect and to also know the rest of them, both in their current and historical versions. But that was not possible. Euskara required a unique common model over the dialectal variants. It was, in many ways, a question of life or death. This unity could only be achieved if we were capable of accepting that the language would lose multiple nuances that were by no means trivial. As a result, there would be some speakers that would feel hurt and offended, but this was something that was unavoidable.

Euskaltzaindia could only aspire to be a guide throughout the process, because it was a shared effort that could not be taken on alone. The objective was twofold: that the dialects not become more removed from each other and that, wherever possible, they should endeavor to draw closer together. The unity of the written language had to be based on the model used in the central dialects, to the extent that the city with the greatest number of inhabitants, Bilbao, was not Basque-speaking, and had to limit itself to superficial issues, since when we spoke of the Basque language we were referring to a diasystem that was not easy to identify, rather than to a unique system. Thus, the proposal had to be confined to aspects relating to the following problems: orthography, the structure of old Basque words; the structure of new Basque words or loanwords; nominal and verbal morphology; and syntax. Some of these issues resulted, however, in the impossibility of making any serious proposal because the the the necessary preliminary studies were lacking. And for other issues it was not possible to make proposals other than at the dialectal level (at least there would be a certain unity among the different variations of the same dialect).

Orthography

Unlike a few previous proposals (that included diacritic marks on several consonants), Mitxelena opted for an orthography that was simplified and stripped of unnecessary frills, the most unambiguous possible: there were no accents; the grapheme "n" would always be written the same regardless of its position; "k" and "z" would be used systematically, not "c"; the "g" would always be velar and not pronounced like the phoneme "/x/", and so on. Moreover, some letters (*c, qu, v, w, y*) were only used to transcribe words and names from other languages, and the proposed alphabet consisted of twenty-two of its "own" letters. Even though a parallelism between the written and spoken language was impossible, Mitxelena proposed a simplification of the model because he assumed that the result of applying any phonological rules within a word must directly transfer to writing.

To illustrate the matter with an example: Aizkorri is the name of a mountain. It is actually a composite name whose etymology is transparent: *haitz* ("stone" or "crag") and *gorri* ("red"), resulting in "haitz + gorri." Consonants such as "tz," "ts," or "tx" were changed in pronunciation, in all the dialects, into "z," "s," or "x," respectively, when they were in front of another occlusive (stop) consonant. In turn, the voiced consonants "b," "d," and "g" were changed to voiceless ("p," "t," and "k") if they came after a voiceless consonant, such as in the case of "z." Thus the application of some basic phonological rules changed the initial "haitz gorri" (the letter "h" was irrelevant here) to Aizkorri, the mountain's name.

There was no unity among writers in these matters: to simplify, some were inclined to use *Aizkorri* and others used *Aitzgorri*. Mitxelena proposed the first step that should be systematically applied within the limits of the word. So, *hutstu* "to empty" arose from *huts* "empty" and *hotztu* "to cool" derived from *hotz* "cold," as it was written by some. Mitxelena proposed that writing be much closer to the spoken register: *hustu, hoztu.* He also proposed that the neutralizations between sibilants observed in some dialects (the lack of distinction between *s, z,* and *x*) should be the opposite, and the model should be capable of clearly distinguishing the writing of those sounds.

The grapheme "h" had always posed specific problems. It was actually a consonant (similar to the English "'h" in "he") but it only survived in the pronunciation of dialects from the French Basque Country. It was not pronounced now in Spain, in the Euskara spoken in the Spanish part. That is, *mahai hau* ("table-this," meaning "this table") did not sound the same between French Basque and Spanish Basque speakers. The former pronounced the consonant, while the latter did not. There were two root causes of this: in the dialects from the Spanish Basque Country, terms that originally had that aspirated consonant had changed it over time to another distinct consonant that was voiced. To take one example, *aho* "mouth" used to sound like "ago" in speech that had apparently lost the "h." On the other hand, in the French Basque Country that continued to preserve the original "h" in its variations, the aspiration extended to other non-intervocalic positions. So, we had *etorri* "to come" in the Spanish Basque Country, without any trace of the "h" consonant, as opposed to *ethorri* in the French Basque Country. It was not at all easy to decide what to do, because any extreme option involved rather drastic changes. Mitxelena opted for the middle ground: restore the "h" to the intervocalic position with all of its consequences (*aho* would not be written as "ago," although it was pronounced this way in some areas), but not use it in the post-consonantal position (*etorri*, but not *ethorri*). In addition, Mitxelena proposed that a list of words starting with that letter be developed.

The palatal consonants derived from the application of phonological rules also posed a problem: depending on the speech, we could have for example *gaña/gaina* "surface," *ollo/oilo* "hen," and *egiñ/egin* "to make," without any homogeneous distribution. In other words, some speakers, always depending on the variations, pronounced these words *gaña, ollo,* and *egiñ* and others *gaina, oilo,* and *egin*. Furthermore, there was no lack of variations that opted for the model *gaña, ollo* (palatals), or *egin* (non-palatal). Thus, the palatalization rule did not always apply in the same contexts. Faced with that situation, Mitxelena proposed that "il" and "in" be used for writing and that the speakers pronounce it the way in which they were accustomed to: in short, a unified and simple writing system in the face of distinct dialects.

The sound represented in Spanish by the letter "j" was introduced quite late on historically (it began to be used under Arab rule of the Iberian Peninsula) and was used in the central dialects of Euskara: so there were words such as *jan* "to eat" that were pronounced either like the initial consonant of "ya" in Castilian Spanish (or the "y" in "you") or like *jamón* ("ham" in Spanish), in which the "j" is pronounced like the "ch" in English renderings of Bach, again, pronounced as in Castilian Spanish. Therefore, writers, depending on their origin, wrote this as "yan" or "jan." Mitxelena proposed that, in these cases, it should be written as *jan* and that everybody should pronounce the word according to their habit.

Certain particles that joined with the verb (*bait,* "because") also marked writing patterns and different pronunciations: for example, *etorri bait da* (to come-because-aux, "because he has come") had been written as *etorri bait da, etorri bai da,* and *etorri baita* (and pronounced as "baida" or baita" according to the speaker). Mitxelena proposed that it be written separately, allowing *bait da* and *baita*.[21]

Some other proposals, which we will not discuss here, on the writing of compound words, punctuation marks, and so forth, appeared in this "Orthography" section. However, the accomplishment of everything noted thus far gave the written language an unexpected unity. It was an important step and an invaluable aid for anyone who wanted to write in Basque.

On Word Form

In the Basque language, words used on a daily basis, and especially in the written tradition, have been integrated into Euskara, regardless of their origin,

---

21. Euskaltzaindia subsequently reformed the issue again and today a unique and definitive form has been imposed: *baita*.

and should be considered Basque. Writing had nothing to do, in principle, with the etymology of a word. The words traditionally used by the majority of speakers had to be incorporated into a shared lexicon.

But there were many terms that were not shared by all the speakers. This lack of unity was due to diverse reasons, as was the solution proposed in such cases. Completely different words were sometimes used, depending on the dialectal variations, to refer to the same concept, as, for example, in the case of *aurkitu* and *ediren* "to find." Here, both words had to be incorporated into the common model because they both enriched the language. Terms could not be rejected from the shared repertory, particularly if those terms had been used in literature (localisms were treated differently). This was regardless of the fact that writers attempted, if you will, to more precisely define the future meaning of each one: "find the key" (*aurkitu*) and "find a new law" (*ediren*) was an illustrative example of what could be done.

On other occasions it was simply phonetic or phonological variations of the same theme: for example, in the case of *berri/barri* "new." In these cases it was better to reject the variations that were too local, although many times they were seen as the language's essence (exaggerated contractions, for example). The variations of a word shared by most dialects had to be respected as such: the Latin *anima* or "soul" resulted in the Basque *arima,* a common word in all of the variations. That version had to be accepted. The same occurred with the words *bekatu* "sin," *bake* "peace," and *errege* "king" (Latin loans *peccātum, pax* (*pacem*), and *rēx* [*rēgem*]), which were rooted in all the dialects. Generally, the most used form would take priority, above all when it coincided among extreme dialects: for example, *burni* "iron" was the form used in the central dialects, but *burdina* was used in the extreme dialects of Bizkaian in Spain and Zuberoan in France; and in this case the extreme dialects took precedence. The elaboration of an orthographic dictionary based on these principles was proposed because even though the differences in other aspects could be small, it was thought that a split in the lexicon was occurring between the dialects used in the French and Spanish areas, influenced by the French and Spanish languages.

New Words

Languages continuously require new words, and there are two methods to incorporate new terms: advantage can be taken of the possibilities that the language itself offers (using compound words, derivatives, suffixes, or prefixes, and so on), or terms can be imported directly from other languages. As a general principle, there is no need to import terms from other languages as long as the language itself possesses them. It is very important, without closing the language off to other possibilities, to endeavor to use all the mechanisms that the language itself offers to create new terms, because doing so strengthens that language.

It seemed that the cultural lexicon (understood in its broadest sense) in the Basque Country should make more use of foreign resources because Basque culture was created more from outside than inside the country itself. This posed a problem though, because the Basque language hardly had any prefixes, which were so abundant in languages linked to societies with great cultural power. Many widely used words had already been incorporated into the language: *psikologia* "psychology," for example. When incorporating terms of this type it was best to preserve the original form as much as possible as they did in French, or to incorporate them in a simplified way while heeding the language's own system, as Spanish did. Except for very technical terms (and proper nouns), a middle path, without resorting to local phoneticisms caused by Spanish or French (like prioritizing *sozialista* "socialist" and not *zozialista*), was more highly recommended. Thus, it seemed that forms such as *psykhologia* should not be used, although there were some writers that also defended that possibility. Words such as *geologia* "geology" posed a pronunciation problem—with the "g" prounced as either "ch" (as in English renderings of Bach) or "y" as in "you" depending on the variations in Spanish or French—or a visual problem (whether it was written with a "g" or a "j"). The proposal was to prioritize the form *geologia*, given that writing was visual, although freedom existed in its pronunciation.

Morphology

The keynote address referred to nominal and verbal morphology, but only as related to the "structure," independent from the content. Given that determinative noun phrases sometimes ended in "a," and that there were also indefinites that ended in that same letter, it was advisable to distinguish when that "a" was part of the word and when it referred to the article (the definite form). Mitxelena also referred to some of the usual forms, giving priority to some variation, and called for the use of the instrumental (*-z*) in Euskara, to distinguish, for example, between "steak *with* potatoes" (accompaniment) and "to kill *with* a sword" (instrument), which generated two different postpositions in Basque. The proposal also called for the need to determine the demonstrative pronoun forms as soon as possible because there was such great diversity between dialects and forms of speech.

With regard to verbal morphology, Mitxelena emphasized the need for preliminary studies before establishing any proposal. As a first step, verbal paradigms from the different variations had to be collected and those that had broken away the least from the rest of the dialects had to be selected. Attention had to be paid to those used in the literary tradition, before forms that, although they were used in oral speech, had a short history. Furthermore, the verb (for example, *ikus* "to see") and its participle (*ikusi* "seen") had to be recognized as it is used in some dialects and had historically been used in others, even though the forms are currently neutralized in some variants. For a short time perhaps, the use of more than one auxiliary verb paradigm could occur.[22]

Syntax

Space precludes a detailed discussion here on matters of syntax, stylistics, word order, and so on. Instead, we will limit ourselves to a few general observations. We must not forget that it was necessary to dive into the tradition and models of the classic writers in Basque, and at that time, just as now, different writing registers had to be equally distinguished: that of poetry was not the same as theater, for example. This would remain a topic to be discussed in the future.

Consequences of the Arantzazu Congress

Mitxelena's proposal, discussed and adopted in Arantzazu, had immediate success in the majority of its approaches, and only a few points were changed afterward. From the perspective that the passing of years gives, we can appreciate that Mitxelena had a vision of the future and approached the question with great common sense. There was certainly much debate on the proposal and some minority groups enthusiastically challenged it, especially those connected with defending the Bizkaian dialect, which was perhaps the furthest from the standard and, additionally, had a great literary tradition. Many of those discussions were catalyzed by proposals related to the use of the grapheme "h," but the process continued and was adopted by all writers.[23] Different committees assumed the preparatory work to make concrete proposals in several areas: orthography, unified postposition forms, verbal paradigms, demonstrative forms, and so on. Indeed, just eight years later, Mitxelena himself expressed his astonishment at the endeavor's success (Mitxelena 1978a). At Euskaltzaindia's subsequent Bergara Congress in 1978 (Mitxelena 1978b), he seemed satisfied with the results of the proposal:

> When I recall Arantzazu and what happened afterward, I am filled with happiness, not sorrow. If I were to say that I have not experienced any kind of sorrow, I would not be lying. Euskatzaindia made the decision it had to make without direction, one that was not made because of thousands of reasons or excuses (shame, fear of what others would say, the desire to maintain a

---

22. As already indicated, the dialects use several forms of auxiliary verbs.
23. See Patxi Goenaga (2000) for an evaluation of this process.

façade of peace in a place where there was no peace. . .). They made the best decision they could, one that was owed to the Basque Country for a long time, even if it would hurt all Basques: they set out deliberately and energetically on the path of unification, without leaving things for later (Mitxelena 2008, 274–75, suspension points in original).

The proposed model was ratified in the 1978 Bergara-Arrasate Congress, after a successful ten-year trial period that originated in the Arantzazu Congress. The Basque language had definitely found its standard model.

Developments accelerated from that moment on. Basque linguistics studies, for example, found its place in the academic world: first at the private University of Deusto, and immediately after at the public UPV/EHU, where Mitxelena was hired as a professor. The fate of Basque was undergoing drastic changes: thousands of students were studying the language at the primary and secondary levels; it enjoyed a significant new presence in radio and television; an important literary production existed; classic authors were translated into Basque; Basque music and its singer-songwriters were enjoying great success, and so on. In 1994 Euskaltzaindia held another congress on the UPV/EHU Leioa campus and cleared the way for other matters related to the standard model, under the management and drive of its standardization committee. The academy, under the academic direction of university professors, promoted work related to Basque grammar, dialectal variations (producing a linguistic atlas), lexicography, and toponymy. During the 1980s the monumental sixteen-volume work, *Diccionario General Básico* (General Basque dictionary) began to be published, originally designed by Mitxelena but directed to its completion in 2005 by Ibon Sarasola, a UPV/EHU professor. The *Hiztegi Batua* (Unified dictionary) was also published in 2000, and the seventh and last volume of *Euskal Gramatika. Lehen Urratsak* (Basque grammar: The first steps) was published in 2011 by several university professors, the most complete descriptive work on Basque grammar known, with the first volume being published in 1985.

Numerous doctoral dissertations have been completed on all types of subjects related to the Basque language, and the Basque Language Institute at the UPV/EHU is conducting several projects on standardization. All the institute's materials (corpus, dictionaries, grammar books, and so on) are available free of charge on the web.[24] Over the course of only a few years the Basque language had quickly traversed, but not without some difficulty, what many other languages had done step by step, with the help of history itself. It was a remarkable achievement.

---

24. See www.ei.ehu.es (Last accessed June 19, 2012).

6

The Current Situation of the Basque Language: Speakers

Miren Azkarate Villar,
the University of the Basque Country (UPV/EHU)

Speaking about a minoritized language's situation requires referencing the "major language" that it coexists with, or has probably coexisted with for a long time; to see the relations that both languages have maintained because they share the same territory. It is possible (and has happened on numerous occasions) for languages that are dominant in particular territories to become displaced by others that have gathered strength; indeed, the wars, invasions, and colonizations experienced in Europe have forged the linguistic map that we know today. Thus, it is important to understand the historical situation of Euskara: Was it once Euskal Herria's only language or, on the contrary, has it always coexisted with some other language? Koldo Mitxelena (2008, 197)[1] focuses clearly on this issue:

> Among us, during the eras that we are familiar with, Euskera has never been our all-embracing vehicle of expression. There has always been another language at its side. Perhaps Euskera was the most beloved of the languages that were being used here in one way or another, perhaps it was the one most closely linked to feelings—the favorite one, or if you prefer, the language of the home—but when we left the home to dedicate ourselves to other tasks, we immediately began to use some other language, for this or that. . . . Some things, and not exactly unimportant things, have always been expressed between us in languages different from Euskera.

---

1. I cite the translation published in Koldo Mitxelena (2008). Mitxelena's original text was entitled *Euskal literaturaren bereizgarri orokorrak*, a lecture given during the 1977/78 academic year and published afterward (Mitxelena 1981).

And in that coexistence of two thousand years, as Mitxelena points out, the relationship had never been balanced; it was enough to just leave home to use the Romance language. It is no wonder, therefore, that following changes during the last century and a half, Spanish and French[2] gained ground: "In the urbanization process correlative to the leap from the rural environment to industrialization, Spanish was imposed over Euskera in many social functions, in cultured functions, and in urban environments" (Baztarrika 2009, 146). The same can be said, of course, with respect to the Northern Basque Country. As Mitxelena says (2008, 198), "In general, the non-Basque speakers of these places could count on support that the Basque speakers in the same places did not have, and for that reason as I mentioned earlier—that is, that the weak always surrenders before the strong—we, the Basque speakers, have been the ones who have conceded in the face of those who were not Basque speakers, and not the contrary." The obligatory conclusion is that Euskara had transferred many of its social functions into a Romance language.

But we now need to analyze what the current situation of Euskara and its speakers is. How have relations between the two hegemonic languages—Spanish and French—and the minority language, Euskara, evolved? The following two figures present data from the *IV Mapa Sociolingüístico* (Fourth sociolinguistic map, Gobierno Vasco 2009a) and from the *Fourth Sociolinguistic Survey,* (Gobierno Vasco 2008a), both published by the Vice-Ministry for Language Policy of the Basque government. The data reveal the current situation of the Basque language in various territories[3] as well as the change it has experienced in the Comunidad Autónoma del País Vasco-Euskal Autonomia Erkidegoa (CAPV-EAE, the Autonomous Community of the Basque Country). These figures, then, serve as a point of departure and arrival, in the sense that they explain the path traveled since 1981 in the recovery of Euskara (Gobierno Vasco 2009a, 36).[4]

As a starting point, during this time frame, there was an increase of more than 15 percent in bilingual speakers (Spanish- or French-speakers who also speak Basque) and a 20 percent decrease in monolingual speakers (non-Basque speakers), to which a 5 percent increase in passive bilinguals was added (this refers to speakers who are able to understand the Basque language, but have trouble expressing themselves in it). Moreover, taking into

---

2. Although Euskara has coexisted with Gascon and with Occitan in the Northern Basque Country, undoubtedly in the last century at least, French has been the hegemonic language with which Euskara has had to "compete."

3. See previous chapters, especially chapter 2, in which Euskal Herria's current configuration within two states (France and Spain), and into two autonomous communities in the Spanish state, is clearly defined.

4. The data corresponds to the fourth sociolinguistic map, although it is presented in a different form.

**Figure 6.1. Evolution of linguistic competence in the CAPV-EAE, 1981–2006
(percent)**

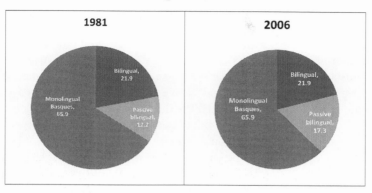

Source: Eustat.

account the language competence in each region (figure 6.2.), compared to a bilingual rate of 35.7 percent of the population in the CAPV-EAE, the significantly lower percentage of bilingual speakers (and corresponding higher rate of monolingual people) in other territories stands out (Gobierno Vasco 2008a, 202).

Figure 6.2. Regional language competence

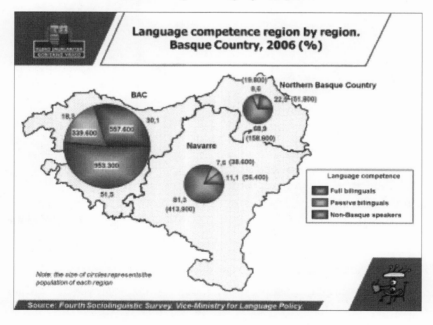

However, there is another variable that should be kept in mind: age. That general 15 percent gain of CAPV-EAE bilingual speakers did not occur proportionally across all the age brackets; furthermore, according to the *Fourth Sociolinguistic Survey* data (Gobierno Vasco 2008a, 21), only 21.3 percent of the speakers included in the 50–65 age group were bilingual and only 25.7 percent were bilingual in the 35–50 age group. The increase was therefore more substantial in the lower age brackets where a 37.3 percent increase was found in the 25–35 age group and, above all, a 57.5 percent increase in the 16–24 age group. If we combine all the data from the *Fourth Sociolinguistic Survey* with that provided by the fourth sociolinguistic map (Gobierno Vasco 2009a, 37), which gathers and compiles data from the population over the age of five, we see that nearly 75 percent of young men and women below the age of fifteen in the CAPV-EAE are bilingual; which, together with the 16 percent of passive bilinguals, means that 90 percent of young people in the CAPV-EAE are, at the very least, able to understand Euskara.

Figure 6.3. Evolution of linguistic competence (< 15 years of age), CAPV-EAE, 1981–2006 (percent)

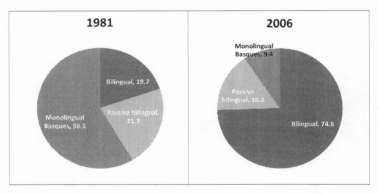

Source: Eustat.

Let us now analyze this data more thoroughly; and also analyze the reasons for the current situation in the three territories: the CAPV-EAE, the Foral Community of Navarre (or Navarre), and the Northern Basque Country. In other words, let us analyze the linguistic policies that were implemented and the results obtained.

The Data: Sociolinguistic Maps and Sociolinguistic Surveys

Aware that precise information was required for the progression of the language that they sought to revitalize in society, first the Secretary General for

Language Policy and then the Vice-Ministry for Language Policy led by the Department of Culture in the Basque government regularly collected data related to the evolution of Euskara. This was done by using the two variables formed by the census and the registry as instruments, even though the information from those sources was not standardized in the different territories. The censuses and registries from the CAPV-EAE and Navarre look at the entire population yet they do not collect identical information, while in regard to the Northern Basque Country, there is no information on language-related questions.

Sociolinguistic Maps

Diverse data on the language were collected every five years in the CAPV-EAE through the cross-referencing of information from both sources (census and registry): that regarding the citizen's language knowledge (data collected since 1981), that relating to their first language (since 1986) and the use of language in the family environment (since 1991), all of this concerning the whole population older than five years of age. The respective sociolinguistic maps were drawn up based on this information. The first, based on the 1986 registry, was created in 1989 and includes an in-depth study of the linguistic situation, taking mother tongue, language competence, and the indicators and typologies developed from both variables into consideration. The fourth sociolinguistic map was the last to be published,[5] based on data from the population and housing census in 2006 (which, as noted, collected data on people older than five years of age). The sociolinguistic maps gave us an expanded view of the evolution of Euskara in the CAPV-EAE: an insight into a twenty-five-year span as regards language competence, twenty years in the case of Euskara as a first language, and fifteen years of recording the extent to which the language was used at home.

In Navarre, on the other hand, only data related to people's language knowledge were collected, yet there was no official census carried out in 2006. Because of this, as Miquel Gros i Lladós (2007, 218) points out "the data chain was interrupted . . . that allowed Euskera's evolution within the Navarrese society to be followed. Likewise, it did not appear that the Navarrese government was going to conduct any type of study or survey in the coming years that would substitute for the questions on language that the five-year census

---

5. The second sociolinguistic map (Gobierno Vasco 1997–1999) covers the sociolinguistic situation in 1991 and population evolution during the 1981–1991 time period, data on percentages of the population's mother tongue, and that tongue's evolution between 1986 and 1991. The third sociolinguistic map (Gobierno Vasco 2005c) analyzes the sociolinguistic situation in 2001 and its evolution during the 1981–2001 time period.

put forth, thus the highly likely positive evolution of Euskera could not be analyzed in-depth." In the Northern Basque Country, the census does not collect any data regarding language.

The Sociolinguistic Surveys

Since 1991 the objective of sociolinguistic surveys held every five years was to collect standardized information about Euskara in its combined territories—the CAPV-EAE, Navarre, and the Northern Basque Country. They examined the population over sixteen years of age, which meant that the younger age brackets were not taken into consideration (those that, due to the influence of effective schooling in Basque, were the most bilingual).

Thus, here I rely on data from four surveys (1991, 1996, 2001, and 2006) that allow one to analyze the evolution of Euskara in its combined territories and also in each separate territory, by means of examining the population's principal characteristics, linguistic competence, language transmission, use of Euskara in certain environments (the family, circle of friends, work, and formal situations, among others), and, finally, attitudes toward the promotion of Euskera's use. These were very similar fields to those that UNESCO considered when measuring the vitality of languages in 2003.[6]

The Data

Adding the data from the fourth sociolinguistic map to that of the *Fourth Sociolinguistic Survey* (Gobierno Vasco 2008a)—in other words, combining the data regarding the population older than sixteen years of age with that of the population older than five years of age, although only in the CAPV-EAE—the following picture emerged in relation to the different environments analyzed.

Language Competence

Data from the *Fourth Sociolinguistic Survey* (Gobierno Vasco 2008a, 202) on the evolution of bilingual speakers within the total population of each territory appears in figure 6.2. It shows how different the language has evolved according to the territory in question, with a clear increase in bilingual people in the CAPV-EAE, a slight increase in Navarre, and a decline in bilingual people in the Northern Basque Country:

---

6. These include, among other aspects, absolute number of speakers, proportion of speakers within the total population, intergenerational language transmission, a community member's attitudes toward their own language, shifts in domains of language use, and governmental and institutional language attitudes and policies, including official status and use. See www.unesco.org/culture/ich/doc/src/00120-EN.pdf (last accessed July 25, 2012).

Table 6.1. Population change age sixteen and over

Region	1991		2006	
	Total	Full bilinguals	Total	Full bilinguals
CAPV-EAE	1,741,500	419,200	1,850,500	557,600
Navarre	420,700	40,200	508,900	56,400
Northern Basque Country	208,900	69,100	230,200	51,800
Basque Country	2,371,100	528,500	2,589,600	665,800

If we also consider the data from the fourth sociolinguistic map we see that in the CAPV-EAE in 2006, 37.5 percent of the people older than age five were bilingual (figure 6.1), although the age group variable was very important in this figure. In other words, half of the population under thirty years of age were bilingual in the CAPV-EAE in 2006 (thirty points more than in 1981), and that percentage increased to almost 75 percent among those younger than fifteen (figure 6.3).

Language Transmission

There are several channels through which a language may be transmitted: family, school, and so on. However, family is considered to be the crucial transmission channel for any language's revitalization; in short, a language that is not passed on in the family is certain to disappear (Fishman 1991, 77; Aizpurua 2002, 145; Baztarrika 2009, 59, 182). Joshua A. Fishman (2001, 11) warns of the danger in underestimating the importance of familial transmission and of the informal functions of a language, which he terms n-P functions, as opposed to formal or P functions.[7] Since language transmission primarily occurs at home (children receive their parents' language), one of the first measures in accomplishing a language's revitalization is to assure familial transmission, which is obviously determined by the parents' linguistic competence. In that regard it is important to remember that Spanish or French is the mother tongue of 78.7 percent of the Basque Country's population, and that

---

7. "A common formulation of the reversing language shift task is to set as a goal the *elevation of Th form n-P to P functions*. The other problem, that of more exclusive Th control of the n-P functions, is less commonly recognised. The two problems are, as we will soon see, intimately linked, however. If Th is not successfully (intergenerationally) maintained at the n-P level (and mother tongue transmission is an informal, spontaneous, intimate n-P function), it will then have no mother tongue speakers within one generation who can use it for n-P functions. In that case, it can *still* discharge certain P functions, but they will have to be acquired anew generation after generation via exposure to a P institution that is under Th-control. Such institutions, like all P institutions, are typically under great n-Th influence, pressure or regulation. Thus, the loss of crucial intergenerational Th-related n-P functions and the difficulty of substituting for them a few institutionally based (rather than intergenerationally transmitted) Th-related P functions, is another reason why it is so difficult to save a threatened language" (Fishman 2001, 11).

the largest number of people whose mother tongue is Euskara is found among the population older than sixty-five (23.5 percent). This percentage decreases as age decreases, although there is an upturn in the population younger than twenty-four years of age in the CAPV-EAE, and also to a lesser degree in Navarre.

It is additionally important to bear in mind that the mother tongue of 30.2 percent of bilinguals is Spanish or French; they are the "new Basque-speakers" (*euskaldun berriak*), those that have learned Euskara in school or in adult classes (in adult education schools that teach Basque, known as *euskaltegiak*). And the majority of bilingual young people in the CAPV-EAE are "new speakers," which is important to bear in mind when considering the opportunities to use Euskara and its ease of use (Gobierno Vasco 2009a, 63–67, 85). In any case, it should be noted that the percentage of young people over twenty years of age with Basque as their mother tongue has increased (15 percent in 1986 compared to 20 percent in 2006); and that the current percentage of full bilinguals (those that speak Euskara at home along with Spanish or French) is greater than in 1986 over all age groups. In sum, then the younger the age, the greater the difference: 5.7 percent of children between the ages of 5 and 9 were fully bilingual in 1986; while this percentage rose to 11.9 percent in 2006.

Regarding family transmission, the data from respondents with children aged 2–9 years old show that when both parents are bilingual, Euskara is the transmitted language in more than 98 percent of the cases in the CAPV-EAE and in Navarre, with the percentage being ten points less in the case of the Northern Basque Country (Gobierno Vasco 2008a, 212). When only one of the parents is bilingual, almost 80 percent received Euskara (or Euskara and Spanish) at home in the CAPV-EAE, almost 70 percent in Navarre, and slightly more than 40 percent in the Northern Basque Country (the large majority of them along with French).[8]

But, as previously noted, there are other important channels that help language transmission: for example, the education system as well as adult education, which I will discuss below when I examine the language policies put into effect in each territory.

Use of Basque

Fishman's (1991) theoretic and practical proposal for helping linguistic communities whose native languages are threatened, and which inspired many language policies in recent years, emphasizes the importance of regularly

---

8. A much more detailed study concerning the CAPV-EAE was recently published by the Basque Government (2008b).

Figure 6.4. Data on parent's language competences

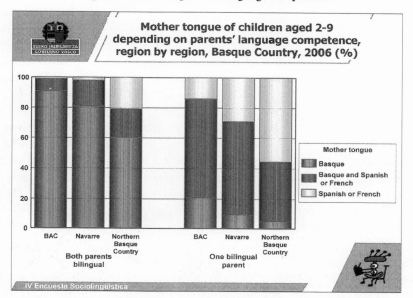

measuring the use of a minoritized language in order to determine the course of its evolution.[9] The use, in turn, must be measured keeping in mind the distinct functions that a language must fulfill (Fishman 2001, 2).[10] That is why, starting in 2001, the Basque government began to measure the use of Euskara in three areas: "home, friends, and the formal domain, the last-named of which has four subdivisions: health care and council services in the public sector, and local shops and banking outlets in the private sector" (Gobierno Vasco 2008a, 215), to which a fourth area was added, the workplace, which was only applicable to people of working age (approximately 50 percent of the respondents). Furthermore, bearing in mind that there were two principal factors that determined use—"the density of the Basque-speaking social network and a speaker's command of the two languages in question" (Gobierno Vasco 2008a, 54)—the sociolinguistic zone variable was included, dif-

---

9. "Due to the time-interval requirement for the most convincing study of language shift, so that the incidence of language use in Time A can be compared, for an equivalent sample of Xmen, with the incidence of corresponding use in Time B, the major tactical problem for the study of LS [language shift] is often that of finding an earlier study that can serve as a benchmark for a currently contemplated comparative study" (Fishman 1991, 41).

10. "Any theory and practice of assistance to threatened languages... must begin with a model of the functional diversification of languages. If analysts can appropriately identify the functions that are endangered as a result of the impact of stronger languages and cultures on weaker ones, then it may become easier to recommend which therapeutic steps must be undertaken in order to counteract any injurious impact that occurs" (Fishman 2001, 2).

ferentiating four sociolinguistic zones, depending on the density of bilingual speakers: Zone 1 (with a bilingual population of less than 20 percent); Zone 2 (with a bilingual population between 20–50 percent); Zone 3 (with a bilingual population between 50–80 percent); and Zone 4 (with a bilingual population that was higher than 80 percent). The data showed that "over the past fifteen years the use of Basque has increased steadily in the [CAPV-EAE], remained constant in Navarre and decreased in the North" (Gobierno Vasco 2008a, 216), but also that the sociolinguistic zone was a decisive influence: in Zone 1, despite having an almost 20 percent bilingual population, less than 10 percent of the people used Euskara in any degree; in Zone 2, this figure rose to slightly more than 30 percent; in Zone 3, more than 60 percent of the respondents used Euskara to some degree or another; and in Zone 4 (with the highest density of bilinguals), 70 percent of those questioned used Euskara as much as or even more than Spanish or French, arriving at almost 90 percent of the population using Euskara at any given time, although not as frequently as Spanish or French.

Nevertheless, it is essential to cross-reference this data with the data regarding the total population in each zone (Gobierno Vasco 2008a, 44): in the CAPV-EAE, half of the population lives in Zone 1; 25 percent live in Zone 2, 19 percent in Zone 3, and only 5 percent live in Zone 4 with the highest density of Basque-speakers. It is a similar case in the Northern Basque Country. In Navarre, which has been officially divided into three linguistic zones— Basque-speaking, mixed, and non-Basque speaking—since the Basque law of 1986,[11] just over half of the population lives in the mixed zone, a third in the non-Basque speaking zone, and only 10 percent in the Basque-speaking zone.

If instead of looking at the total population, we analyze how bilingual speakers are divided by zones, we see that 51 percent live in Zone 2, while only 9 percent live in the highest density zone (Zone 4); by contrast, 32 percent lived in Zone 2 in 1981, and 15.4 percent resided in zones with higher densities of Basque speakers. It is therefore obvious, as Baztarrika remarks (2009, 202), that "today's bilinguals, contrary to what occurred twenty years ago, are concentrated in zones in which there are less opportunities to use Euskera."

Regarding the environments in which Euskara is used, figure 6.6[12] shows that in the bilingual population between the years of 1991and 2006, Euskara was used less in the home during 2006, data that was also corroborated by the fourth sociolinguistic map (Gobierno Vasco 2009a). One can easily under-

---

11. See chapter 2.
12. Developed for the publication of the *Fourth Sociolinguistic Survey* (Gobierno Vasco 2008c).

stand this if we remember that there are increasingly more bilinguals that acquired Euskara outside of the home, and that increasingly more bilinguals live in Spanish-speaking zones. It is not the same with regard to children (also easily understood by looking at the language transmission data). Nevertheless, the use of Euskara has increased substantially in formal domains and in the workplace.

Figure 6.5. Evolution of bilingual speakers who use Basque as much as or more than Spanish or French by environments, 1991–2006 (percent)

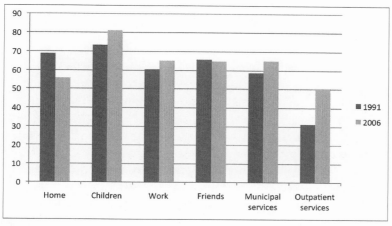

Source: Eustat.

The fourth sociolinguistic map (Gobierno Vasco 2009a, 75–83, 86) offers more detailed data concerning the use of the language at home in the CAPV-EAE, and specifically data that shows that the level of home use hardly changed over fifteen years. Keeping in mind the increase of bilinguals in those last few years, there are more and more bilinguals that use Spanish in the home. However, this data needs to be analyzed in light of Basque-speakers' first language (remember that more than half of bilingual young people have acquired the language in school) and according to the respective sociolinguistic zone:

Eighty percent of bilinguals whose first language was exclusively Spanish prefer to use that language within the family, while only 2.4 percent prefer Euskera. In contrast, 64 percent of Basque speakers due to familial transmission mainly use Euskera at home, and 10 percent mainly use Spanish. Looking at the sociolinguistic zone, 88 percent of bilinguals that live in the first sociolinguistic zone (less than 20 percent bilingual) use Spanish above all else at home. It is only starting with the third zone that bilinguals begin to mostly use Euskera within the family, 55 percent in the third and 71 percent in the fourth zone (Baztarrika, 2009, 207).

Finally, bearing in mind the age variable, in the CAPV-EAE the largest percentage of the population that use Euskara as much as or more than Spanish is found among those younger than twenty-five years old (23.5 percent). It is a similar situation in Navarre, although only 6.7 percent of young people use Euskara regularly there. However, in the Northern Basque Country, people over sixty-five use Euskara the most (18.5 percent). In sum, "the younger the group, the lower the figures for language use until we get to the youngest group. The use index for the 16-to-24 group improves slightly in comparison to the preceding age groups" (Gobierno Vasco 2008c, 111).

Attitudes toward Efforts to Promote Basque

If, as we will see later, the will of the people is the key factor that can determine the success or failure of any language plan and policy for the promotion of a language, in the Basque case as well, "The decisive factor for the change produced in Euskera's situation is the citizens' attitude and behavior" (Baztarrika, 2009, 164).

There are three attitudes worth highlighting when analyzing how measures regarding the promotion of Euskara are received by society: the favorable attitude of the majority toward adopting measures for promoting Euskara (measured by the successive sociolinguistic surveys); the effort that numerous people have made to acquire the Basque language; and the overwhelming majority of mothers and fathers that chose, for their sons and daughters, educational models that in their view are the most effective in assuring the acquisition of Euskara (I will analyze these last two points in connection with applied language policies).

Figure 6.6 shows the evolution of people's attitudes toward promoting Euskara between 1991 and 2006 in each territory: this was clearly mostly favorable in 1991 and increased over the course of fifteen years, while approximately 10 percent of the population remained opposed to adopting measures for promoting the minoritized language.[13] Those that favored the language's promotion also increased in Navarre, but failed to reach 40 percent. Meanwhile, still in Navarre, despite decreasing in number, the percentage of those opposed to active promotion policies for Euskara was only slightly lower than those that displayed a favorable attitude. Once again it was the Northern Basque Country that produced more disheartening data, as it was the only territory in which the number of those opposed to adopting promotional measures increased.

---

13. Those that are interested in studying this issue more in depth should consult the work of Amorrortu, Ortega, Idiazabal, and Barreña (2009).

Figure 6.6. Evolution of attitudes regarding the promotion of the use of Basque by territories (percent)

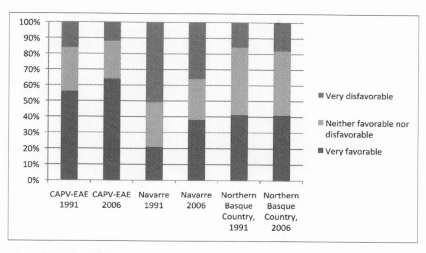

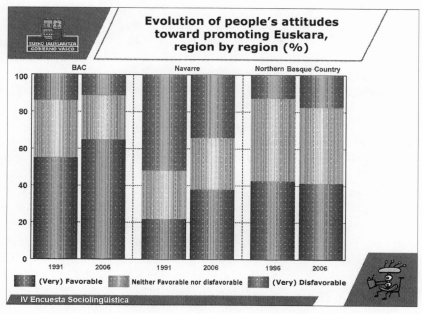

Having analyzed the data related to knowledge, use, and attitudes, we will now examine the nature of the language policies carried out in each territory and that, in large part, explain the different situations that exist in Euskal Herria (the Basque Country).

The Language Policies

In all societies in which two or three languages coexist or, put another way, in societies where linguistic diversity exists, there is also some type of language policy: "The nature of it is another thing, but something always exists. So much so that the absence of a language policy also constitutes a type of language policy" (Baztarrika, 2009, 51). Indeed, as Mitxelena stated more than thirty-five years ago (1985a, 187), "tolerance, *laisser faire, laisser passer* in terms of language, has always been and is probably still today, the most practiced policy . . . this policy, like economic liberalism, is a means just as effective as any other—more effective actually, since it entails omission, not an action whose responsibility someone has to take charge of—of favoring some languages and passing over others: it is, therefore, a policy, not a lack of policy."

The CAPV-EAE [14]

Of the three territories, it is, without a doubt, the CAPV-EAE that promotes a language policy that seeks to recover the Basque language, based on a legal framework that is analyzed in this same book. The criteria that have inspired this language policy were recorded in several documents such as the *Criterios básicos para la política del euskera* (Basic criteria for the Basque language policy, Gobierno Vasco 1993), *Futuro de la política lingüística* (The future of the language policy, Gobierno Vasco 2005b), and *Basis for a Language Policy for the Early 21st Century: Towards a Renewed Agreement* (Gobierno Vasco 2009b). The first of these contained statements that still apply today: the aim is linguistic standardization, and this implies that "the minoritized language must be recovered and the features secured, because they have been neglected or they have been lost, and to reach an equality in society as well as in its territory" (Gobierno Vasco 1993, 7). Furthermore, a language policy that desires to achieve this objective must establish priorities, consider tiered objectives, and be flexible: "a plan that responds to every moment, to every situation, to society's wishes, to the availability of mediums, difficulties, and limitations" (Gobierno Vasco 1993, 15). Flexibility and progressiveness were recurring terms in the documents of the Basque institutions. To be sure, any language's promotional policy must be based on political decision-making, but above all, on social will.

A language policy based on the aforementioned principles, whose priorities are transmission, family, youth, all the fields covered by education, encouraging more Basque-speakers and adult literacy in Euskara, the communication media, public administration, and the workplace (Gobierno

---

14. For a more detailed analysis, see Miren Mateo (2005).

Vasco 1993, 22–31) was detailed in the *Plan General de Promoción del Uso del Euskera* (General Plan for Promoting Basque Use,Gobierno Vasco 1999). This plan was built around three areas: language transmission, the social use of Euskara (service provision in the language), and the quality of the language; and it examined specific objectives and proposals for action to achieve the three strategic objectives.

The Basque institutions' language policies were modeled on Fishman's "reversing language shift" (1991), a term that was reflected in *Criterios básicos para la política del euskera* (Gobierno Vasco, 1993). Fishman proposes eight degrees that make up his Graded Intergenerational Disruption Scale (GIDS)—which he compares to the Richter scale used to measure the intensity of earthquakes—that would serve to measure the intensity of the threat to a particular minoritized language (Fishman 1991, 87–109). Following Fishman's model,[15] programs were implemented to introduce the language into the schools; to teach adults the language; to promote the use of Euskara in social and labor environments; [16] and to encourage its use in public administration.[17] These were implemented with the aim, as Xabier Aizpurua (2002, 153) acknowledges, to identify the most efficient and viable measures, and once identified, to establish these as priority measures. Moreover, according to Fishman (2001, 14): "threatened languages must establish both a priority of functions and of linkages between functions in order to derive the maximal benefit from their relatively weak resource base and unfavorable resource competitive setting."

Among the measures adopted over the course of twenty-five years, I would highlight decree 138/1983, July 11, issued by the Department of Education and Culture (Gobierno Vasco 1983), which regulates the use of the two official languages in nonuniversity education, and establishes three educational models in compulsory education: Model A (instruction in Spanish, teaching Euskara as an additional subject), Model D (instruction in Euskara with Spanish as an additional subject), and Model B (that involves using both official languages as vehicular languages of instruction); from these choices, parents select the linguistic model that they want their children educated in.

The almost thirty years that have gone by since the decree was passed[18] have seen a large number of parents select the models where the most Basque

---

15. Fishman himself includes Euskara among the case studies in his work dealing with the "reversing language shift" model. See "The Cases of Basque and Frisian" (Fishman 1991, 149–86).

16. The Lanhitz program (www.euskara.euskadi.net/r59-734/es/ (Last accessed June 19, 2012)).

17. There were four consecutive plans, the last of which covered the 2008–2012 time period, to be completed with the criteria established by the Basque government. See Gobierno Vasco (2008c).

18. A detailed evaluation of the first fifteen years by territory, by type of elementary and high school (both public or private), and by educational year, as well as data on teacher-training programs and the creation of materials can be found in Mikel Zalbide (1998).

is spoken, D and B, to the detriment of Model A, especially in early childhood and primary education. As Baztarrika observes (2009, 185): "the choice is clear: Model A has declined from 80 percent in the 1982–83 academic year to barely 19 percent in 2009–2010, while during this same time Model D has gone from 12 percent to 58 percent." Universities, especially the public Universidad del País Vasco/Euskal Herriko Unibertsitatea (University of the Basque Country, UPV/EHU), have also witnessed the introduction and development of Euskara. Today nearly 60 percent of students decide to take the university entrance exams in Euskara; and more than 40 percent of first-time enrolled students at the UPV/EHU choose to pursue their studies in Basque.[19] This leads Baztarrika (2009, 185) to conclude that, "In 15–20 years, a large proportion of the elite that Euskadi will count on will also speak Euskera. It does not seem unreasonable, therefore, to think that it will link Euskera with modern values, and that, to the same extent, Euskera will gain specific weight in urban environments and professional sectors, thus strengthening its social recognition."

The efforts made in primary, secondary, and university education have been complemented by the creation of specific educational institutions to teach Euskara to adults: euskaltegis , coordinated by HABE (Helduen Alfabetatze eta Berreuskalduntzerako Erakundea, the Institute for Literacy and Re-Basquization of Adults),[20] in which some 40,000 adults learn or improve their Euskara every year.

The key to the growth of Euskara is in the data in figures 6.1 and 6.3: specifically, bilinguals under forty-five years old (including passive bilinguals) are more numerous than monolingual Spanish-speakers; and of those people younger than fifteen, 75 percent are bilingual, while monolingual Spanish-speakers do not even add up to 10 percent.

Nevertheless, already in 1993 there was an awareness of schools' limitations in creating new Basque-speakers,[21] limitations that have been noted and underscored by several authors (Aizpurua 2002; Zalbide 1998, Gobierno Vasco 2005b, 2009b, and so on). In reality, there are two types of limitations, although essentially the first determine the second: the extent to which young

---

19. Those who are interested in finding out more on this matter should consult the master plan for Euskara at the UPV/EHU for the period 2007/2008–2011/2012 (UPV/EHU 2007, www.euskara-errektoreordetza.ehu.es/p267-content/es/contenidos/informacion/plan_informa/es_plan/adjuntos/plan_director.pdf (Last accessed June 19, 2012). However, the recent implementation of the single district system that negates priority entrance of CAPV-EAE students into the UPV/EHU may result in a decreased demand for Euskara due to an increased number of students from other autonomous communities enrolling in this university.

20. A public institute created by Basque parliamentary law 29/1983.

21. "Regarding the Reversing Language Shift, it is known that the schools themselves, for example, do not possess the sole capacity to revive a language" (Gobierno Vasco 1993, 19).

Basques learn Euskara in school and the extent to which they use it thereafter. Today there is evidence that even the proficiency in Euskara of those enrolled in Model D varies considerably, depending on the sociolinguistic environment in which these students find themselves. In his research on the question, Mikel Zalbide (2000, 50--56) tackles the issues of both knowledge and use: according to him, proficiency in Euskara differs greatly even among those students enrolled in Model D, depending on their mother tongue and the density of bilinguals in their surroundings. Concerning use, during the first years of enrollment, Model D students whose mother tongue is Euskara use the language; but upon entering into adolescence, the language of their *cuadrilla* (circle of friends) or peer group, or that of the neighborhood or public environment in which they socialize becomes more influential. One must conclude, then, that,

> Our education system, with the exception of Model A, facilitates students becoming Basque-speakers up to a minimal level. And that represents a great achievement. In any case, Models B and D do not guarantee, by themselves and only by themselves, children and young people becoming Basque-speakers, given the educational system's clear limitations. It is obvious that other efforts must be simultaneously carried out in diverse social domains: family, leisure, enterprise, etc. The educational system, despite exceptions, does not resolve—nor can it—the problem of authentic learning of the language. (Gobierno Vasco 2009b, 20)

This is why programs have been initiated that promote students' use of Euskara outside of the classroom, in extracurricular activities during their leisure time (Gobierno Vasco 2004);[22] because, as Fishman (2001, 14) states, it is necessary to combine school efforts with the family-neighborhood-community environment: "school language efforts are often not linked to home-family-neighborhood-community functions. Threatened languages cannot afford functionally diffuse or free-floating efforts."

Navarre

In contrast to the situation in in the CAPV-EAE, "The whole issue of Euskara in Navarre seems imbued with a restrictive character" (Rodríguez Ochoa 2001, 591), or as Jose Mª Legarra and Erramun Baxok (2005, 28) state, "In short, the intention [in Navarre] is to relegate Basque exclusively to optional subjects

---

22. Along the same line, in reflecting on an appropriate language policy for the twenty-first century, it was established that "in any case, a special effort should be made in Spanish-speaking areas, in order to guarantee the use of Euskara in extracurricular activities. For that, it is necessary to promote cooperation protocols between schools and neighborhood, town, and city associations, in an attempt to offer the student appropriate networks to continue using Euskara in informal domains" (Gobierno Vasco 2009b, 52).

and to make sure it disappears from the administrative sphere." In Navarre, one might say that society itself has been and continues to forge ahead of its institutions. In other words, it is Navarrese society itself that demands Model D classrooms in the mixed zone, [23] because in Navarre the advancement of Euskara is also taking place among the youngest population also, thanks especially to the schools. If from 1991 to 2006 there was an increase of 16,200 bilinguals (a change of 9.5 to 11.1 percent), "Growth in the number of bilinguals has taken place in all age groups below thirty-five. This increase is particularly marked in the youngest part of the population. Today 19.1 percent of the population between 16–24 are fully bilingual, as are 12.5 percent of the population between 25–34 years of age" (Gobierno Vasco 2008a, 142).

Bearing in mind that in Navarre the teaching of Euskara in any of the models (A, B, or G)[24] is only obligatory in the Basque-speaking zone and that in the other two zones it depends on parental demand, the evolution of instruction in Navarre has been as follows (Aldasoro 2001, 613):

Table 6.2: School models in Navarre

	1988/89	2000/01
Model D	13.34 percent	25.25 percent
Model A	5.48 percent	26.67 percent
Model G	81.18 percent	48.08 percent

Source: Aldasoro (2001). Aldasoro (2001) does not include data from Model B because the percentage of students enrolled in this model is negligible.

Even though in the Basque-speaking zone, 85.26 percent of students are educated in Model D, while in the mixed zone 28.18 percent attend a Model D school and 22.4 percent a Model A school, the Navarrese institutions have not promoted teaching in Euskara nor have they facilitated the opening of Model D classrooms; still "the social response continues to be positive and enrollment in the bilingual educational models continues to increase slowly, but progressively" (Legarra and Baxok 2005, 28). At any rate, the Universidad Pública de Navarra/Nafarroako Unibertsitatea Publikoa (the Public University of Navarre, UPNA/NUP) still does not have any standardization plan for Euskara.

As in the CAPV-EAE, Navarre has also been aware of school limitations and because of this has created strategies and programs for using Euskara in the classroom as well as in informal contexts; among these is the "lagunarteko hizkera" (colloquial speech) program, "where during a monitored activity,

23. See chapter 2 for an analysis of the Basque law and the linguistic division of Navarre.
24. Model G, which is specific to Navarre, does not offer Euskara even as a subject in school.

students come to understand and use expressive language in informal situations" (Aldasoro 2001, 616). Together with the schools, each year the euskaltegis help between five and six thousand adults begin to learn or improve their knowledge of the Basque language (Aldasoro 2001, 613).

Schools and euskaltegis testify to the adherence of Navarrese society to Euskara, an adherence that is much more visible in the Basque-speaking and mixed zones. In this respect, Miquel Gros i Lladós (2007, 190–91) points out the importance that the Basque substratum has in the social consciousness:

> An objective factor like the historical presence of Euskara in a region is just one more fact, rather than circumstantial evidence, in explaining the language's resilience. The regions that kept Euskara alive have maximum enrollment rates in Euskara, and those that were marked by language replacement [in other words, losing Basque] have between 70 and 90 percent of their children speaking Basque. Next, the regions that lost Euskera during the twentieth century demonstrate a majority percentage of Basque-speakers among their juvenile population. The numerous regions that saw their native Euskara fade away throughout the nineteenth century are all within a range in which about half of their children speak Basque again (between 65 and 35 percent) . . . The regions that were totally or partially Basque-speaking until the sixteenth or eighteenth century show a percentage of Basque-speaking children that is between 50 and 30 percent . . . Lastly, and logically, the regions where Euskera barely had a historical presence during the Middle Ages are those that demonstrate the weakest recovery indexes, always below [a rate of] 30 percent of Basque-speaking children, percentages that continued to drop to under 10 percent the more one advances into the Ribera, a region where there is no reliable documented Euskara presence.

Northern Basque Country

This is undoubtedly the territory that presents the most worrying data. It is a territory in which the *laisser faire, laisser passer* policy has predominated until quite recently and in which, once again, attempts to revive the language have fallen mostly to society rather than institutions. Legarra and Baxok conclude that:

> It is evident that general language planning is needed for the Basque language. Limited solutions do not produce good results. Over the last thirty years in the Northern Basque Country, Basque language associations have grown out of all proportion: the Ikas pedagogical movement, Basque-medium schools, itinerant teachers, AEK (an organization coordinating literacy in Basque and Basque learning programs for adults), Basque language radio stations, bilingual classrooms, summer camps and others. Nevertheless, the number of young Basque speakers in the 16–25 age group has fallen from 27 percent

to 11 percent. In contrast, in the Basque Autonomous Community (BAC), the Basque language has made a significant advance from 21 percent to 33 percent among young people and has jumped to 62 percent among school children. The difference between the two regions lies in language planning. (2005, 34–5)

The effort made by a group of about forty people—professors, Euskaltzaindia (The Academy of the Basque Language) academics, elected representatives, and representatives from different cultural associations—to lay the foundation for language planning ended with the 2004 creation of the Public Bureau of the Basque Language; a public interest organization sponsored by the state of France, the Aquitaine Regional Council, the département of Pyrénées Atlantiques, the Syndicat Intercommunal in support of Basque culture, and the Basque Council of Public Office-Holders.[25] Its mission consists of defining and initiating a public and concerted language policy in favor of the Basque language, and to mobilize the financial means necessary to carry out the planned actions. In late 2006 a language policy project was approved that had the central objective of securing completely bilingual speakers, especially among the younger generations. And in this objective of gaining bilingual speakers, the factors noted above were acknowledged (and repeated): motivation, knowledge, and use. The focus is, then, on the importance of familial transmission and on education, for children as well as for adults, on communication mediums, the world of leisure, and on toponymy.

As regards the field of education—a key area in the CAPV-EAE and also largely in Navarre for increasing bilingual people—for years in the Northern Basque Country, the only education in Euskara was that offered by ikastolas or Basque-medium secondary education schools (twenty-seven in all), in which more than two thousand students were taught. Bilingual classrooms emerged in 1983 in public schools and in 1986 in private schools. However, in total, only 22.3 percent of children were taught in an immersion model (ikastola) or in a bilingual model ("Ikas bi") during the 2003–2004 school year; both public and private schools offered three hours of Euskara per week for those that wished to learn the Basque language; and 72 percent did not receive any type of instruction in Euskara. Nevertheless, the creation of the Public Bureau of the Basque Language, and the efforts made to implement a language policy that promoted Euskara, have begun to bear fruit: 32.4 percent of people older than sixty-five are bilingual; 26.8 percent of 50–64 year olds are bilingual; 17.5 percent in the 35–49 age group; 11.6 percent among those

---

25. See www.mintzaira.fr/fr/oplb.html (Last accessed June 19, 2012).The steps taken between 2000 and the creation of the Public Bureau of the Basque Language in 2004 are outlined in Legarra and Baxok (2005).

in the 25–34 age group; and 16.1 percent of young people between the ages of 16–24 are bilingual (almost 5 percent more than in 2001). That 16.1 percent signifies that the trend of losing bilingual speakers as one descends the age groups had stopped and has begun a slow, but hopeful, recovery. This was the data that made Max Brisson, then President of the Public Bureau of the Basque Language, entitle the Northern Basque Country chapter, "alarming statistics amidst rays of hope" (Gobierno Vasco 2008a, 73).

Future Challenges

The data that we have seen speaks for itself of the effort made to increase the number of bilingual people, or people that possess sufficient knowledge of Euskara, and of the success achieved. We have also seen the efforts made in the CAPV-EAE to spread the use of Euskara into environments that, until now, were unknown. From this viewpoint, Euskara has gained social functions that, as Mitxelena said, it had not possessed throughout its history. However, one should also recall the changes produced in Basque society as a whole in order to be able to accurately value the increase in the knowledge of Euskara, especially among young people (Gobierno Vasco 2008a, 199–200): specifically, one should note the progressive aging of the Basque population, due to higher life expectancy as well as declining birth rates (in the CAPV-EAE and in Navarre, between 1991 and 2006, the population over sixty-five increased almost 50 percent); and the increase in immigration, above all in the CAPV-EAE (2 percent in 1991, 5 percent in 2006) and in Navarre (2 percent in 1991, 10 percent in 2006); changes pointed out by several authors (Aizpurua 2002, Gros i Lladós 2007, Baztarrika 2009). The first of these changes has meant that, in absolute numbers, there has been no great increase in bilingual numbers because, as we have seen, the largest increase, with a significant difference, occurred in the younger age brackets, those whose significance has diminished in the population pyramid. The second change has meant that attracting immigrants to the world of Euskara has become one of the action priorities adopted by institutions. The 2001 survey states that "Similarly, now is the time to offer newly-arrived immigrants the resources and facilities they require for learning and using the Basque language" (Gobierno Vasco 2003, 20). In this regard, the AISA program excelled in introductory courses for immigrants.[26]

But, without a doubt, the major future challenge is use. Without renouncing the importance of increasing knowledge, promoting use needs to take priority, above all keeping in mind that Euskara is acquired in school as a second language by more than half of young people. The importance of use was

---

26. See www.habe.euskadi.net/s23-4728/es/contenidos/noticia/aisa/es_12745/aisa.html (Last accessed June 19, 2012).

first noted in the data from the third survey: "We urgently need to establish strategies aimed at ensuring that bilingual speakers, for whom Basque is not their first language, can consolidate and improve their language competence, in an effort to encourage them to use Basque more often in their daily lives" (Gobierno Vasco 2003, 20). For that, "the first challenge before us . . . relates to the use of Euskera, and proposals must be aimed at that challenge, cooperation must be promoted in that direction, and exemplary references must be placed within that perspective" (Gobierno Vasco 2005b, 19). In this regard, the document *Basis for a Language Policy for the Early 21st century: Towards a New Agreement* Gobierno Vasco 2009b, 16) notes two tasks that cannot be postponed: strengthening the use of Euskara in informal environments; and social recognition of a new Basque-speaker's contribution to maintaining the language. We must accept that we are moving toward a society in which there will be increasingly more bilingual people, but with different degrees of proficiency in Euskara. The challenge is, precisely, to encourage each person to use Euskara in some way.

In order to promote use, we need to take dual action. Language policy at the beginning of the twenty-first century should give high priority to Euskara's vital niches, because language requires preeminent spaces to develop: "It is in such vital niches, and in no other place, where the language to be revitalized must find enough strongholds in that which concerns its intergenerational transmission as well as in the language's communicative functions, and in its reference values. If such vital niches are not cared for, created and, if possible, extended, any other effort will most likely be in vain" (Gobierno Vasco 2009b, 16). Yet efforts to revitalize the language cannot be limited to Euskara's vital niches alone. Many young people encounter limitations because Euskara is their second language, because they live in Spanish-speaking zones, and because their relational networks primarily function in Spanish. Thus, a special effort has to be made in the Spanish-speaking areas in order to guarantee the use of Euskara in extracurricular activities, so that the language learned at school as a second language can become the "intimate language," which is also needed to live and socialize in Euskara away from school.[27] In fact, the primary key to the future resides in "guaranteeing family transmission particularly ensuring that bilingual children who are under thirty in twenty-five years times use Basque as a family language" (Gobierno Vasco 2009b, 54). The major challenge, therefore, is the use, in formal environments, but above all, in informal settings.

---

27. According to Fishman (2001, 14), "post- and out-of-school functions for threatened language must also be increasingly assured for adolescents and young adults (e.g. clubs, sports teams, hobby group, etc.), otherwise these young post-scholars will have no further use for their threatened language until their own pre-parental period, by which time they may well have to relearn it."

However, we must not forget that, above any other factor concerning use, the most important requirement is the willingness to use Euskara. As Mitxelena (1985b, 196–97) comments, minoritized languages "if they have been preserved, if they are to continue living, it is due to the devotion that has been given to them by people of all ages and diverse conditions. In English that is often called *language loyalty.*" Proficiency, the network of daily relationships, and the mother tongue are all important factors that affect use, but the most important is adherence to the language (Baztarrika 2009, 201).

As regards a final reference to the other two territories, there is no doubt that the future challenges are also the same in Navarre and in the Northern Basque Country. But in Navarre's case, keeping in mind the progress that Euskara has experienced, especially among those younger than fifteen years old, there is an urgent need to revise the division of the territory into linguistic zones. Utilizing the same parameters from 1986 (a higher than 5 percent Euskara presence was the criterion for including regions and municipalities in the mixed zone; a rate higher than 10 percent was needed to be included in the Basque-speaking zone), today the municipalities included in the mixed zones (and in the Basque-speaking zone) would be much higher. For Gros i Lladós (2007, 211) "The data show that both linguistic zones—the Basque-speaking and the mixe—have doubled the minimum percentages of Euskera's presence needed to be declared part of that zone." Although the challenge of use will continue to be a crucial factor, a "resizing" of the linguistic zones will favor the continued gain of bilingual persons through the schools.

7

Linguistic School Models in the Basque Country

JULIAN MAIA, the University of the Basque Country (UPV/EHU)

The Basque Country/Euskal Herria[1] as a whole can be considered a trilingual country, divided into two bilingual parts. Three languages are relatively widely used in the territory of its seven historic provinces: while to the north of the Pyrenean political border (Iparralde in Basque) Euskara and French are spoken, to the south (Hegoalde) Euskara and Spanish are used.

Euskara is a language of pre-Indo-European origin and has been established since prehistoric times in the whole of the territory of Euskal Herria (which means "country or people of Euskara"). In this sense, it can be considered the country's "own" language. Spanish and French are languages that are historically associated with the Spanish and French states. Both states have implemented, on an ongoing basis, an active linguistic policy of promoting their official language, while Basque has been ignored (when not persecuted). In general terms, the application of this policy has made Euskara the "L" language in the diglossic relationship it maintains with French and Spanish, which are the dominant languages in their respective state spheres.

The seven provinces that make up the historical extension of the cultural Basque Country (Euskal Herria) belong politically to two different states and constitute a threefold politico-administrative reality. The four provinces located in the Spanish state make up two distinct autonomous communities: on the one hand, the Comunidad Autónoma del País Vasco-Euskal Autonomia Erkidegoa (CAPV-EAE, the Autonomous Community of the Basque Country), with the three provinces of Gipuzkoa, Bizkaia, and Araba; and on the other, the province of Upper Navarre, which constitutes on its own the Comunidad Foral de Navarra-Nafarroako Foru Komunitatea (the Foral Community of Navarre or CFN-NFK). The three provinces north of the Pyrenees—Lapurdi, Behe-Nafarroa, and Zuberoa in Euskara—do not make up

---

1. The ambiguity of the name "Basque Country" is explained in chapter 1.

a political or administrative community of their own,[2] but instead, together with Béarn, form part of the Département des Pyrenées Atlantiques, located in its turn in the French region of Acquitaine. In what follows, therefore, I will refer to three communities differentiated by their politico-administrative status: the French Basque Country or Iparralde to the north of the Pyrenees and the CAPV-EAE and CFN-NFK to the south.[3]

In the mid-twentieth century, Basque society found itself immersed in an undisguised process of linguistic substitution: knowledge and use of the dominant languages (Spanish and French) was spreading, at the same time that the number of Basque-speakers was falling and the whole complex of social functions channeled through that language was being undermined. In the 1950s and 1960s, Euskara had no significant presence in the educational systems of any of its territories. In this context, in the era of General Franco's dictatorship in Spain (1939–75), a noteworthy movement in defense of the Basque language developed in the peninsular Basque territory or Hegoalde (Euskaltzaindia 1977). Upon Franco's death in 1975, the Spanish state's recently created autonomous communities acquired a certain political decision-making capability, which made it possible to establish a new orientation for linguistic policy in relation to Basque in the two autonomous communities of the Spanish state where it is used: the CAPV-EAE and the CFN-NFK. In the French state, Basque was practically ignored by the authorities. However, in recent years, although to a lesser extent than in the CAPV-EAE and the CFN-NFK, a change in the value assigned to Euskara has also been taking place in the French Basque Country or Iparralde.

The fact of belonging to different political entities entails the existence of different realities and approaches in aspects such as the linguistic policy applied with respect to Basque. The Spanish and French states share the trait of promoting their respective official state languages (Spanish and French), while they differ in the policy applied with regard to the minority languages in their territories, one of which is Basque. At a second level, the governments of Euskal Herria's three politico-administrative communities apply different linguistic policies with respect to the languages of their territories, in which these policies are implemented amid diverse sociolinguistic and educational realities, within the general legislative framework of the respective Spanish and French states. At the same time, together with the institutional arena and the communications media, the educational system is customarily one of the basic institutional pillars of linguistic policy.

---

2. Although many Basques refer to the three collectively as Iparralde, which means "northern part" in Euskara.

3. Many Basques call the area made up of the latter two territories Hegoalde, which means "southern part."

As a consequence of the new linguistic policy applied in recent years in the Basque Country's different administrative communities, there has been a very noticeable increase in the demand for bilingual Basque-Spanish and/ or Basque-French education.[4] This has served to promote the development of the Basque language without prejudicing knowledge of Spanish or French in their respective territories of reference. It must be kept in mind that, as a result of the linguistic policies actively or passively applied in the French and Spanish states, (practically) everyone in the Southern Basque Country (CAPV-EAE and CFN-NFK) speaks Spanish, just as all citizens of the Northern Basque Country know French; this is not the case with Basque, known only by a minority of the population (see the data on this in chapter 6).

In the next section, I will present an overview of some basic aspects of linguistic policy and discuss the educational systems in the three communities, focusing on the educational models used from the perspective of the presence of Basque in this arena. For each community, I will consider as points of reference such elements as the basic legal framework, the linguistic characteristics of the different educational models, the evolution in demand for the different models, and the evaluation of the results, in order to conclude with a reflection on the new challenges related to language that Basque society is facing in its educational system.

The Basque Language in the Bilingual Educational System of the Basque Country

Although the concept of bilingual instruction or bilingual education has been subject to a variety of refinements and has been the object of a number of conceptual restrictions with which I agree (see Siguàn and Mackey 1987; Serra and Vila 2000), for the purposes of this study I will consider all educational models that include the presence of the country's marginalized language (Euskara), including those that only provide for teaching *of the Basque language*.

Despite the politico-administrative division of the territories of Euskal Herria, some similarities exist with regard to the educational systems in those territories and the presence of Euskara in those systems. On the one hand, the levels and stages into which these educational systems are divided are similar in the three territories. Table 7.1 shows the similarities between the Spanish system (applied in Hegoalde or the CAPV-EAE and the CFN-NFK) and the French system (applied in Iparralde).

---

4. In this study, when I refer to bilingual education, it will always be in the context that one of the languages is Euskara. Consequently, I will not be considering bilingual educational models in other languages (for example, the Spanish/English bilingual models that currently exist).

Table 7.1. Levels of the non-university educational systems of the Spanish (Hegoalde) and French (Iparralde) states

Hegoalde	Level	Age	Iparralde	Level	Age
Non mandatory	Preschool education	2–6	Non mandatory	École maternelle	2–6
Mandatory	Primary education	6–12	Mandatory	École élémentaire	6–11
	Obligatory secondary education	12–16		Collège	11–15
Non mandatory	Obligatory postsecondary education	16–18	Non mandatory	Baccalauréat	15–18

In each of the three territories, three networks of schools exist: the public network, the private religious network, and the network of ikastolas (community-organized schools teaching in Basque). There are also a number of non-religious private schools.

Euskara is present in the educational system in two basic modalities, according to the role it plays in educational tasks. In some cases, it is merely a curricular subject (the language is understood only as an object of teaching and learning), while in others it is used as the principal channel of academic content (Euskara as a means of instruction or channel of teaching and learning for other curricular content). In other words, we can speak of two concepts:

Table 7.2. Similarities among the models for the teaching of Euskara and teaching in Euskara in the three politico-administrative communities into which Euskal Herria is divided

	Teaching *of* Euskara[*]	Teaching *in* Euskara	
		Teaching in Two Languages	Teaching in Euskara
Iparralde	"Awareness." Students: 995	"Equal-time." Students: 6,608	"Immersion." Students: 1,940
CFN-NFK	Model A. Students: 13,564	Model B. Students: 161	Model D. Students: 15,714
CAPV-EAE	Model A. Students: 12,828	Model B. Students: 54,403	Model D. Students: 143,735

Sources: Académie Bordeaux 2010; Gobierno de Navarra, *Guía de estudios* and *Estadística de datos básicos*; Eustat (Basque Statistics Institute).

*. The data for the Northern Basque Country (Iparralde) refer to the premier degré (primary education) level, made up of both *école maternelle* (nursery school) and *école élémentaire* (elementary school). Those for the CFN-NFK and CAPV-EAE correspond to students in *educación infantil* (preschool) and *educación primaria* (primary education).

teaching of Euskara and *teaching in Euskara*. Both modalities are present in the three historical Basque communities, by way of the different linguistic models adopted in the educational arena. Table 7.2 shows the similarities in the approaches to Euskara in the educational systems of the different communities (along with the data for students at the primary level (between six and eleven years old) for the 2010–2011 academic year).

Bilingual Instruction in the Iparralde

Unlike the case of the Basque autonomous communities in the Spanish state, Euskara does not currently enjoy the status of being an official language under French law. The French state is a signatory to the European Charter for Regional or Minority Languages (Council of Europe 1992), but it has not met the conditions for this charter to take effect.[5] Taking as a reference point the movement that began in Hegoalde in the 1950s, the first ikastola in the French Basque Country was created in 1969,[6] for which purpose its backers formed a nonprofit association under a 1901 French law (Euskal Herriko Ikastolak-Euskaltzaindia 2010). In 1969, the French administration also assigned three specialist teachers of Euskara for the educational system (Aldasoro Lecea 2001). Following various ups and downs, the legal situation of the ikastolas and of bilingual education as a whole in the different networks of the French educational system has improved notably. In 2004, the Public Bureau of the Basque Language was created as a public-interest group under French law, through an agreement among state, regional, departmental, and local institutions (www.mintzaira.fr/fr/oplb.html).[7]

Three networks make up the educational system of Iparralde: the public network, the Catholic or religious network, and the network of ikastolas grouped together in the Seaska organization. The Basque language is treated in three different ways in the French educational system: a) "awareness" or "introductory instruction" for one to three hours a week, in which basic elements of Euskara are taught (this *sensibilisation* approach is primarily offered in the public system); b) equal-time bilingual Euskara-French education, in which both languages are used as a means of instruction in primary education, while at the secondary level, Euskara is taught as a subject and one or two other subjects are also taught in Basque (this approach is found in the public system and in private religious schools); and c) an immersion program in Basque, a model developed by the Seaska network of ikastolas, in which

---

5. The list of signatory states can be consulted in Council of Europe (1992).

6. The first initiative dates back to 1964. For historical, pedagogical, and organizational details, see www.seaska.net/web/default.php (Last accessed June 19, 2012) and also Euskal Herriko Ikastolak-Euskaltzaindia (2010).

7. Information on its legal status can be consulted in EEP-OPLB (2004).

Euskara is the principal means of instruction through which all curricular content is channeled, while French is treated as a subject in the school curriculum (Euskararen Erakunde Publikoa-Office Publique de la Langue Basque, EEP-OPBL 2005; Académie Bordeaux 2010).

The number of students enrolled in "awareness instruction" reached 1,400 in the 2004–2005 academic year, although this number fell to 995 registered students in the 2010–2011 academic year. The decline of enrollment in this modality in recent years has been offset by an increase in the demand for bilingual French-Euskara instruction in the public and private religious networks. Table 7.3 shows the evolution of enrollment in equal-time and immersion bilingual classrooms at the *prémier degré* (primary) level.

Table 7.3. Evolution of Enrollment in equal-time and immersion bilingual instructional models

Academic year	2001–02	2002–03	2003–04	2004–05	2005–06	2006–07	2007–08	2008–09	2009–10	2010–11
Equal-time students	3,725	3,955	4,335	4,620	4,557	5,318	5,752	6,052	6,319	6,608
Immersion students	1,385	1,418	1,450	1,460	1,480	1,535	1,625	1,715	1,816	1,940

Source: Académie Bordeaux (2010).

The total figures for teaching in two languages (equal-time plus immersion in Euskara) are increasing significantly in Iparralde, with the result that the use of Basque as a means of instruction (teaching *in* Euskara) is growing. Between the 2004–2005 and 2010–2011 academic years, the number of nursery and elementary schools (students up to eleven years old) offering bilingual instruction increased from 108 to 146, entailing a sustained percentage increase from an initial figure of 42 percent to 57 percent of the total schools in the three networks. The number of students being taught in two languages also saw significant growth, in both absolute numbers and percentage terms, in comparison to non-bilingual education: from 24 percent in 2004–2005 to 34 percent in the 2010–2011 academic year. The data can be seen in table 7.4

Table 7.4. Evolution of the number of schools imparting and students receiving bilingual (B) and non-bilingual (NB) instruction (2004–2005/2010–2011)

	2004–5		2005–6		2006–7		2007–8		2008–9		2009–10		2010–11	
	B	NB	B	NB	B	NB	B	NB	B	NB	B	NB	B	NB
No. of schools	108 (42%)	147 (58%)	112 (44%)	143 (56%)	120 (47%)	136 (53%)	130 (51%)	126 (49%)	132 (51%)	125 (49%)	138 (54%)	117 (46%)	146 (57%)	111 (43%)
No. of students	5,931 (24%)	18,295 (76%)	6,213 (26%)	18,074 (74%)	6,718 (28%)	17,629 (72%)	7,145 (29%)	17,286 (71%)	7,579 (31%)	16,971 (69%)	7,958 (32%)	16,691 (68%)	8,380 (34%)	16,292 (66%)

(Euskararen Erakunde Publikoa—Office Publique de la Langue Basque, EEP-OPLB 2010).[8]

Bilingual Basque/Spanish Instruction in the Spanish State

Article 3 of the 1978 Spanish Constitution establishes that Spanish is the official language of the state and that the other "Spanish" languages will also be official in their respective autonomous communities. It likewise stipulates that all Spaniards have "the duty to know and the right to use" that language. The legislation that shapes both linguistic policy as a whole and its educational components in the CAPV-EAE and the CFN-NFK has been developed on the basis of this article. In the next section, I will discuss various aspects related to the educational arena in both the CAPV-EAE and the CFN-NFK.

Foral Community of Navarre

The 1982 constitutional law on the reinstatement and improvement of the *foral* system in Navarre (Ley Orgánica de Reintegración y Amejoramiento del Régimen Foral de Navarra) establishes in Article 9 that "Spanish is the official language of Navarre" and immediately adds that "Basque will also have the status of an official language in the Basque-speaking zones of Navarre" (Jefatura del Estado Español 1982).

Article 2 of *foral* law 18/1986, dated December 15, 1986, on Basque, considers Spanish and Basque as Navarrese languages and consequently recognizes the right of all Navarrese citizens to know and use them. This article specifies that Spanish is the official language of Navarre and that Basque "is also" an official language, but with territorial limitations. Article 5 establishes that Navarre is divided into three linguistic zones (Gobierno de Navarra 1986): (a) the Basque-speaking zone, made up of sixty-three municipalities (9.3 percent of the total population); (b) a mixed zone containing fifty-two municipalities, among them the capital, Iruñea-Pamplona (54.5 percent of the population); and (c) the zone termed "non-Basque-speaking," made up of the rest of the Upper Navarrese municipalities (36.2 percent of the population).[9]

Perhaps the most significant characteristic of this law is that it configures the linguistic rights of Navarrese citizens as a function of the linguistic zone in which they live (unlike the case in the CAPV-EAE). As far as the educational system is concerned, this Basque law establishes that "all citizens have the right to be taught in Basque and in Spanish at the various educational

---

8. Data for previous years can be consulted in Stuijt/Sánchez (2008).

9. Gobierno de España. Instituto Nacional de Estadística (2011): Censo de 2010. Internet: http://www.ine.es/ (last accessed June 15, 2011).

levels." Nevertheless, the subsequent chapters of the act establish distinctions as a function of linguistic zone.

In the Basque-speaking zone, the act establishes that students are to be taught in the language of their choice, and that the teaching of Basque and Spanish are mandatory, in order that, at the end of their basic schooling, students manifest a sufficient level of "capacity" in both languages. In the mixed zone, on the other hand, "Basque will be taught to those students who desire it, in such a way that at the end of their school careers, they may be able to obtain a sufficient level of knowledge of that language." Finally, in the non-Basque-speaking zone, "the teaching of Basque will be supported and, as applicable, financed in whole or in part by the public authorities with the aim of promoting and encouraging it, in accordance with demand." In this region, the possibility of teaching "in Basque" is not mentioned (Gobierno de Navarra 1986).

Subsequently, a *foral* decree (Gobierno de Navarra 1988) regulated the incorporation and use of Basque in non-university education in Navarre. The decree treats the three sociolinguistic zones into which the *foral* community has been divided in a differentiated way; the law distinguishes between the "teaching of" and "teaching in" Basque, and the basic characteristics of the different models of instruction with regard to the territory's languages are established. The modality of "teaching in Euskara" in the non-Basque-speaking region is not taken into consideration in the decree, on the understanding that this is not a possible option in reality (nevertheless, six ikastolas currently exist in that zone, with a total of 1,115 students in the 2010–2011 academic year).

For preschool (*educación infantil*) and primary (*educación primaria*) education, three linguistic models incorporating (to some extent) the Basque language were initially established: A, B, and D. In model A, teaching is in Spanish, and Euskara is considered a curricular subject, assigned around 15 percent of school hours (four hours a week) at the preschool and primary levels. Model B in its initial formulation was intended for the Basque-speaking zone; teaching is done in Euskara, with a progressive introduction of Spanish in the upper grades. This model has had very little acceptance and currently appears to be on its way to disappearing. In model D, all teaching is in Euskara except for Spanish and foreign languages, which are treated as curricular subjects. In addition, in the case of Navarre, there is also a model G (without any presence of Euskara at all in the school curriculum), which has been widely accepted, unlike the case of the CAPV-EAE, which has not shown any demand for such an option.[10]

In mandatory secondary education (*Enseñanza Secundaria Obligatoria*

---

10. For the initial formulation of the models, see Gobierno de Navarra (1988); for the current situation, see the Navarrese government's guide to academic programs (*guía de estudios*) (Gobierno de Navarra, undated).

or ESO, students between twelve and sixteen years old) today, there are three models from which to choose: G, A, and D. The characteristics of these models are similar to those of their homonyms in the lower grades. In addition, since the 2006–2007 academic year, variants of these models exist with an enhanced presence of English in the school curriculum.

Navarrese society's acceptance of the teaching of Euskara and teaching in Euskara can be observed in the enrollment data for the last few years (see Gobierno de Navarra. *Estadística de datos básicos*, undated). The following aspects are worth noting: (a) most students are enrolled in model G, which does not make any provision for Euskara, although this majority is slowly declining, from 61 percent of enrollment in 2000 to 56 percent in 2010–2011; (b) enrollment in model A oscillates between 18 percent in 2000 and 16 percent in 2010–2011; (c) the programs with an enhanced English presence have been growing since their introduction in the 2006–2007 academic year, while the combined demand for the "pure" G and A models is in slow but constant decline;[11] (d) in the 2010–2011 academic year, models A and G taken together (including the models with an enhanced presence of English) accounted for 76 percent of total enrollment (a large majority, and very different from the case of the CAPV-EAE); (e) the models that have shown themselves to be most effective for students obtaining real Basque-Spanish bilingual proficiency (models B and D) maintain a combined demand reaching 24 percent of the total enrollment in 2010-2011 (in fact, model B attracts less than 0.2 percent of demand).[12]

The absolute and percentage data for the evolution of the demand for the different models over the last decade can be seen in table 7.5, grouped in two large groups, as a function of their efficiency in ensuring the bilingual competence of the attending student. The paltry variation in the percentages combines with a small increase in the demand for models with a greater presence of Euskara (in reality, model D).

Table 7.5. Evolution of enrollment demand at the nonuniversity levels in Navarre, grouping models G+A and B+D (2000–2010)

	2000–1	2002–3	2004–5	2006–7	2008–9	2009–10	2010–11
Models G+A	63,219	64,531	65,933	66,483	69,131	72,747	73,798
	(79%)	(78%)	(78%)	(77%)	(76%)	(76%)	(76%)
Models B+D	16,465	17,790	18,695	20,532	22,154	22,831	23,173
	(21%)	(22%)	(22%)	(23%)	(24%)	(24%)	(24%)

Source: Gobierno de Navarra. Estadística de datos básicos, undated

11. I have grouped the models with an enhanced English presence together with their base models of reference (G, A, and D).

12. According to a 2006 sociolinguistic survey, the Navarrese population over sixteen years old that identifies itself as bilingual in Euskara and Spanish, to varying degrees, oscillates between 11 and 18.8 percent of the total population (Eustat 2010).

Autonomous Community of the Basque Country

Among the different administrative entities into which Euskal Herria is divided, the CAPV-EAE is undoubtedly the area that has taken the most decided action to defend and promote Euskara. Starting from a situation in which a marginalized language was used by a very limited amount of the population (see chapter 6), a linguistic policy was established in the 1980s that, without notable detriment to Spanish (known by the entire population), took offering the population of the three provinces within its borders the opportunity to learn Euskara as its objective (see, among others, Baztarrika 2010 and Zalbide 2010).

The 1979 Statute of Autonomy of the Basque Country establishes in Article 6 that Euskara, the Basque people's own language, will have, like Spanish, the status of an official language in the CAPV-EAE and that "all inhabitants have the right to know and use both languages." It likewise stipulates that the measures and means to ensure that knowledge will be supervised and regulated (Jefatura del Estado Español 1979).

The so-called 1982 law on the normalization of the use of Euskara established the foundation for the increased use of the Basque language in (among other spheres) the educational arena. In the second chapter of this act, the right of all students in the territories of the CAPV-EAE to be taught in Euskara is recognized, at the same time that the mandatory nature of the teaching of the official language not chosen is regulated. Article 17 establishes that the government will take the necessary measures to guarantee that students have a real possibility of "possessing a sufficient practical knowledge of both official languages upon completing their mandatory education" (Parlamento Vasco 1982).

Following previous studies and drafts (Zalbide 2010), in July 1983, the Basque government issued a decree establishing the different linguistic models through which the aims proposed for the educational system were to be attained. In response to the autonomous community's linguistic heterogeneity and the different sensitivities that might exist, three models including the two official languages were proposed for basic education: A, B, and D (Gobierno Vasco 1983). In addition, students who are justifiably exempted from having to study Euskara constitute the so-called model X.

In model A, all subjects (except Euskara) are basically taught in Spanish. Euskara is treated as an ordinary subject, with around four hours a week dedicated to its study. In the event that the students attain a sufficient level of proficiency in Euskara, the possibility exists of teaching another subject in Basque to them. In model B, both Spanish and Basque are used to teach the other subjects. In the original formulation, the idea was for Spanish to be used for the main subjects such as reading, writing, and mathematics, while

Euskara would be used for the others; in reality, model B has taken a variety of forms in practice. The legal formulation for model D stipulates that all subjects—except Spanish language—will basically be taught in Euskara. Here, Spanish is assigned around four hours a week (Gobierno Vasco 2010b).[13]

In (non-mandatory) secondary education, the models are reduced to two, A and D, with characteristics basically similar to the corresponding models in the lower grades. Although model B (both languages as the channel for learning) does not legally exist at this level, in practice the possibility exists of enhancing model A with one or another curricular subject in Euskara. Taking into account the objectives for which it aims, bilingual education in the CAPV-EAE resembles the typology of an enrichment model (Fishman 1976, Serra and Vila 2000).

The decisive factor in the CAPV-EAE in implementing and effectively developing the models has been the wishes of parents and guardians, with the result that the sociolinguistic environment, which was also taken into consideration at the beginning of the process, has been relegated to secondary importance in practice. In fact, models B and D are applied in varied sociolinguistic contexts and enroll students who speak various languages at home, so that their results are quite heterogeneous, according to the different intervening variables.

In the CAPV-EAE, demand for models B and D, which really use the two official languages as the means of instruction, is very high. Table 7.6 contains the data for the evolution of enrollment at all non-university levels in the CAPV-EAE between 2000 and 2010. The supremacy of the bilingual models, B and D, is evident: in the 2010–2011 academic year, the two models together accounted for 75 percent of total reported enrollment.

Table 7.6. Evolution of the number of students enrolled at nonuniversity levels in the CAPV-EAE by linguistic model (2000–2010)

	2000–2001	2001–2002	2002–2003	2003–2004	2004–2005	2005–2006	2006–2007	2007–2008	2008–2009	2009–2010	2010–2011
Model A	119,954 (37%)	114,219 (36%)	109,945 (34%)	107,698 (33%)	103,979 (32%)	99,862 (30%)	95,902 (28%)	93,426 (27%)	92,569 (26%)	93,591 (25%)	92,332 (24.5%)
Model B	67,838 (21%)	66,932 (21%)	67,205 (21%)	67,967 (21%)	69,941 (21%)	71,284 (21%)	72,479 (21%)	74,077 (21%)	75,274 (21%)	75,813 (21%)	75,301 (20%)
Model D	132,735 (41%)	136,092 (43%)	139,849 (44%)	145,783 (45%)	154,164 (47%)	163,054 (49%)	171,154 (50%)	179,076 (51%)	187,543 (52%)	196,140 (53%)	205,774 (55%)
Model X	1,950 (1%)	1,963 (1%)	1,898 (1%)	1,882 (1%)	1,863 (1%)	1,846 (1%)	1,900 (1%)	1,947 (1%)	1,993 (1%)	2,013 (1%)	2,006 (0.5%)

Source: Eustat

13. For the definition of the models, see: http://en.eustat.es/ci_ci/documentos/opt_0/tema_300/elem_1521/definicion.html#axzz22qwUsZE3 (last accessed July 30, 2012).

Here, we see the continuous growth of model D (teaching in Euskara, with Spanish as a curricular subject), which accounts for over half of all students if we take all non-university levels as a whole. Model B (teaching in the two languages, Spanish and Euskara) remains constant with slightly more than 20 percent of total enrollment. Model X (without any presence of Euskara in the school curriculum) accounts for less than 1 percent of enrollment (0.5 percent in 2010).

In addition, the tendency to choose bilingual models is greater at the lower levels, something that appears to indicate that the choice of models B and D will maintain its current trend, although the maintenance of social consensus plays an important role here (Zalbide 2010). Table 7.7 shows the absolute and percentage enrollment data for the 2010–2011 academic year in terms of the different mandatory educational levels (preschool, primary, and mandatory secondary education).

Table 7.7. Total Enrollment in the mandatory levels of education in the CAPV-EAE (2010–2011 academic year)

2010–2011 Academic Year	Total students	Model A	Model B	Model D	Model X
Preschool (2–6 years old)	94,818	3,898 (4%)	21,530 (22.7%)	68,945 (72.7%)	445 (0.5%)
Primary (6–12 years old)	117,193	8,722 (7.4%)	32,903 (28.1%)	74,730 (63.8%)	838 (0.7%)
Mandatory secondary (12–16 years old)	70,516	10,884 (15.4%)	19,718 (28%)	39,390 (55.9%)	524 (0.7%)

Over the course of recent years, a number of evaluations based on a variety of criteria have been conducted, with the aim of studying the results produced in the educational system by way of the different models (Sierra 2008). The overall results of the CAPV-EAE bilingual educational system are superior in Spanish to those obtained with regard to Euskara.

In 2005, the Basque government, through the Basque Institute for Research and Evaluation in Education conducted a study (Gobierno Vasco 2005a) with the objective of evaluating whether or not the knowledge of Euskara among students in their last year of mandatory education reached level B2 of the common European framework of reference for languages (Council of Europe 2001). It found that 54 percent of students surpassed the level analyzed. By models, about 33 percent of students in model B passed the test, as well as about 68 percent of students in model D (after a pilot test, the decision was made not to administer the test to students in model A, since they did not have the minimum level for it). It must be taken into account that the linguistic models are implemented in varied sociolinguistic conditions and among students with various home languages. Nevertheless, as a whole, these results indicate that a significant percentage of the student population, at the end of their mandatory education, does not attain the level of proficiency in Euskara desired and stipulated by law.

In 2007, a study titled *Nivel B1 de Euskara en Educación Primaria* (Euskara Level B1 in Primary Education) was published (Gobierno Vasco 2007), the objective of which was to analyze whether or not the level of Euskara among students in the sixth year of primary education (twelve years old) reached level B1 of the same common European framework of reference mentioned previously. The overall results showed that about 49 percent of students passed the test, while 51 percent did not. The analysis in terms of linguistic models showed that 39 percent of students in model B passed the test, while about 67 percent of students in model D did so.

Since 2009, the Basque government has conducted two "diagnostic evaluations" of students in their second year of mandatory secondary education (fourteen years old). On a scale of three levels of proficiency (beginning, intermediate, and advanced), over a third of students failed to score above the beginning level in Euskara (see table 7.8).

Table 7.8. Percentage of students per level of linguistic communicative proficiency in Euskara in the CAPV-EAE (2009 and 2010)

Diagnostic evaluations: Euskara	Year of evaluation: 2009			Year of evaluation: 2010		
	Beginning	Intermediate	Advanced	Beginning	Intermediate	Advanced
	38.1%	43.6%	18.4%	33.5%	42.4%	24.1%

Source: Gobierno Vasco (2010a and 2011a).

Separating out the results according to models, we observe that the results of model A for proficiency in Basque are significantly lower than those of model B, and that these, in their turn, are lower than those of model D. In 2010, over 85 percent of model A students failed to get beyond the beginning level, and only around 3 percent had an advanced level of proficiency. The comparative data for 2009 and 2010 can be seen in table 7.9.

Table 7.9. Percentage of students in each linguistic model per level of performance in linguistic communication in Euskara in the CAPV-EAE

	Diagnostic evaluation: 2009			Diagnostic evaluation: 2010		
	Beginning	Intermediate	Advanced	Beginning	Intermediate	Advanced
Model A	85.2%	12.7%	2.1%	78.6%	18.3%	3.1%
Model B	38.4%	45.8%	15.8%	36.8%	43.9%	19.3%
Model D	26.4%	50%	23.6%	22.5%	46.6%	30.9%

Source: Gobierno Vasco (2010a and 2011a)

The diagnostic evaluation report noted that "it is evident that these results are entirely governed by the influence of the students' linguistic model of schooling." (Gobierno Vasco 2011a, 23).

Taking an average score of 250 points adopted in 2009 as a point of reference for measuring the evolution of the data in subsequent years, the results for model A are notably lower than that value and also notably lower than those obtained in the other models. The average scores for students in the three models can be seen in table 7.10.

Table 7.10. Evolution of the average score in Euskara obtained by students in each linguistic model in the CAPV-EAE (reference score: 250)

2009 average (reference level): 250 points	Model A	Model B	Model D
2009	189	251	265
2010	201	255	272

Source: Gobierno Vasco (2010a and 2011a).

In the case of competence in Spanish, the levels of performance are better in all models: in 2010, only around 12 percent of students were at the beginning level, while 88 percent of students were at the intermediate or advanced levels (see table 7.11).

Table 7.11. Percentage of students per level of communicative proficiency in Spanish in the CAPV-EAE (2009 and 2010)

Proficiency in Spanish	Year of evaluation: 2009			Year of evaluation: 2010		
	Beginning	Intermediate	Advanced	Beginning	Intermediate	Advanced
	16%	54.7%	29.3%	12.1%	59.3%	28.6%

Source: Gobierno Vasco (2010a and 2011a).

As far as the scores obtained are concerned, with an average score of 252 points in 2010, the differences among the different groups considered varied between scores of 223 and 261 (see table 7.12). The greatest differences, nonetheless, do not appear to depend on the instructional model, but rather on socioeconomic and cultural factors; if these are taken into account, the differences are reduced, although those in favor of state-subsidized private institutions remain significant.

Table 7.12. Average score in Spanish by type of school in the CAPV-EAE

2010 average score: 252	A public	A state-subsidized private	B public	B state-subsidized private	D public	D state-subsidized private
	223	258	243	261	249	255

Source: Gobierno Vasco (2011a).

At the same time, students' linguistic proficiency in Spanish does not appear to be negatively affected by bilingual instruction. Indeed, the reverse is the case. The PISA (Programme for International Student Assessment) report compiled by the Organisation for Economic Co-operation and Development (OECD) in 2009 includes data from sixty-five states, in addition to separate samples for a number of regions and autonomous communities. On the overall measure of reading proficiency, Spain scored 481 points, while the CAPV-EAE obtained 494 points, one point above the OECD average (493 points), but significantly above the Spanish average.[14] It should be noted that the reading-comprehension tests were administered in Spanish for 84.4 percent of the CAPV-EAE sample (Gobierno Vasco 2011b).

Basque in the University System

The educational systems in the different parts of the Basque Country have made very notable progress in the direction of offering bilingual education. One can also see the results of bilingual policies in the university sphere.

In the three politico-administrative communities, there are seven universities: the Universidad del País Vasco/Euskal Herriko Unibertsitatea (University of the Basque Country, UPV/EHU), Mondragon Unibertsitatea (Mondragon University, MU), the Universidad Pública de Navarra/Nafarroako Unibertsitatea Publikoa (The Public University of Navarre, UPNA/NUP), the Université de Pau et des Pays de l'Adour (University of Pau and the Pays de l'Adour, UPPA), the Universidad Nacional de Educación a Distancia (National Distance Education University, UNED), the Universidad de Navarra (University of Navarre), and the Universidad de Deusto/Deustuko Unibertsitatea (University of Deusto), with the last two belonging to different religious organizations. Here I will focus on data for the UPV/EHU, due to its qualitative and quantitative importance in relation to the development of university programs in Euskara, and from the UPNA/NUP and UPPA, due to their status as public universities representing other communities in which different linguistic policies are applied.

During the 2009–2010 academic year, the roster of teaching and research staff at the UPV/EHU included 1,819 bilingual positions (34.2 percent) and 3,479 non-bilingual positions (65.8 percent). A professor who occupies a bilingual position teaches in Euskara, although he or she may also do so in Spanish. In all degree-granting programs of study taken together, there were a total of 14,054 first-cycle credits (leading to a diploma degree or the first half of an undergraduate degree), of which 11,698 were also offered in Euskara;

---

14. See www.oecd.org/document/61/0,3746,en_32252351_32235731_46567613_1_1_1_1,00.html (Last accessed June 19, 2012).

among the mandatory courses of the second cycle (the second half of an undergraduate degree), 3,429 out of a total of 6,025 credits were offered in Euskara (UPV/EHU 2010). Among other cases, the degree programs in pre-school and elementary education can be completed entirely in Euskara. University entrance exams can be taken in Euskara or in Spanish. At the UPV/EHU, more than eight thousand students took the exam in 2010 and 2011, and in both cases, somewhat over 60 percent opted to do so in Euskara.

A study conducted at UPNA/NUP indicated that in 2006, about 21.3 percent of students took the university entrance exams in Euskara. Separately, in the 2006–2007 academic year, 1,484 students said they knew Euskara well (about 21.7 percent of the university's total student body), while that figure rose to about 23.8 percent (420 students) among new entrants (UPNA 2007).

Finally, at the UPPA, in France, a few subjects are offered and taught in Basque within its program of Basque studies.

The Future of the Models

The linguistic models currently in existence were designed and implemented under specific conditions at a specific time. In short, a linguistic policy that only took into account the state language (Spanish or French) was being applied in society and the educational system was practically monolingual. At the same time, during the dictatorship in Spain, trustworthy democratic information about society's sensitivities was lacking in relation to the attitude it might show toward the use of Euskara. In addition, the Basque Country's varied sociolinguistic make-up suggested correspondingly differentiated approaches according to the characteristics of the surrounding environment: while in some parts of the Basque Country, Euskara maintained a healthy vitality, its presence in others was scant or even non-existent. Likewise, society lacked clear reference models that could serve to organize the educational system and the presence of more than one language within it.

Thirty years later, in the early twenty-first century, significant experience in implementing a bilingual system in the educational arena is available. At the same time, society has evolved and now has different characteristics. As a result, such transformations also entail a change in the linguistic panorama present in the classroom and call for a debate on and the search for solutions adapted to the new realities.

The system of models constructed during the last quarter of the twentieth century was a response to a situation in which two languages basically existed at the start of a child's school education (Euskara and Spanish or French), with the final objective of the process of mandatory education being mastery of the two official languages. Studying a foreign language in the classroom was also taken into consideration, but the level to be achieved by the students was not seriously discussed, nor was there a notable demand by society in this regard.

However, the educational system today differs in several ways regarding languages and their educational treatment. On the one hand, there are more languages in the classroom: in addition to the two official languages, present in different proportions in the different regions of the Basque Country in their standard and dialectal varieties, others have appeared that are making their way into the system as a consequence of immigration and that also have their origins in highly diverse cultural and linguistic contexts, in comparison both to one another and to those previously present. Faced with this new reality, the educational system needs to articulate a response, for which there are no previous models directly applicable to the new situation.

On the other hand, in a globalized world, growing international interaction and the spread of the new information and communication technologies (ICTs), especially the internet, mean that society is ever more aware of the growing need for a certain level of communicative competence in an international language. This reality favors the introduction of English in schools, with more specific and tangible objectives and demands than those assigned up to now to the foreign language(s) already present in current school curricula.

The educational system of the Basque Country, as a consequence, has the task of continuing to articulate a response to the challenges posed by Basque society's new linguistic situation, which can be synthesized into two ideas: firstly, a multiplicity of languages of origin in the classroom, and then, as an objective to be attained at the end of a student's school career, a generalized knowledge of three languages: the two official languages (Euskara and Spanish or French) and a language valid for international communication on the global level (English). In effect, then, the system of models described here has served to move from a monolingual system (in Spanish or French) to a bilingual Basque-Spanish or Basque-French system. And at present, there are proposals for a transition from a bilingual system to a system that is multilingual in terms of the language of origin and trilingual in terms of the linguistic communicative proficiency objectives to be achieved in the course of mandatory schooling.

This change that is being demanded from the educational system is taking place, meanwhile, at the same time that data is becoming available about the results of the bilingual system currently in place. Studies evaluating the current system of models indicate that model A is clearly ineffective for obtaining the proficiency in Euskara established by law. Models B and D obtain better results, but their students still do not achieve (in statistical terms) a level of communicative proficiency in Euskara comparable to that in Spanish, posing the need to consider possible ways to improve the system.

At the same time that the data being obtained from evaluation of the current system is supplying dynamic information on its effectiveness or suitability, we cannot lose sight of the global change that is underway in society and that is introducing a greater degree of complexity into the system as a whole. Today, the current and future heterogeneity of users and professionals of the institutions that make up the educational system is being emphasized, underlining the need to find appropriate answers for each context. For this reason, the initiative of educational professionals is being appealed to at the same time that greater functional autonomy for schools is being proposed. Along these lines, it appears that the linguistic models will have to become more flexible according to the sociolinguistic characteristics of their environment.

In this way, the educational system manifests growing complexity and diversity in linguistic matters. The starting point is a more heterogeneous situation in the classroom, and the aim is to achieve a specified level of communicative proficiency in three languages. This new situation requires more in-depth attention to methodological aspects in order to optimize the teaching and learning processes in the school environment. Along these lines, approaches such as content and language integrated learning (CLIL), already used to some extent in its bilingual version, are being proposed, in combination with what is known as the integrated language approach, which appears destined to undergo significant development. These aspects will be integrated into the linguistic project of each school, where, taking into account the characteristics of the local environment, the criteria should be developed for the teaching and use of languages in the learning process, and the approach to be taken to those languages will be determined.

In this complicated context, there is debate over aspects such as the ideal time to introduce the third language and the amount of instructional time to be devoted to each language, due in part to the different sensitivities that exist: while some sectors express concern that the increasing presence of English in the educational system may harm the normalization of Euskara, delaying or preventing generalized knowledge of Euskara in society, others want to move forward as quickly as possible in the mastery of English, relegating the issue of Basque to a secondary plane.

As a consequence, debate exists with regard to different aspects related to the approach to be taken to each language in the school environment, even if there does not appear to be significant disagreement about the need for communicative proficiency in an international language. As examples, I would highlight the fact that the Federation of Ikastolas, a movement at the forefront of the public defense and promotion of Euskara, is proposing generalized trilingualism (even quadrilingualism) as an objective of its linguistic project (Euskal Herriko Ikastolen Konfederazioa 2009), and separately, the Basque government is promoting a trilingual educational framework, in which several schools are already involved.

Finally, I should note that different sensitivities exist in the society of Euskal Herria with regard to the official languages, but I want to emphasize the idea that Euskara must serve as an element of cohesion and not of rejection or discrimination, for which purpose it is important to maintain a certain level of social consensus on this subject (Baztarrika 2010, Gobierno Vasco 2009b, Zalbide 2010).

8

The Basque Language in the Minds of Native and Nonnative Bilinguals

ITZIAR LAKA, MIKEL SANTESTEBAN, KEPA ERDOCIA, AND ADAM
ZAWISZEWSKI, University of the Basque Country (UPV/EHU)

An Overview of the Bilingual Mind

Bilinguals outnumber monolinguals: according to some recent estimates, between 60 and 75 percent of the world's population is bilingual. It has been argued that the capacity to learn more than one language is an adaptive trait in human evolution (Hirschfeld 2008), and given what we know of interactions between human groups, is not unlikely that people throughout history have more often than not known more than one language. Language research initially tended to restrict itself to the study of monolinguals, and there was not much interest in the study of bilingualism, because it was generally (though tacitly) assumed that the representation and processing of a given language was not affected by another one, whether acquired simultaneously or later in life. Recent findings have completely overturned this assumption, and suggest instead that research beyond monolingualism holds a great potential for generating knowledge about the psychological nature of the human language faculty and the way in which language is organized in our minds.

François Grosjean, a pioneer researcher on bilingualism, warns in his foundational paper (1989) that the bilingual is not two monolinguals in one person. Current work on the cognition of bilingualism shows the extent to which this statement is true because mental differences that relate to being bilingual or monolingual are being discovered. Some of these differences involve cognitive abilities that lie outside linguistic systems, such as the

* Our research is supported by the Spanish Ministry of Education and Science (BRAINGLOT CSD2007-00012/CONSOLIDER-INGENIO 2010, FFI2009 09695/FILO, FFI2008-00240/FILO, FFI2010-20472/FILO), and the Basque government (IT414-10).

capacity to ignore irrelevant information when changing tasks, or a certain degree of resilience toward symptoms of neurodegeneration. Other differences between monolinguals and bilinguals involve the interplay of the two linguistic systems they use: we now know that bilinguals are simultaneously activate both languages, and must select or inhibit one at a time; we also know that the cost involved in having two lexicons instead of one are experimentally detectable. The developmental patterns of preverbal bilingual babies—who can very early on detect that more than one language is spoken in their environment—are also different from those of their monolingual counterparts. Ultimately, the main differences between monolingual and bilingual minds eventually emanate from the intensive cognitive training undergone by bilinguals in their lifetimes, given the frequency and speed at which they switch from one language to another.

From a more narrowly linguistic point of view, people with more than one language in their brains provide crucial evidence regarding the neurocognitive nature of the human language faculty. Thus, for instance, aspects of grammar are sensitive to *when* in life they are acquired, and also to *what* was known before, so that native speakers and nonnative speakers do not process certain aspects of the same grammar in the same way, even at high levels of language proficiency and given frequent use of the language. In contrast, vocabulary appears insensitive to when it is learned and what the words of a previously acquired language look like: given high proficiency in the language, nonnative speakers are native-like with respect to vocabulary processing (see Laka 2012a for a review).

Broadly speaking, neurocognitive studies of language and bilingualism reveal that the patterns of activation related to language processing are consistent across languages and native speakers; research shows that the processing of different languages occurs in much of the same brain tissue (Kim et al. 1997, Perani et al. 1998), and in recent work we have also found that the processing of Basque by native speakers generates electrophysiological signals that are equivalent to those generated by the processing of other languages (Erdozia et al. 2009; Díaz et al. 2011). When differences between languages are found, they obtain in bilinguals and they correlate with differences in proficiency levels attained in each language, and differences in age of acquisition for each language. This strongly suggests that age of acquisition and language proficiency are determinant factors in the neural underpinnings of language and bilingualism, so that early and proficient bilinguals do not "separate" languages in the brain, but as age of acquisition of the nonnative language increases and proficiency decreases, the nonnative language tends to be located in more extended and individually variable areas.

Given these findings, neurobilingualism has teneded to focus research on the impact of language proficiency and of the age at which a language is acquired. Less attention has been devoted to the impact of the degree of similarity of the grammars located in one brain and the differences among different types of grammatical phenomena. As our knowledge advances, language diversity emerges as a likely relevant factor to be kept into account, and as the volume and level of detail of the studies carried out increases, it also becomes increasingly clear that, although all these factors have often been studied separately, there are strong connections between them: proficiency in the language, age of acquisition, and grammatical similarity are likely to be intertwined rather than separate factors. These are the topics that our research focuses on, as we strive to contribute to the general knowledge on bilingualism by exploring in detail Basque-Spanish bilinguals in our community.

Activation and Control of the Two Languages in the Bilingual Brain

The brain activates all the languages it knows when it has to use language. In particular, bilinguals activate both of their languages when they have to use one (Desmet and Duyck 2007). The simple hypothesis that bilinguals have two separate lexicons—one for each language, so that when they use one language only its lexicon is activated—has been proved wrong by many studies: both lexicons are active whenever the bilingual speaks, either in one or the other language. In a pioneering study, Walter Van Heuven, Ton Dijkstra, and Jonathan Grainger (1998) find that the lexical items from a bilingual's native language are active while the bilingual is engaged in recognizing words from a nonnative language. Further studies have shown that this activation of the lexical items occurs irrespectively of the language for different types of bilinguals and language-pairs. Further evidence that the native language is activated when using the nonnative one had been uncovered by a large number of studies (including Costa, Caramazza, and Sebastián-Gallés 2000; Colomé 2001; Duyck 2005; Duyck et al., 2004; and Schwartz et al. 2007), by means of many different phenomena. It has also been repeatedly shown that the nonnative language is active when the native one is used (see for instance Duyck 2005, and Van Hell and Dijkstra 2002, among others). Similar results have been obtained in studies in which participants, instead of reading, heard the words they had to recognize (for instance Marian, Blumenfeld, and Boukrina 2008; Marian, Spivey, and Hirsch 2003), and in studies in which participants had to actually say the words (Costa, Santesteban, and Caño 2005; Kroll, Bobb, and Wodniecka 2006; Costa, Albareda, and Santesteban 2008; and Santesteban and Costa 2006).

The most important evidence supporting the parallel activation assumption comes from the so called cognate facilitation effects reported in both comprehension and production modalities. Cognates are those words that are formally (orthographically and phonologically) similar across languages (for example, the words *botella* and *botila* meaning "bottle" are cognate words of Spanish and Basque, respectively). In studies of lexical access during comprehension and production, cognate words have been reported to be faster to learn and more resistant to forgetting (for example, De Groot and Keijzer 2000), less likely to fall into tip-of-the-tongue states (Gollan and Acenas 2004), faster to produce (Costa, Caramazza, and Sebastián-Gallés 2000), and more sensitive to cross-linguistic priming (Van Hell and De Groot 1998).

According to some researchers, the cognate effect arises because retrieving phonemes belonging to cognate words is facilitated by concurrently activating the corresponding translations (Costa, Caramazza, and Sebastian-Galles 2000; Costa, Santesteban, and Caño 2005). For instance, in production, the phonological content of a cognate word would be activated by its corresponding lexical representation and, given the phonological overlap, also by its translation. In contrast, the phonological representation of a non-cognate word would be actrivated only by the corresponding lexical representation. In other words, when a Spanish-Basque bilingual aims to produce a cognate word like *botila*, the parallel activation of its Spanish translation *botella* would facilitate retrieval of the phonemes shared by both words, because these phonemes will be activated by both the target word and its cognate. In contrast, when the word to be produced is a non-cognate like *labana* ("knife," in Basque), its Spanish translation *cuchillo* would also be activated, but would not be able to facilitate retrieving the phonemes of the target word *labana*. This is because the target word and its translation do not share any phoneme, so that retrieving the phonemes of the target word *labana* would not receive extra activation from its translation word *cuchillo* (Costa, Caramazza, and Sebastian-Galles 2000; Costa, Santesteban, and Caño 2005; Gollan and Acenas 2004).

This discovery naturally leads us to the question of how bilinguals manage to produce the words of the target language and prevent words from the non-target language from being uttered. If all the languages of the bilingual are active when language is processed, then there must be some further cognitive operation that controls what language is used at a given time.

Proposals as to how bilinguals control their languages in order to produce the one they want to use generally agree that bilingual lexical access must involve some kind of attention control mechanism (Costa 2005; Costa, Miozzo, and Caramazza 1999; Finkbeiner, Gollan, and Caramazza 2006; Green 1998; Kroll, Bobb, and Wodniekca 2006; La Heij 2005). Some researchers argue that, in order to avoid competition between the simultaneously activated lexical items of the target and non-target languages, language control in bilinguals entails the active inhibition of the linguistic representations of the non-target language; this is known as the inhibitory control model proposed by David Green (1998). However, others argue that bilingual speakers do not need to actively inhibit the linguistic representations of the non-target language. Instead, Albert Costa, Michele Miozzo, and Alfonso Caramazza (1999) suggest that the lexical nodes of the non-target language are activated but do not act as competitors during lexical access. In other words, according to the so-called language specific selection model, the bilinguals' language control mechanism allows them to ignore the activation of the non-target languages' lexical items by not considering them for selection.

The most important evidence in favor of the language specific selection model and the absence of cross-linguistic competition during bilingual lexical access comes from the picture-word interference paradigm. In this paradigm, participants are asked to name pictures while ignoring printed words. Here, it has been repeatedly demonstrated that speakers need more time to name a picture (such as a table) presented with a semantically related distractor word as *chair* than a semantically unrelated word such as *dog*. This "semantic interference effect" has been taken as evidence for the existence of lexical competition during lexical access in monolinguals. Hence, Costa, Miozzo, and Caramazza (1999) suggest that, if a semantically related word in the target language interferes in the lexical access process, the target's translation would be the strongest possible distractor. However, highly proficient Catalan-Spanish bilingual speakers were shown to be faster to name a picture of a table (*taula*, in Catalan) when the printed distractor word was its Spanish translation *mesa* than with an unrelated word like *perro* ("dog," in Spanish). Hence, Costa, Miozzo, and Caramazza (1999) interpret these "translation facilitation effects" as evidence of the absence of competition of the non-target language during bilingual lexical access.

The most revealing evidence for inhibitory mechanisms in bilinguals has been provided by Renata F. I. Meuter and Allan Allport (1999) in an experiment on language-switching, in which participants were asked to name a picture in one language or another, depending on the color of the picture. In their experiment, Meuter and Allport (1999) asked low proficient bilinguals to name digits in their L1 (French, Spanish, German, Italian, and Portuguese), and in their L2 (English) in switch and non-switch trials. This study shows that low-proficient bilinguals take longer to switch from their less dominant nonnative language to their native one than the other way around; an effect that has been termed the "asymmetrical switching cost." At first glance, this result may appear counterintuitive because it implies that it is "harder" to change from the language you do not know so well to the language you know better than it is to change from the language you know better to the language you do not know so well. However, this is the pattern of results predicted by the inhibitory control model. This is because, as Green (1998) suggests, the amount of inhibition applied to one language depends on the proficiency level with which that language is spoken: the more proficient one is in a language, the more inhibition has to be applied over it in order to favor the other language. Moreover, the more inhibition is applied to a given lexicon, the longer and the harder it will take to overcome it in a subsequent trial. Hence, when low proficient bilinguals have to speak in their weaker, nonnative language, the native language is activated and therefore it has to be very strongly inhibited. As a consequence of the strong inhibition applied to it, if later these low proficient bilinguals want to speak in the dominant native language, they need to undo the strong inhibition applied to words in their native language. In contrast to this, changing from the strong native language to the weaker nonnative language does not require undoing such a strong inhibition, because words in the weaker language need not be so strongly inhibited.

Albert Costa and Mikel Santesteban (2004) further test the language switching performance of low- and high-proficient bilingual speakers, and suggest that bilingual speakers might make use of both language selection mechanisms. More specifically, these authors replicated the asymmetrical language switching cost patterns in a group of low proficient Spanish-Catalan bilinguals (who had more difficulty in switching from L2 to L1 than vice versa). Additionally, as would be predicted by the inhibitory control model, high proficient Spanish-Catalan bilinguals showed a symmetrical language switching cost pattern while switching between their two strong languages. However, in contrast to the predictions of the inhibitory control model, these high proficient bilinguals *also* showed a symmetrical language switching pattern while switching between their strong L1-Spanish or L2-Catalan and their weak L3-English (Costa and Santesteban 2004; Costa, Santesteban, and Ivanova 2006). Based on these results, these authors suggest that, although low proficient bilingual speakers rely on inhibitory processes to select words in the intended language, a shift from inhibitory to language specific selection mechanisms occurs in the case of high proficient bilinguals. Additionally, Costa, Santesteban, and Ivanova (2006) show that a symmetrical language switching was obtained in a group of high-proficient Spanish-English translators that acquired their L2 at a late age (after ten years old), and by a group of high-proficient Spanish-Basque bilinguals who acquired Basque at an early age, suggesting that neither L2 age of acquisition (AoA) or linguistic distance (how different the two languages of the bilingual are) play a role in the shift from inhibitory to language specific selection mechanisms.

Thus, while the switching performance of low-proficient bilinguals leads to an asymmetrical pattern, depending on language dominance, in proficient bilinguals it yields a symmetric pattern. This does not only apply to the dominant languages, but also to non-dominant, languages that one might learn later in life.

Why Study Basque-Spanish Bilingual Syntactic Processing?

In recent decades, a rapidly growing body of studies using experimental methods and neuroimaging techniques has explored syntactic processing, and as a result, findings from linguistics and the neurosciences are progressively converging and finding common ground (Moro 2008; Pullvermüller 2002). However, the vast majority of language processing and neuroimaging studies focus on rather similar languages (English, Spanish, Italian, French, German, or Dutch, for instance). In other words, with the exception of a few recently emerging studies on Japanese, Chinese, and Korean, the languages most intensively studied share many central design properties.

In linguistic theory, a significant expansion of the language pool investigated and systematic cross-linguistic inquiry were crucial to uncovering the interplay between universal and variable aspects of the language faculty (Greenberg 1963; Chomsky 1981). Research on language representation and processing in the brain must similarly also engage in cross-linguistic studies so that we can differentiate language-particular effects from universal invariant properties of language processing by the brain, and thus properly understand the interplay between the two. In order to achieve this goal, it is necessary to conduct studies and gather evidence from a wide array of languages pertaining to different typological groups, and it is particularly important to study bilinguals whose languages have opposite parametric specifications; in other words, bilinguals who speak typologically very different grammars, like Basque-Spanish bilinguals.

One main goal of our research strategy is to contribute to uncovering the impact of variable versus universal design properties of language in its representation and processing by the brain. In particular, we seek to understand whether (and how) different typological/parametric properties of language impact on the neural representation of a speaker's knowledge of language; in other words, how opposite grammatical properties are represented and put to use in the bilingual mind. To address this central research question, we selectively target instances in which grammatical specifications are opposed in value for the two languages of the bilingual population we study (Spanish/Basque), and compare them to instances in which the specifications of the two grammars converge.

Here, we will review a series of experiments we have designed and conducted targeting three central domains of linguistic variation across languages: word order (the head-parameter: head-final/head-initial languages), the argument marking system (ergativity versus accusativity), and verb agreement types (subject agreement versus object agreement). These three domains have either hardly been studied from a neurocognitive perspective, or in some cases have never been considered at all before. Thus, we are in a position to inquire into phenomena that have not been previously addressed, working at the frontiers of our knowledge.

There are 6,912 languages in the world today (according to Ethnologue's last count, at www.ethnologue.com), showing both great diversity and significant similarities. In the second half of the twentieth century, with the birth of generative grammar and the cognitive sciences, significant advances were made regarding the invariant universal design aspects of human language. But language variability is still not sufficiently well understood from a theoretical (explicative) perspective, despite the wealth of valuable descriptions of linguistic types provided by modern linguistic typology (Newmeyer 2005). Noam Chomsky's (1981) principles and parameters model (henceforth P&P) constitutes a promising attempt to provide a principled account for the interplay and nature of the variant and invariant aspects of grammar (Baker 2001, 2003). Though there are still deep gaps in our understanding, and despite the fact that the model has been challenged and is far from verified, P&P still provides the only verifiable model for language variation (Yang 2003; Moro 2008). This makes parametric theory a particularly suitable model for experimental research; and the model can thus serve as empirical test for neurocognitive models of language (see Friederici 2002; Bornkessel and Schlesewsky 2006, among others). For instance, the declarative/procedural (DP) model (Ullman 2001, 2004), claims that the computational component (grammar) belongs to the procedural system. Since the DP model argues that procedural cognitive processes have limited neuronal plasticity, it predicts that syntactic parameters in particular should show age-related effects.

Ever since Eric Lenneberg (1967) suggested that there is a critical period for language acquisition, the impact of age of early linguistic experience on adult neural representation and processing has been a much debated issue, particularly regarding bilingualism. Whether adult knowledge of a nonnative language is represented and processed as the native language has been intensely debated for almost two decades (White 2003), and we hope that our research will be able to contribute significantly to understanding this issue, both given the type of bilingualism we can study in the Basque Country, and also given the type of experimental techniques we employ. As we will see, these can give us very fine-grained measures that are not otherwise detectable regarding neural processing of language.

In our research, one aspect we explore is precisely the representation and processing of the syntactic component in adult Basque-Spanish bilinguals. In recent years we have undertaken a systematic study of adult Spanish/Basque bilinguals, exploiting the fact that Spanish and Basque have opposite values for several parameters (see Bosque and Demonte 1999 for a thorough description of Spanish grammar; and Hualde and Ortiz de Urbina 2003, and de Rijk 2008 for a description of Basque). We investigate whether the specific grammatical phenomena targeted in our experimental work give rise to differences in the neural representation and processing of bilinguals of various types. Since nothing is known about how Basque grammar is processed in the brain, we first determine how the phenomena under study are processed by natives of Basque (and also Spanish, as regards cases in which there are no previous studies on the particular topic we address), and once we obtain those results from native speakers, we explore how nonnative speakers who learned Basque at different ages represent and process these same phenomena. In order to proceed systematically, we start by studying nonnatives with high proficiency levels and early ages of acquisition of Basque. Basque-Spanish and Spanish-Basque bilinguals are particularly suited to contributing to our understanding of bilingual language processing, because bilingualism is pervasive in all realms of Basque society and because the two languages have the same or opposite values for different syntactic properties.

Table 8.1. Parametric settings of Basque and Spanish. "Plus" values represent a positive value of that choice in the linguistic parameter and "minus" values a negative value

	Verb agreement	Argument alignment	Word Order			
	Yes	*No*	*Nominative*	*Ergative*	*Initial*	*Final*
Spanish	+	−	+	−	+	−
Basque	+	−	−	+	−	+

The Impact of Age and Proficiency in the Bilingual Brain

Studies on bilingual language processing currently provide a somewhat confusing picture: while some studies report that if a second language is not acquired early, it is not processed native-like, others report that age does not have an effect on bilingualism, so that proficient bilinguals are like natives regarding language processing.

Regarding the first group of results, we should refer to the pioneering work of Christine M. Weber-Fox and Helen J. Neville (1996): this uses the event-related potentials' technique to test various groups of Chinese-speakers who had acquired English at different ages. Regarding syntax, participants who were exposed to English after the age of eleven showed a different processing pattern (different electrophysiological activity of the brain) from that found in native speakers. However, vocabulary-related phenomena elicited the same brain signature in all participants, whether natives or nonnatives who had arrived in the United States at different ages. The study concludes that syntax shows maturational effects related to the age of language learning, whereas vocabulary-related tasks do not. A significant impact of early exposure to the language is also reported by Anja Hahne and Angela D. Friederici (2001) for native Japanese who learned German at a mean age of twenty-seven. Their brain signatures did not look like the native speakers' when they were processing German grammar, but they did when they were engaged in vocabulary-related tasks. Subsequently, many studies have reported similar findings (such as Hahne 2001; Chen et al. 2007). All these studies conclude that certain aspects of syntax are sensitive to early experience.

Regarding the second group of results, there is also a wide sample of studies that find that very proficient nonnative speakers show the same electrophysiological brain signatures as native speakers, independently of the age at which they learned their second language. For example, Angela D. Friederici, Karsten Steinhauer, and Erdmut Pfeifer (2002) show that native German-speakers of a mean age of twenty-four, who were taught an artificial language named Brocanto, displayed the same brain signatures elicited by their native language when they processed the newly learned one. Rossi and colleagues (2006) investigated Italian-speakers who had learned German at around eighteen years of age and had either high or low proficiency in German. High-proficient speakers responded similarly to natives, but low proficient speakers did not. Sonja A. Kotz, Phillip J. Holcomb, and Lee Osterhout (2008) similarly report that Spanish natives who are high-proficient speakers of English (learned at about five years of age) process English sentences like natives. These results strongly suggest that high proficiency leads to equivalent neurophysiological activity in syntactic processing despite a delay in exposure to the nonnative language.

How can these apparently contradictory results be reconciled? Our hypothesis is that high proficiency allows for native-like processing only when there are no new parametric values involved in the acquisition of the nonnative language. A detailed and linguistically informed review of reported age-induced differences reveals that they always involve a grammatical feature in the nonnative language that is not present in the native one (for a detailed discussion of the literature in this respect see Zawiszewski et al. 2011). We hypothesize that when the native language lacks a specific syntactic trait, nonnatives do not become native-like even if they achieve high proficiency. Thus, if we review the studies that have investigated the impact of age and proficiency in language processing in light of the P&P model, we observe that early exposure effects are found only when the first and second language had opposite parametric values, and we also discover that proficiency results in native-like processing when the two languages share the same value for that specific parameter.

How do Spanish-Basque Bilinguals Process Two Very Different Grammars?

There are fewer studies on syntactic processing in non-monolinguals in comparison to studies on lexical processing, but in recent years this area of research has experienced enormous growth. While evidence on nonnative syntactic processing is still sparse, "even so existing data clearly indicate that syntax is a phenomenon that deserves full consideration" (Kotz 2009, 68).

If the studies that have examined the role of age versus proficiency in language processing are reviewed focusing on the syntactic phenomena they explore, differences in processing attributed to AoA tend to be found when the native grammar of the participant diverges significantly regarding the phenomenon tested in the nonnative grammar, and high proficiency tends to yield native-like processing when the syntactic phenomenon tested in L2 has an equivalent correlate in the L1 of the participants.

If we consider Weber-Fox and Neville (1996), Mueller et al. (2005), Shiro Ojima, Hiroki Nakata, and Ryusuke Kakigi (2005), Chen et al. (2007), we observe that age effects were obtained whenever very proficient nonnatives were processing a syntactic phenomenon that had no equivalent correlate in their native language: in the case of Weber-Fox and Neville (1996), they were obtained when testing native Chinese-speakers processing subjacency effects in English Wh-questions; Chinese lacks overt Wh-movement (it is a Wh in-situ grammar), while English is an overt Wh-movement language, so that the syntactic phenomenon tested involved a parametric property absent in the native language of the participants (see Cheng 1997); in Mueller et al. (2005), the phenomenon tested was classifier morphology, which German lacks completely. In Ojima, Nakata, and Kakigi (2005) and Chen et al. (2007), the phenomenon tested was verb agreement, in natives of grammars that lack verb-agreement relations.

In light of this, the results from ERP studies suggest that it is diverging grammatical phenomena that might be sensitive to age of exposure, rather than superficial morphosyntactic differences. Both age and proficiency have been hypothesized and scrutinized as relevant factors conditioning L2 processing, but perhaps less attention has been paid so far to the issue of what syntactic phenomena are tested, and why. In linguistics, one view of cross-linguistic variation holds that specific grammars result from combinations of a set of linguistic parameters. Thus, syntactic variation would result from differences in the values of this combination of parameters (see Chomsky 1981 and Baker 2001, 2003 for overviews), and the acquisition of syntax would consist in determining the values of these syntactic parameters for the input language.

We thus investigated to what extent the linguistic distance between L1 and L2 can influence nonnative language processing, and in order to do so, we tested Basque native speakers and very proficient L2 Basque speakers whose native language is Spanish. We focused particularly on three conditions that involve syntactic parameters: (i) sentence word order (the head parameter), (ii) case morphology, and (iii) verb agreement. (i) Basque and Spanish diverge with respect to the value assigned to the head parameter. Whereas Spanish is head-initial, so that heads of phrases precede their complements, Basque is head-final: heads of phrases follow their complements, as in Turkish or Japanese:

(1)   Basque   Spanish
   a. $[_{PP}[_{DP}[_{NP}$liburu] a] rekin]   b. $[_{PP}$ con $[_{DP}$ el $[_{NP}$ libro]]
      book-the-with   with the book

   c. $[_{VP}[_{DP}[_{NP}$liburu] a] irakurri]   d. $[_{VP}$ leer $[_{DP}$ el $[_{NP}$ libro]]
      book-the read   read the book

(ii) These two languages also diverge with respect to argument alignment: Spanish is a nominative-accusative language, like English, while Basque is an ergative-absolutive language. Thus, in Basque, intransitive subjects (2a) look like transitive objects (2b) while transitive subjects have a different case-marker and agreement morphology (2b). In Spanish, subjects have the same form and agreement regardless of whether they are transitive or intransitive, and objects are different (2c,d):

(2)   a. gizon-a etorri da
         man-the arrived is
         "the man has arrived"

      b. emakume-a-k gizon-a ikusi du
         woman-the-erg man-the seen it-has-her
         "the woman has seen the man"

      c. el hombre ha venido
         the man has arrived
         "the man has arrived"

      d. la mujer ha visto al hombre
         the woman has seen acc-the man
         "the woman has seen the man"

In fact, the very characterization of notions like "subject" and "object" is built upon nominative-accusative grammars, as the description of ergativity above in terms of "subject/object" makes apparent. There is no morphologically consistent class of "subjects" in ergative languages, at least not one that matches that class in nominative languages.

The head parameter and the nominative/ergative alignment are two fundamental syntactic parameters in which Spanish and Basque diverge. However, Spanish and Basque converge in having (iii) verb agreement. Both languages have subject agreement, and Basque also has object agreement, as shown in (2b and 3).

(3)   zu-k ni ikusi na-u-zu
        you-erg me seen me-root-you
        "you have seen me"

To our knowledge, the impact of argument-alignment on L2 processing has not been systematically investigated so far. Previous ERP studies on case morphology, all of them carried out on nominative-accusative languages, showed that case violations elicit a centro-parietal positivity (P600) in 500-800 ms time window, usually preceded either by a left anterior negativity (LAN) or by an N400 component in 300-500 ms time window. Basque provides us with the opportunity to test whether these effects hold also in ergative case-systems; some previous results reported by Díaz et al. (2011) suggest that the electrophysiological signatures elicited by ergative case violations do not differ from those found in nominative languages, eliciting a comparable P600 component. (See Laka 2012b and Laka and Erdozia 2012 for a review of results on native processing of Basque word order and ergativity.)

Regarding verb-agreement, nonnatives performed the behavioral task with similar accuracy levels and displayed an equivalent biphasic N400-P600 pattern as a response to the ungrammatical stimuli, like natives had in previous experiments (Zawiszewski and Friederici 2009; Díaz et al. 2011). Regarding ergative case morphology, specific to Basque adn absent in Spanish, behavioral and ERP measures revealed significant differences between native and nonnative speakers. In the grammaticality judgment task performed along with the ERP session, nonnatives made significantly more errors than natives, despite their overall high language proficiency and early AoA. As for the ERP results, ungrammaticality elicited a broad negativity in both groups, but only the native group showed a P600 effect between 600-800 ms at the critical word position. Zawiszewski et al. (2011) offer two possible interpretations of these results: (i) the lack of P600 in the nonnatives could reflect transfer from their native grammar (Spanish) so that participants interpreted the absolute case as an equivalent of Spanish nominative case, and as a consequence did not process the sentence as containing a grammatical violation; (ii) nonnative speakers could have neglected case information and relied on other extragrammatical factors such as animacy to infer the thematic role of the ungrammatical noun phrase.

Regarding the third syntactic property, the head-directionality parameter that governs the order of words in phrases, Spanish and Basque differ fundamentally in the same way as English and Japanese: Spanish and English are head-initial languages, while Japanese and Basque are head-final languages. We found a different brain signature (by means of ERP signal) for native and nonnative speakers who had an early AoA (three years) and high levels of language proficiency. Previously, Erdocia et al. (2009) demonstrated that processing canonical SOV (subject-object-verb) word order is faster and easier than processing the non-canonical OSV (object-subject-verb) word order for native speakers, and regarding brain electrophysiology, OSV sentences showed increasing negativities at both subject and object positions and a P600 effect at verb position. These results demonstrate that OSV sentences are costlier to process than canonical SOV for native speakers of Basque (Laka 2012b; Laka and Erdozia 2012). Early and proficient Spanish-Basque bilinguals also employ more processing effort to process OSV sentences as compared to SOV ones. Spanish-Basque bilinguals performed indistinguishably from natives in the behavioral experiment, but ERP signatures departed from those observed in natives, suggesting on the one hand that behavioral measures are not accurate enough to detect this type of subtle differences in neural language processing that ERPs can detect; and on the other, that natives and nonnatives employ different neural resources to process sentence word order in Basque.

Concluding Remarks

All told, our findings indicate that divergent parameters have a significant impact in nonnative syntactic processing even at high proficiency and low AoA. Natives and nonnatives behave alike in tasks that involve equivalent linguistic phenomena for Basque and Spanish such as verb agreement condition and semantic condition, but differ in tasks that involve diverging syntactic parameters such as the head parameter and argument alignment (nominative/ergative). The results indicate that, in particular, not all linguistic differences have the same impact in nonnative language processing, and they suggest that divergent parameters have a deeper impact in nonnative syntactic processing than other seemingly variable but superficially different aspects of language variability.

Our data lend support to the hypothesis that linguistic distance is one fundamental source behind native/nonnative contrasts in the neural syntactic computation of proficient bilinguals. We obtained indications that linguistic properties that systematically diverge between the native and the nonnative language of the bilingual yield a distinct processing signature different to that of natives, even in the case of early and very proficient bilinguals. Whether this distinct signature is due to an effect of transferring the parametric setting from the native language onto the nonnative one (transfer), or whether it is due to difficulty in setting two opposite values for one linguistic parameter in the bilingual, and the extent to which these two possibilities are mutually exclusive or necessarily concurrent, cannot be determined given the available evidence, and future work is required to further unravel the ultimate nature of the language-distance effect.

9

Current Basque Literature

Jon Kortazar, the University of the Basque Country (UPV/EHU)

A Panorama of Current Basque Literature

Among the historians and analysts of Basque literature, a consensus exists about the importance of the passage of the Statute of Autonomy for the Basque Country in 1979 and the implementation of the law on the normalization of the use of Euskara in 1982 for the subsequent development of literature in Basque, given that the legislators addressed the teaching of language and literature in the schools of the Basque Country. This resulted in an unprecedented presence of the publishing world in Basque society. In other words, the need to create and develop textbooks in Euskara and their subsequent distribution provided publishing houses with a significant financial base that would allow them to grow exponentially.

From the 1980s on, consequently, a series of events occurred that led to the creation of a literary environment based on those publishing houses' stability and institutions were created that would serve to support the various protagonists of the Basque literary world. First came the creation of the Euskal Idazleen Elkartea, (Association of Basque Writers, EIE) in 1982 (www. idazleak.org), followed by the Euskal Itzultzaile, Interpretari eta Zuzentzaileen Elkartea/ Asociación de Traductores, Intérpretes y Correctores en Lengua Vasca (Association of Translators, Interpreters, and Copyeditors in Basque, EIZIE) in 1987 (www.eize.org), as platforms for defending the rights of the professionals they served. Other associations also appeared, such as the Bertsozale Elkartea/ Asociación de Amigos del Bersolarismo (Association of Friends of *Bertsolaritza*—improvised oral Basque poetry), also in 1987 (www. bertsozale.com).

* This study is part of a research project financed by the Basque government under number IT 495/10 and by the Universidad del País Vasco/Euskal Herriko Unibertsitatea (University of the Basque Country, UPV/EHU) under number GIC 10/100.

This panorama might begin by stating one fact: since the 1980s, narrative prose in Basque has acquired the preeminence that poetry has had at other times. Literature's access to the schools created a demand for texts intended for young readers, one that would permanently modify the literary panorama and the way in which the writing and reading of Basque literature is structured. The officialization of literature in teaching had notable effects. Indeed, one might speak of an unparalleled development of children's and young people's literature in Basque, as an initial way to reach beginning readers, with the result that this genre became one of the pillars on the basis of which both the Basque-language market and the creativity of its authors developed. In a first stage in the 1980s, the sudden appearance of literature in the schools gave rise to concern about the type of reader who was being developed. The provision of reading material that students were supposed to read in school led to talk about a "captive reader" who was required to turn to the texts chosen by his or her teacher.

The development of what has been called genre literature is another of the most significant consequences in this framework for explaining the Basque literary panorama. Cruime fiction has been well received by readers, although it has not been a field for literary ambition, and the authors of this genre have dedicated themselves to importing formulas already established in other literatures, such as those of the United States and France. Travel books have been very widely welcomed by Basque-language readers; and, together with these, comic novels focusing on the experience of learning Euskara or the lives of Basque university students have also been published.

Literature of this kind thinks first about the reader, about creating a transparent literature that is easily understood by the reader and can be read with enjoyment. This coincides with one of the maxims of postmodernity: attention to the reader as the first literary premise. However, this is not the only factor in the creation of a mass-market literature. Publishing houses, in their process of professionalization, try to recover the investment made in a book. The importance of sales and the transformation of culture into a market have thus had a significant impact on Basque literature, as in the case of other literatures. In the course of this process, homogenization has taken place both with regard to content and with regard to the chosen language itself, which seeks rapid communication with the reader and not to entail difficulty in reading. All these elements, however, have also produced positive effects that we should take into account in discussing the panorama of Basque literature.

Among these effects, one should mention the creation of a recognizable Basque literary canon. Several writers who began their careers in the late 1970s have become points of reference for Basque literature today, whether because of their impact outside the Basque Country or their presence on the Basque literary scene and their recognition among Basque authors and readers.

This canon, as has been the case in other neighboring literary systems, has maintained a certain degree of stability in recent years. At the center of the literary system is the work of Ramon Saizarbitoria (born in 1944), Anjel Lertxundi (1948), Bernardo Atxaga (1951), Joseba Sarrionandia (1958), and on another level, the work of Arantxa Urretabizkaia (1947) and Joan Mari Irigoien (1948), the latter of whom perhaps had a greater presence in the canon in the 1980s and early 1990s. The stability of this group of writers, considered crucial in the current panorama, is due to a variety of factors: the reception of their work by the reading public, whether due to its content or to its approach to language; continuity in their novelistic careers; the impact of their work outside the Basque Country; and the innovative elements they brought to Basque literature at the time of their appearance on the literary scene.

Poetry's share in the canon has been declining over the years, although the presence of highly regarded writers such as Juan Mari Lekuona (1927–2005), Bitoriano Gandiaga (1928–2001), and Xabier Lete (1944–2010) is worth mentioning, at the same time that we cannot forget the impact of the poetic work of some of the writers previously mentioned: for example, Bernardo Atxaga and Joseba Sarrionandia are the authors of well-regarded works of poetry.

Even if the image of the canon remains highly stable, and the cited names will hardly be absent from any quick reference to Basque literature, one should begin by pointing out a change in that same canon due to three fundamental factors that add nuance to this portrait: the emergence of authors of mass-market literature who are continuously read in secondary schools such as Jon Arretxe (1963), Julen Gabiria (1973), and Fernando Morillo (1974); the presence of an ever more numerous and widely read new generation of women writers like Karmele Jaio (1970) and Uxue Alberdi (1984); and, above all, the growing recognition obtained by two young writers: Kirmen Uribe (1970) and Unai Elorriaga (1973).

The stability of the literary system and the canonical landscape that I have just outlined has two significant consequences. The first is the practical disappearance of so-called writers of a single work—those authors who turned to literature with the aim of defending their language and their identity, but who did not see literary work as a profession—with the result that today's Basque writers are writers with an extensive history and lengthy literary careers.

The second consequence is the variety of aesthetic approaches that can be observed in current Basque literature. If we look at narrative, for example, we see that a realistic aesthetic dominates the field at present, with a range of nuances within that broad characterization. From the critical, ironic, and sarcastic realism of Ramon Saizarbitoria, to the realism aiming at a reevaluation of history practiced by Bernardo Atxaga, by way of Anjel Lertxundi's realism of moral reflection, almost any variation can be found among these authors. What is called the "Basque question"—violence and its consequences, and the presence of its victims—is addressed in short stories like those of Jokin Muñoz (1963) and Iban Zaldua (1966), representatives of the generation of writers born around 1963, the birth year of many Basque writers. The union of fiction with references to reality is also present in the work of Xabier Montoia (1955), and dirty realism is an aesthetic with a wide following among Basque writers.

In the current Basque literary panorama, it is customarily pointed out with some frequency that several generations of writers are publishing at the same time, and it is added (I believe not entirely accurately) that this is something new in the history of Basque literature.

In summary, one can argue that today's Basque literature is experiencing a favorable period of development, with some problems that we will discuss below. There are authors active today across a wide generational spectrum, from those born in the 1930s to those born in the 1980s. This range of authors' ages suggests the possibility of a reading public of similar extension, although the central canon of important authors is made up of those born between 1940 and the early 1950s, with the exception of Joseba Sarrionandia. The importance of this variety of authors resides in the fact that it offers readers widely representative texts with a variety of content. Works designed to be read and consumed immediately fit into the classic literary genres: crime fiction, comic novels, travel novels, novels about university life, erotic novels, and so on. However, references to topics of other kinds can also be found in novels and stories, such as historical memory (Jokin Muñoz), the historical novel (Juan Mari Irigoien; Aingeru Epalza, 1960), the narrative of contention and ellipsis (Pello Lizarralde, 1956), works about the personal histories of characters and about their individual relationships (Arantxa Iturbe, 1964), the creative novel that arises from the crisis of its characters (Lourdes Oñederra, 1958), an interest in the literature of the absurd (Karlos Linazasoro, 1962), the defense of autobiographical memory (Juan Kruz Igerabide, 1956), the creation of a feminist consciousness (Arantxa Urretabizkaia), narrative experimentation (Harkaitz Cano, 1975), an interest in naive narrative forms (Unai Elorriaga), and stories closely tied to current events (Xabier Montoia). In other words, there are multiple ways to approach literary subject matter as a reflection of the complex forms acquired by contemporary life in the Basque Country.

An important element in the configuration of the Basque literary system is centered on the attention given to works translated into Euskara. Translations of classics of European and world literature have led the system to promote two aspects that one should briefly note: first, translators have had to recreate in Basque forms of expression present and commonly used in other languages; and second, translations offer models for reflection about literary creation and have to be capable of responding to the demands posed by the professionalization of the sector. Basque-language writing has advanced in the rigor of its construction, in the adoption of techniques already used in other languages, and in reflection about the registers and styles that can be used in new versions in Euskara, after having passed over the threshold of translation and drawn near to new creative moments.

Toward these ends, two collections have served to impart a seal of quality to this activity. The collection *Pentsamenduaren Klasikoak euskaraz* (Classic Works of Thought in Basque) began in the 1990s and has published over 130 titles by classic authors from around the world (www.ehu.es/ehg/klasikoak). Another collection, *Literatura Unibertsala* (World Literature), has translated numerous literary classics into Euskara: a hundred books between 1990 and 2002, and another fifty-two in a second series from 2002 to 2010.

This panorama, which has positive aspects, has developed in an era of postmodern aesthetics in which elite and popular culture are coming together and melding, with the result that mass-market literature such as genre novels and bestsellers is accepted as literature, and in which the industrial and marketing elements have been reinforced. Literature is no longer only what is defined as such in academic and critical circles; instead, the object of mass consumption is accepted as such. Consequently, several factors of socialization are used in defining what qualifies as literary.

Referring to the literary system in Spain, Jordi Gracia and Domingo Rodenas de Moya (2009, 15) sketch the following panorama:

The literary map has fragmented, and readers have grown in number, although they are scattered over the different provinces of this map, and all this is occurring in the context of great difficulties in the way of a critical intelligentsia seeking to take action in society, in the face of arguments that are no longer of a practical nature, but rather a *business* one. In a scenario in which the role of the humanities in secondary and higher education has been reduced and literature too often limited to entertainment (for readers) or to a mere commercial product (for publishing middlemen, increasingly managers rather than editors), it is unsurprising that intellectuals' capacity for influence is limited.

Some of these characteristics, given concrete form in a context of nostalgia for literary modernity, can be observed in the Basque literary system, beginning with the fragmentation of literary aesthetics. Cultural elements such as a greater number of readers (within the scale of Basque culture and the number of Basque-speakers, and in open competition with new forms of leisure and with the introduction of the internet and its consequences for the use of free time), the appearance of commercial and industrial motivations in the world of the book (in the past, people read out of political commitment, but this form of cultural integration has now disappeared), reduction of the place of the humanities and literature in education, creation of an entertainment market, and reinforcement of the figure of the editor or the director of a literary collection are all characteristic elements of a time in which the democratization of culture and of reading is accompanied by other conditions perhaps less accepted by a critical mass (Tortosa 2009).

In any event, one modern theme continues to be present in the general panorama of Basque literature. I am referring to the treatment of identity and the so-called national question or Basque conflict, the persistence of violence in a European society. Basque-language writing is identified with defense of national identity, just as in the nineteenth century, literature was established as one of the ways in which a nation was defined. Certainly, very few writers today engage in an explicit defense of identity by means of their textual creations, and the autonomy of literature is an idea that predominates over those books that defend Basque identity. However, forms of expression that defend the Basque nation and its independence, for example, have not disappeared. The metaphor for this defense might be the search for a utopian location that represents an independent Euskadi (Basque Country), as in the poetry of Koldo Izagirre.

The topic of the so-called Basque conflict has greater analytical reach. In Ramon Saizarbitoria's first works such as *100 metro*, (1976)/*Cien metros* (1979)/*100 meters* (1985),[15] in the mention of violence in Anjel Lertxundi's *Hamasigarrenean aidanez* (On the sixteenth, they say, 1983), and in Mario Onaindia's (1948–2003) biographical novel *Grand Placen aurkituko gara*, 1983/*Grande Place*, 1985, it appears to point toward an ethical examination of violence in order to disown it. The issues have gradually come to be channeled in such a way that from description, allegory, or apology, the focus has moved to an examination of the effects of violence on society in works such as *Bizia lo*, 2003/*Letargo* , 2005 (Lethargy by Jokin Muñoz. It is not a topic that is absent from the narrative of Bernardo Atxaga—in works such as *Zeru horiek*, 1995/*Esos cielos*, 1996/*The Lone Woman*, 1999 and *Soinujolearen semea*, 2003/*El hijo del acordeonista*, 2004/*The Accordionist's Son*, 2007—who distances himself from the violence and deplores its consequences. Something similar is also found in *Bilbao-New York-Bilbao* by Kirmen Uribe (2008 in Euskara/2009 in Spanish/forthcoming in English).

---

15. All titles and years of publication for any book mentioned will be given first for the original Basque edition, followed by Spanish and English translations if applicable. If a title appears in italics, it refers to a published work.

I am confident not only in the health of narrative prose, but also in that of Basque literature in general, although lyric poetry has suffered under market forces that have pushed it to the margins of the system, and theater has suffered the same fate to an even greater extent. Few theatrical works are published, and fewer are performed (only two works were publicly staged in 2010).

If theatrical performances have been decreasing, Basque actors have found in television a vehicle for continuing their acting careers. Television has had the virtue of making some actors who got their start in theater well known. Consequently, works performed on television deserve a more hopeful prognosis with the shift of acting to that medium, a genre about which very little is said in surveys of Basque literature, despite the presence of works with the chronological staying power of the soap opera *Goenkale*, created by the Pausoka production company; it began broadcasting in October 1994, and its three-thousandth episode was broadcast in July 2010.

As noted, postmodern aesthetics promote the absence of aesthetic hegemony and assigns greater meaning to a more varied range of production in terms of content and textual realizations. Together with the authors who make up the literary canon, and who, in another special characteristic of the Basque literary system, maintain close ties to their publishing houses (when they are not their owners), new authors are also appearing—especially in the narrative genre—who are renewing the forms of literary expression.

Of course, this does not lessen the sensation of confusion produced by a market in which sales are primary and disposable literature dominates, in which narrative fluency is preferred to depth and the narrative of action over that of reflection. Other characteristics such as plain language and simple syntax contribute to defining a state of the question that has both bright spots and shadows.

Finally, I would like to address the topic of innovation in literature. Perhaps for sociological and historical reasons (the long period of time since the death of Franco in 1975 has been one of political stability), the canon of Basque literature, as is also the case in other systems, has remained stable around the figures already discussed; a stability that is not unconnected to the control that some of the mentioned authors exercise over their publishing houses. It may be the case that in the last few years, we have been witnessing a slight change in the literary canon in relation to two axes of literary presence.

A new generation of young women writers (Karmele Jaio; Eider Rodriguez, 1977; Irati Jiménez, 1977; Uxue Alberdi) has changed the system's readership figures, and many of their works come with a cover band indicating that they are in their fifth, sixth, or seventh edition, achievements of a new system that grants literary works the presence of their readers. Mass-market literature and the literature of social experimentation are represented among them.

Moreover, Kirmen Uribe's sudden—and fortunate, some scholars note—appearance on the scene has brought with it a debate about his literary work that demonstrates the possibility of opening the closed Basque canon to new names. His universally acclaimed volume of poetry, *Bitartean heldu eskutik* (2001)/*Mientras tanto dame la mano* (2004)/*Meanwhile Take My Hand* (2007), with translations into French and English, was a novelty both in the number of copies sold and in the vitality it brought to the musty world of Basque lyric poetry. Furthermore, his novel *Bilbao-New York-Bilbao* created new paths for Basque narrative, and the debate around it made clear the conservative attitude of his detractors in that new and untidy quarrel of ancients and moderns.

National Prizes and the Basque Literary System

The National Literature Prizes, which are awarded annually by the Spanish Ministry of Culture in several categories (narrative, poetry, drama, and literature for children and young people), have offered an important platform for making Basque writers known beyond the borders of the Basque literary system alone.

For Basque literature and for its international recognition, National Prizes in the narrative category have been decisive because they have meant that Basque writers have obtained decisive publicity for their literary careers and have had the doors of the international market opened to them. The National Prizes were established in 1926 and from 1977 on, they changed course and objective and soon accepted in their competition works written not only in Spanish, but in any of the four languages recognized as official in the 1978 Spanish Constitution. In 1986, for example, Alfredo Conde won with a work written in Galician, *Xa vai o grifón no vento* (1984)/*El Griffón* (1987)/ *The Griffon* (2000). As can be read on the website of the Ministry of Culture of the Kingdom of Spain (www.mcu.es/libro/CE/Premios/presentacion.html), "Their objective is to stimulate literary creation by publicly recognizing the efforts of authors whose works have been judged especially distinguished by a jury of experts in each category. The efforts to promote the dissemination of culture by particular entities and professionals are likewise recognized."

The linguistic plurality and cultural diversity that characterize Spanish society, the great variety and richness of Spanish, Catalan, Galician, Valencian, and Basque literature, are promoted by the Ministry of Culture in all their manifestations related to the book. This is reflected in the composition of the juries, which include a representative of each of the institutions that safeguard Spain's official languages (Ministerio de Cultura).

The door was opened, therefore, for works written in Basque to also obtain the award. A historical precedent existed in the figure of the poet Gabriel Aresti (1933–1975), who won the National Prize in 1968, named on that occasion for José María Iparragirre (1820–1881), a nineteenth-century Basque poet and lyricist.

In this new phase, Bernardo Atxaga, Unai Elorriaga, and Kirmen Uribe won the National Prize for Narrative, respectively, in 1989 for *Obabakoak* (1988 /1989/1992), in 2002 for *SPrako tranbia* (2001)/*Un tranvía a SP* (A streetcar to SP, 2003), and in 2009 for the novel *Bilbao-New York-Bilbao* (2008/2009). Anjel Lertxundi won the National Prize for Essay-Writing in 2010 for *Eskarmentuaren paperak* (2009)/*Vida y otras dudas* (Life and other doubts, 2009). Meanwhile, since Mariasun Landa (1949) won in 2003 in the Children's and Young People's Literature category for *Kokodrilo bat ohe azpian* (2002)/*Un cocodrilo bajo la cama* (A crocodile under the bed, 2004). Reactions to the prize within the Basque literary system have included a variety of nuances and even debates.

The distinction won by Bernardo Atxaga in 1989 was the cause of great rejoicing and a feeling of self-satisfaction in the work that was being done in Euskara. Atxaga's work has been translated into many languages: Albanian, Asturian, Catalan, Spanish, Danish, German, French, Galician, Greek, Croatian, Hebrew, Dutch, Japanese, Norwegian, Polish, Portuguese, Russian, Swedish, Arabic, Turkish, and English, with a recent republication of *Obabakoak* in the United States in 2010. This made a small literature visible in the world's culturally most important languages. The book put Basque literature on the map. The number of translations that *Obabakoak* enjoyed meant that works written in Euskara had an impact they had never known before. It was the first time in the history of Basque literature that this minor literature, which drew nourishment from outside influences, could approach the status of a major literature, exercising influence and becoming worthy of imitation (Kortazar 2005).

Obabakoak was a symptom of the complex paradigm into which the Basque literary system was entering. On the one hand, it indirectly maintained a political position, the symbolic confirmation of the configuration of the Comunidad Autónoma del País Vasco-Euskal Autonomia Erkidegoa (CAPV-EAE, the Autonomous Community of the Basque Country) within a wider Spanish state made up of autonomous communities, a constitutional structure that had been reinforcing its position since the end of Franco's dictatorship and Spain's democratic consolidation. The book served to acknowledge that things were being done well in Euskadi, which could show off a work that reached beyond linguistic and cultural borders. On the other hand, it was the fruit of a new cultural conception that was in the process of formation in the CAPV-EAE and served to underline the cultural impetus that the new autonomous Basque government was giving to society.

It was part of a current that modified the image of the Basque writer and demonstrated the internationalization of Basque literature, with the result that Atxaga was confirmed as a Basque and international writer. Ur Apalategi describes the process in his *La Naissance de l'écrivain basque* (The Birth of the Basque Writer, 2000). In this cultural context, a Basque writer who wanted to become a professional and write full-time, not an amateur who writes and publishes in occasional bursts, would have to adapt to the strategies that shaped the market. Internationalization was one of the paths that Basque writers would follow. They all have the ambition of being translated and entering into broader and more diverse dynamics than those offered by the limited Basque literary system.

Mariasun Landa has also seen her work translated into several languages: Spanish, Catalan, Galician, English, Korean, and Russian. Her international impact has been less, as is also true of her work's symbolic importance within the system. The last two prizes were awarded so recently that the authors have not had time for an international tour, something that Kirmen Uribe did do with his volume of poetry *Bitartean heldu eskutik*, translated into Spanish (two editions), French, and English, with an edition in the United States. *Bilbao-New York-Bilbao* has been published in Spanish (2009), Galician and Catalan (2010), and Portuguese (2011), with editions soon to appear in English, French, and Japanese.

Some authors, who firmly defend a literature of identity and look to the system's interior, denying the influence that an external institution like the Kingdom of Spain with its prizes could have within the system, have proposed a boycott of the prize and questioned its impact. They affirm that the prize distorts a work's significance and that a work that lacks significance within the system obtains publicity that, in their opinion, it does not deserve. In response, one should note that all the prize-winning works had obtained significant resonance before obtaining the prize; or in other words, the prize was a confirmation of opinions already circulating within the Basque literary scene. Atxaga, Uribe, and Landa, not to mention Lertxundi, were well-known authors within the system before obtaining the prize, and their award-winning works had passed the system's own test before receiving the prize.

Finally, a division has been created between on the one hand the authors who have received the prize and who represent two generations, that of the "seniors," born around 1950 (Lertxundi, 1948, Atxaga, 1951), and the "juniors" (Uribe, 1970, Elorriaga, 1973), and on the other, those who have not received it and who are part of the generation born around the 1960s.

Undoubtedly, however, life exists beyond the National Prizes. Ramon Saizarbitoria's literary work, for example, is highly regarded in Basque literary circles, despite or precisely because of his flight from the conditions imposed by the market and his publication of rich and dense work at very widely spaced intervals. Of course, he also just missed out on winning in 2001 for *Gorde nazazu lurpean* (2000)/*Guárdame bajo la tierra* (Bury me beneath the earth, 2002).

A Survey of Authors and Works

I will begin my survey, for purely chronological reasons, with a look at the work of Saizarbitoria, one of the Basque novelists most representative of contemporary Basque narrative. His work has aimed openly at rupture, although he has always sought to reflect some of the most important aspects of the human condition. For that reason, the depth of style with which he treats the great human problems in his works has made his literary production very highly regarded in extensive literary circles, both in the Basque Country and beyond. This is especially so in well-informed critical circles, given that his current narrative work, distanced from market conditions, is not intended for mass consumption.

His narrative work is divided into two extensive periods: between 1969 and 1976 he published three novels, after which he maintained a lengthy silence of nineteen years, before returning to publishing between 1995 and 2000. He is currently writing a new novel.

In the first period (Hernández Abaitua 2008), the themes of his work surveyed some of the moral issues of the society of the time: the legalization of abortion and its impact on women. Gisèle Sergier, the protagonist of *Egunero hasten delako* (Because it begins every day, 1969), suffers the paradox that abortion is legal in some cantons of Switzerland, the country in which the author was living at the time the novel was composed, and not in others, something that leads to a reflection on the changes in legality from one region to another within a single country. The novel plays with the levels of narration; on one level, a charlatan character comments on ethical and political issues with anonymous interlocutors, creating a fluid monologue, while on a second level Gisèle experiences the conflicts discussed by the anonymous conversationalist, either in her narrated story or internally. The linkage between the two levels is a semantic one: Gisèle experiences the problems that the conversationalist raises theoretically. Clearly influenced by John Dos Passos's novel *Manhattan Transfer* (1925), the novel *100 metro* (1976), the publication of which was delayed by problems with the censors (copies of it were seized), recounts the final moments of an activist before he is killed in the Constitution Plaza in Donostia-San Sebastián. In this brief and complex, simple and profound novel, however, there are also two levels of narration: the story of the man, Jose, who is going to die (there is perhaps a suicidal drive behind his acts) and who in his flight remembers (fragmentarily) his life; and a view of the city and its inhabitants, who over the course of the novel show increasing indifference to its central event, the protagonist's death, an action that can consequently be interpreted as useless and in vain. The author's interest in psychoanalysis, which would grow in his subsequent novels and stories, appeared already in this text.

The second cycle began with a major work, *Hamaika pauso* (1995)/*Los pasos incontables*, The uncountable steps, 1998), focusing on the last executions of the Franco regime in September 1975. A complex work, it breaks with linear narrative, as is habitual in this author, in order to make the central event into the novel of a generation, a metaphor for Basque society, which did not know how to say no and let itself by kidnapped by armed violence. The novel mixes reality (the author uses the names of real people or changes them slightly) and fiction; or rather, various degrees of fiction, since one of the characters within the work, Abaitua, writes a novel titled *Hamaika pauso* (Eleven steps), which is not the one that we are reading, and a remarkable exercise of memory is created. In addition to the psychoanalytic element so common in this author, the topic of the social, personal, and communicative differences between men and women appeared in this work.

This concern would govern his next novel, *Bihotz bi. Gerrako kronikak* (1996)/*Amor y guerra* Two hearts: War stories, 1999). Also structured on two levels, it combines the story of an adulterous affair set in the present with stories of the 1936 Spanish Civil War. The war referred to in the title is both the civil conflict and the war between the sexes.

The exhumation of corpses, an act full of psychoanalytic echoes, gave unity to *Gorde nazazu lurpean* (2000), a collection of five stories. The five stories reflect on the weight of history, memory, and the changes that the protagonists undergo when what has been kept hidden in the darkness comes to light. In this twist of his narrative trajectory, Saizarbitoria works with elements used in his previous works such as the narrator's doubts, the importance of memory, the psychoanalytic approach, and the difficulty of communication and coexistence between men and women.

Anjel Lertxundi received the National Prize for Essay-Writing in 2010 for his work *Eskarmentuaren paperak,* following a highly productive career. His narrative work can be divided into several phases. In the first phase, Lertxundi renewed the Basque story with works such as *Aise eman zenidan eskua* (You easily gave me your hand, 1980). In a second phase, he turned away from allegory and took the path of the modern novel. *Hamaisegarrenan aidanez* (1983) won the Jon Mirande Prize for novels and was his first great success. It brought new life to the crime fiction novel in order to take an in-depth look at issues such as that of violence in Basque society. After the success of Ataxaga's *Obabakoak* in 1988, Lertxundi took a more experimental approach, one further from conventional narrative patterns, as in *Carla* (1989).

Lertxundi's great narrative cycle was produced between 1994 and 1998, with two high points. In 1994, he published his most celebrated work, the novel *Otto Pette* (*Las últimas sombras*, The last shadows, 1996), set in an allegorical Middle Ages that serves the author as a space for reflection on power and human relationships. This work reflects his profound knowledge and mastery of the language in which he writes, in which he seeks to transmit a Basque language that can be used to express any kind of register. The work was published in Spanish in Barcelona, entailing a further step in the promotion of the writer, who tackled some of the great themes of European literature such as the demon and Faust in *Piztiaren izena*, (1995)/*La noche de la bestia* (The night of the beast, 2002) and the eternal wanderer in *Azkenaz beste* (1996)/*Un final para Nora* (An end for Nora, 1999) and *Argizariaren egunak* (1998) /*Los días de la cera* (The days of wax, 2001). These three works were published by Alfaguara, one of Spain's most important publishing houses.

After 2002, Lertxundi returned to a more traditional narrative method and a novel closer to the situation of Basque society with *Zorion perfektua* (2002)/*Felicidad perfecta* (2006)/*Perfect Happiness* (2007). A young women witnesses an ETA murder, and the social consequences and the treatment of the act in the press serve as a backdrop against which the author projects his ethical and moral reflections on political violence. Ill-treatment of women is reflected in *Zoaz infernura, laztana* (2008)/*Vete al infierno, cariño* (Go to hell, my dear, 2009), and his recent work *Etxeko hautsa* (2011)/*Trapos sucios* (Dirty rags, 2011) takes up the issue of reflection on the period of Spain's transition to democracy.

Following this career, which earned him numerous and varied marks of recognition, his essay *Eskarmentuaren paperak* (2009) gathered a series of fragments, similar to maxims, proverbs, and distilled thoughts; in the work, the author offers a vision of the world in relation to very different topics: life, books, an ironic perspective on current events, with Montaigne as the chief point of reference in an act of writing continually in the process of invention.

Mariasun Landa has renewed children's and young people's literature through critical realism. The author of an extensive body of work (around thirty published works), she is considered to have passed through several phases in her literary career (Barbancho 2008). In the first phase, she took an approach close to that of critical realism, with the use of fantastic elements, but situated within real contexts (*Txan fantasma/Chan el fantasma*, 1984/ *Karmentxu and the Little Ghost*, 1996). With *Iholdi* (1988), she moved in the direction of minimalism. *Galtzerdi suizida* (2001)/*El calcetín suicida* (The suicidal sock, 2004) reflected a third phase in her work, taking the short novel as its point of departure, with a consequent increase in the complexity of the situations. *Krokodriloa ohe azpian* (2002) (2004) is one of her most recent successes, in which the author has combined a psychoanalytic perspective with a young person's reality.

Bernardo Atxaga represents the image of a professional writer with extensive international impact within the Basque literary system. His fundamental merits, in addition to the quality of his literary work, reside in his sustained capacity to project that work known beyond the borders of the language, in such a way that he has been the main promoter of Basque literature and its internationalization.

His initial work manifested avant-garde leanings and an interest in a minority and experimental literature, as expressed in *Ziutatzeaz* (About the city, 1976) and *Etiopia* (Ethiopia, 1978), which was considered a poetic work that broke with previous work more closely related to social poetry and renewed the imaginary and the library of Basque poetry from a surrealist perspective. In a second phase he opted for a literature that united nostalgia for rural childhood with aspects of the literature of fantasy and magic, learned from authors such as the Argentine writer Jorge Luis Borges, at the same time that he showed himself very much open to the influence of oral literature. *Bi anai* (1985)/*Dos hermanos* (1995)/*Two Brothers* (2001) is a clear representative of this period in his artistic production. The story of two brothers, which ends tragically, it spoke of cruelty in the rural world and the possibility of the magical transformation of the characters into animals. This current terminated in the author's best-known work, *Obabakoak* (1988), a collection of twenty-six stories, some of them previously published but included here in a network of meanings that, taken as a whole, maintains the reader suspended in a marvelous world built from the old formulas of traditional storytellers.

Following the success of the Obaba cycle, Atxaga decided to change register. In a number of statements, he has stressed the importance of children's and young people's literature as a laboratory for experimentation. Correspondingly, in 1991, he published *Behi euskaldun baten memoriak/Memorias de una vaca* (Memoirs of a Basque cow, 1992), a book in which he used animals as protagonists, as if in a fable, in order to move in a realist direction and take up the topic of the 1936 Spanish Civil War, with reference in this case to the postwar period and the life of anti-Franco resistance fighters in that period.

This book served as an introduction to the author's great novelistic cycle on the Basque Country's recent history, beginning with *Gizona bere bakardeadean* (1993)/*El hombre solo* (1994)/*The Lone Man* (1996). It is the story of a man, Carlos, who has abandoned the armed struggle and, with a group of friends, manages a hotel near Barcelona where the Polish soccer team stays during the soccer World Cup in Spain in 1982. Carlos gives refuge to an ETA couple, leading to a tragic ending. If that novel narrates the end of a group of friends who were militants in an armed group and recounts the end of illusion and the acceptance of the collapse of illusions, *Zeru horiek* (1995) centers on the figure of Irene, a woman who accepts leaving prison and wants to enetr society once more despite the rejection she is going to suffer in her family and social environment. In this novel, Atxaga took another step in his contemplation of social activity in the Basque Country and the evolution of its armed groups.

The most ambitious work in this cycle of historical novels is *Soinu-jolearen semea* (2003). The novel aims to recount seventy years of the history of the Basque Country. With a tone close to that of autobiography, Joseba, the friend of the accordionist's son, David, rewrites his memoirs. These begin in 1957, at the moment at which he begins to feel and to be conscious of nationalist sentiments. The work then jumps to a narrative of the Spanish Civil War (1936–1939), with the participation of David's father in the conflict and the repression, including the insertion within the narrative of a novella about the fate of an uncle from the New World, one of the constants in Atxaga's narrative writing. The novel recounts David's years as a university student, his participation in the armed struggle, and his flight from that commitment. Within the brief compass of a complex novel, Atxaga creates a synthesis of the history of Basque society from 1936 to the present.

His latest narrative contribution has revealed a new change in his narrative interests. In *Zazpi etxe Frantzian* (2009)/*Siete casas en Francia* (2010)/ *Seven Houses in France* (2011), the action takes place in the Belgian Congo and is intended as an implacable critique of colonization.

Kirmen Uribe first became known with a multimedia text, *Bar Puerto. Bazterreko ahotsak* (2001)/*Bar Puerto. Voces desde el margen* (2010)/*Bar Puerto: Voices from the Edge* (2010). This poetic account of the disappearance of a neighborhood in the town where Uribe was born at the beginning of the twenty-first century juggled and united a variety of aesthetic modes including photography, video, music, song, and the recitation of poetic texts, in order to arrive at a unity of meaning. The text brought together diverse forms of communication in order to retain the memory of the neighborhood's inhabitants, who were recorded on video and who, in the text's representation, recall a world in which life was not easy: *Bar Puerto* aimed to be a compressed history of the twentieth century. He published *Bitartean heldu eskutik* (2001) in the same year, and his success has been constant since that moment. In the exiguous world of Basque poetry, the book sold out its first edition in a month, and from that time forward, its editions, sales, and translations into other languages have been on the increase.

At first glance, Uribe's poetry is characterized by three elements: the simplicity of his language, his narrative approach to poetry, and his autobiographical pose. However, any attempt to reduce his poetry to a single formula is a fruitless task. The poetic text grows in richness on each reading, because in the end, it offers a hymn to life, to a changing, exultant way of life beyond all limitations. Uribe's poetic text takes as its foundation some of the premises of postmodernity such as the affirmation that it is impossible for language to encompass reality, and makes use of certain key themes to shape the book's overall composition: the body as a new language for being in the world; memory as a way of anchoring oneself in identity; love and sex; a gaze directed toward others and toward an "I" become multiple in a changing reality; the borders of language; understanding and interaction between literature and other arts; life that flourishes in the most difficult moments of his father's death, and so on. Uribe writes a poetry that appears simple, but that can only take form after having distilled much reading and given life to a powerfully moving voice.

His novel *Bilbao-New York-Bilbao* (2008) tells the story of a plane trip from Bilbao to New York during which he recalls his family's history over four generations: the generation of his grandfather, his father, himself, and the presence of his partner's child. We find ourselves, then, once again faced with the concentrated history of the twentieth century from the viewpoint of a small community. The work is structured on the basis of four axes of composition: the play between biography and autofiction, the importance of the creation of family history as an axis for interpreting a time, the play between fiction and reality, and the use of new literary forms. It can be considered a novel about memory, but at the same time, it is a literary text that reflects on the way to create a novel and leads the reader through multiple tiny stories. This novel could not be understood without taking into account the possibilities that the use of the internet and its influence have opened for literary writing. The use of forms that owe their existence to the online world explains some of the constants in this text made up of small fragments. Postmodernity and globalization are the foundations on which the book is constructed.

SPrako tranbia (2001) by Unai Elorriaga won its author the National Prize in 2002. The novel centers on a new topical focus: the solitude of the elderly and the nearness of a world that, originating in the protagonists' illness (possibly Alzheimer's), gives rise to a dreamlike world of solidarity. The characters move in a world of sensations and dreams, with the result that the text finds its roots in a fantastic aesthetic that owes much to the narrative of Julio Cortázar, but descending into the depths of the absurd and the description of a world of sensations. Elorriaga's writing has been described as an aesthetic that does not renounce the avant-garde and that seeks to surprise the reader by way of the absurd, with touches of innocence. This way of writing is demonstrated in his subsequent works: *Van't Hoffen ilea* (2003)/*El pelo de Van't Hoff* (Van't Hoff's hair, 2004) and *Vredaman* (2005 and Spanish translation in 2006, and in English translation as *Plants Don't Drink Coffee* in 2009).

His most recent work, *Londres kartoizkoa da* (2009)/*Londres es de cartón* (London Is made of cardboard, 2010), maintains some of the characteristics of his previous work, but it has involved a leap in his conception of writing. Strange environments and hidden allusions to literary works remain, but the action is located in the asphyxiating world of a dictatorship, in which the inhabitants climb up onto the rooftops as they await the arrival of a woman who has disappeared. A hearkening-back to avant-garde writing is combined with the author's interest in mental illness and experimentation with different types of writing, from narrative to the transcription of a book of laws and regulations on which this phantasmal dictatorship is founded.

References

Abney, Steven Paul. 1987. "The English Noun Phrase in its Sentential Aspects." Ph D. diss. Massachusetts Institute of Technology.

Académie Bordeaux. 2010. *L'enseignement du Basque dans l'Académie de Bordeaux. Année Scolaire 2010/2011.* Document provided by Mixel Esteban, official representative of the Euskararen Erakunde Publikoa-Office public de la langue Basque (EEP-OPLB), June 2011.

Aginako, Julen, et al. 1999. *Herri Batasuna: 20 años de lucha por la libertad 1978–1998.* N.p.: Herri Batasuna, 1999.

Aizpurua, Xabier. 2002. "Euskara: bizirik irautetik biziberritzera." In *Hizkuntza Biziberritzeko Saioak. Experiencias de inversión del cambio lingüístico. Récupération de la Perte Linguistique. Reversing Language Shift.* Eremu urriko Hizkuntzei buruzko VII. Nazioarteko Biltzarra. VII Conferencia Internacional de Lenguas Minoritarias. VII Conférence Internationale des Langues Minoritaires. 7th International Conference on Minority Languages 1999. Vitoria-Gasteiz: Servicio Central de Publicaciones del Gobierno Vasco. At www.kultura.ejgv.euskadi. net/r46-17894/es/contenidos/informacion/argitalpenak/es_6092/adjuntos/ EREMU.PDF.

Aldasoro, Eduardo. 2001. "La evolución de la enseñanza en euskera en Navarra. Una perspectiva pedagógica." *Revista Internacional de Estudios Vascos* (RIEV) 46, no. 2: 593–624. At www.euskomedia.org/PDFAnlt/riev/46/4605930624.pdf.

Altube, Seber. 1929. *Erderismos.* Bermeo: Euskaltzaindia.

———. 1949. "La Unificación del Euskera Literario." *E-J* 3, 2–3 zb: 183.

Amorrortu, Esti, Ane Ortega,, Itziar Idiazabal, and Andoni Barreña. 2009. *Actitudes y Prejuicios de los castellano hablantes hacia el euskera.* Vitoria-Gasteiz: Servicio Central de Publicaciones del Gobierno Vasco. At www.kultura.ejgv.euskadi. net/r46-17894/es/contenidos/informacion/argitalpenak/es_6092/adjuntos/ Actitudes%20y%20prejuicios.pdf.

Apalategi, Ur. 2000. *La naissance de l'écrivain basque. Evolution de la problématique littéraire de Bernardo Atxaga.* París: L'Harmattan.

Apalauza, Amaia. 2010. "Nafarroako Ipar-mendebaleko hizkeren egitura geolinguistikoa." Ph.D. diss. University of the Basque Country (UPV/EHU).

Arana, Sabino de. 1965. *Obras Completas.* Bayonne and Buenos Aires: Sabindiar-Batza.

Aranzadi Zientzi Elkartea. 1983. *Euskalerriko Atlas Etnolinguistikoa.* Donostia-San Sebastián: Aranzadi Zientzi Elkartea.

Artiagoitia, Xabier. 2002. "The Functional Structure of the Basque Noun Phrase." In

Erramu Boneta: A Festschrift for Rudolf P. G. de Rijk, edited by Xabier Artiagoitia, Patxi Goenaga, and Joseba A. Lakarra. Bilbao: Anejos de ASJU.

Arzoz Santisteban, Xabier. 2006. "Estatuto jurídico del euskera en Navarra." In *Estudios sobre el estatuto jurídico de las lenguas en España*, edited by José Manuel Pérez Fernández. Barcelona: Atelier.

Atxuri [pseudonym]. 1949. "Euzkaid, nombre consagrado."*Alderdi* 33 (December).

Aurrekoetxea, Gotzon. 1986. "Euskal Herriko Hizkuntza Atlasa (EHHA): Inkesta metodologia eta ezezko datuak." Euskera 31, no. 2: 413–24.

———. 1995. *Bizkaieraren egituraketa geolinguistikoa*. Bilbao: UPV/EHU.

Aurrekoetxea, Gotzon, and Xarles Videgain, eds. 1992. *Nazioarteko Dialektologia Biltzarra. Agiriak*. IKER 7. Bilbao: Euskaltzaindia.

Axular, Pedro. 1643; 1954. *Gero, bi partetan zatitua eta berezia*. Edited by Manuel Lekuona. Zarauz: Itxaropena.

Azkue, Resurrección Ma. 1969. *Diccionario Vasco-Español-Francés*. Bilbao: La Gran Enciclopedia Vasca.

Baker, Mark C. 2001. *The Atoms of Language*. New York: Basic Books..

———. 2003. "Language Differences and Language Design." *Trends in Cognitive Sciences* 7, no. 8: 349–53.

Barbancho, Iñigo. 2008. "Galtzerdi suizida (2001)." Euskal Literaturaren Hiztegia, Idazlanak. At ehu.es/ehg/literatura/?p=435.

Baztarrika, Patxi. 2010. *Babel o barbarie. Una política lingüística legítima y eficaz para la convivencia*. Irun: Alberdania.

Bluntschli, Johann, and Karl Brater, eds. 1857. *Deutsches Staats-Wörterbuch*. Volume 1. Stuttgart and Leipzig: Expedition des Staats-Wörterbuchs.

Bonaparte, Louis Lucien. *Carte des sept provinces basques, montrant la délimitation actuelle de l'euscara*. London: Stanford's Geographical Establishment, 1863.

———. 1883. *Carta lingüística del Príncipe Louis-Lucien Bonaparte, publicada en el número 116 (tomo IX) de la revista bascongada 'Euskal-Erria'*. San Sebastián: J. R. Baroja.

———. 1991. *Opera Omnia*. 4 volumes. Bilbao: Euskaltzaindia. At www.euskaltzaindia. net/dok/iker_jagon_tegiak/6934.pdf.

Bornkessel, Ina, and Matthias Schlesewsky. 2006. "The Extended Argument Dependency Model: A Neurocognitive Approach to Sentence Comprehension Across Languages." *Psychological Review* 113, no.4: 787–821.

Bosque, Ignacio, and Violeta Demonte. 1999. *Gramática descriptiva de la lengua española*. Madrid: Real Academia Española; Espasa Calpe.

Burzio, Luigi. 1986. *Italian Syntax: A Government-Binding Approach*. Dordrecht: Reidel.

Camino, Iñaki. 1997. *Aezkoako euskararen azterketa dialektologikoa*. Pamplona: Gobierno de Navarra.

———. 2003. "Hego-nafarreraren egituraz." *Fontes Linguae Vasconum* 94: 427–68.

———. 2004. "Irizpide metodologikoak egungo Euskal Dialektologian." *Euskera* 49, no. 1: 67–102.

———. 2009. *Dialektologiatik euskalkietara tradizioan gaindi*. Donostia: Elkar.

Cardaberaz, Agustín. 1761. *Eusqueraren berro onac: eta ondo escribitceco, ondo ira-curtceco, ta ondo itzeguiteco Erreglac.* Iruñea: Libruguille Antonio Castillaren Echean.

Caro Baroja, Julio. 1943. *Los pueblos del norte de la Península Ibérica.* Madrid: Consejo Superior de Investigaciones Científicas, Patronato "Menéndez y Pelayo."

Castells, José Manuel. 1976. *El Estatuto Vasco.* San Sebastián: Haranburu.

Chen, Lang. 1997. *On the Typology of Wh-questions.* New York and London: Garland.

Chen, Lang, Hua Shu, Youyi Liu, Jingjing Zhao, and Ping Li. 2007. "ERP Signatures of Subject–Verb Agreement in L2 Learning." *Bilingualism: Language and Cognition* 10, no. 2: 161–74.

Chomsky, Noam. 1981. *Lectures on Government and Binding.* Dordrecht: Foris.

Clark, Robert P. 1984. *The Basque Insurgents. ETA, 1952–1980.* Madison: University of Wisconsin Press.

Cobreros Mendazona, Edorta. 1989. *El régimen jurídico de la oficialidad del euskera.* Oñati: IVAP.

Colomé, Àngels. 2001. "Lexical Activation in Bilinguals' Speech Production: Language-specific or Language-independent?" *Journal of Memory and Language* 45, no. 4: 721–36.

Comrie, Bernard. 2008. "Basque, Romance, and Areal Typology: What do We Learn from the World Atlas of Language Structures?" In *Lenguas en diálogo: El iberorromance y su diversidad lingüística y literaria, ensayos en homenaje a Georg Bossong,* edited by Hans-Jörg Döhla, Raquel Montero Muñoz, and Francisco Báez de Aguilar González. Madrid: Iberoamericana; Frankfurt am Main: Vervuert.

Corcuera Atienza, Javier. 2006. *The Origins, Ideology, and Organization of Basque Nationalism, 1876–1903.* Reno: Center for Basque Studies, University of Nevada, Reno.

Costa, Albert. 2005. "Lexical Access in Bilingual Production." In *Handbook of Bilingualism: Psycholinguistic Approaches,* edited by Judith F. Kroll and Annette M.B. De Groot. New York: Oxford University Press.

Costa, Albert, Bárbara Albareda, and Mikel Santesteban. 2008. "Assessing the Presence of Lexical Competition Across Languages: Evidence from the Stroop Task." *Bilingualism: Language and Cognition* 11: 121–31.

Costa, Albert, Michele Miozzo, and Alfonso Caramazza. 1999. "Lexical Selection in Bilinguals: Do Words in the Bilingual's Two Lexicons Compete for Selection?" *Journal of Memory and Language* 41: 365–97.

Costa, Albert, Alfonso Caramazza, and Nuria Sebastian-Galles. 2000. "The Cognate Facilitation Effect: Implications for Models of Lexical Access." *Journal of Experimental Psychology: Learning Memory, and Cognition* 26, no. 5: 1283–96.

Costa, Albert, and Mikel Santesteban. 2004. "Lexical Access in Bilingual Speech Production: Evidence from Language Switching in Highly Proficient Bilinguals and L2 Learners." *Journal of Memory and Language* 50, no. 4: 491–511.

Costa, Albert, Mikel Santesteban, and Agnès Caño. 2005. "On the Facilitatory Effects of Cognate Words in Bilingual Speech Production." *Brain and Language* 94: 94–103.

Costa, Albert, Mikel Santesteban, and Iva Ivanova. 2006. "How do Highly Proficient Bilinguals Control their Lexicalization Process? Inhibitory and Language-Specific Selection Mechanisms are both Functional." *Journal of Experimental Psychology: Learning, Memory, and Cognition* 32, no. 5: 1057–74.

Council of Europe. 2001. *Common European Framework of Reference for Languages: Learning, Teaching, Assessment.* Strasbourg: Council of Europe.

———. 1992. *European Charter for Regional or Minority Languages*, Strasbourg, 5.XI.1992. On the Internet at: http://conventions.coe.int/treaty/en/Treaties/Html/148.htm (last accessed June 21, 2011).

Daranatz, Jean Baptiste. 1931. "Correspondance du Capitaine Duvoisin." *Revista Internacional de Estudios Vascos* (RIEV) 22: 310–37.

De Groot, Annette M. B., and Rineke Keijzer. 2000. "What is Hard to Learn is Easy to Forget: The Roles of Word Concreteness, Cognate Status, and Word Frequency in Foreign-language Vocabulary Learning and Forgetting." *Language Learning* 50, no. 1: 1–56.

De Rijk, Rudolf P. G. 2008. *Standard Basque: A Progressive Grammar.* Cambridge MA: MIT Press.

Desmet, Timothy, and Wouter Duyck. 2007. "Bilingual Language Processing." *Linguistics and Language Compass* 1, no. 3: 444–58.

Díaz, Begoña, Nuria Sebastián-Gallés, Kepa Erdocia, Jutta Mueller, and Itziar Laka. 2011. "On the Cross-linguistic Validity of Electrophysiological Correlates of Morphosyntactic Processing: A Study of Case and Agreement Violations in Basque." *Journal of Neurolinguistics* 24, no. 3: 357–73.

Documentos Y. 1979. Volume 2. San Sebastián: Lur.

Dressler, Wolfgang U. 2005. "Word-formation in Natural Morphology." In *Handbook of Word-Formation*, edited by Pavol Štekauer and Rochelle Lieber. Dordrecht: Studies in Natural Language and Linguistic Theory.

Duyck, Wouter. 2005. "Translation and Associative Priming with Cross-lingual Pseudohomophones: Evidence for Nonselective Phonological Activation in Bilinguals." *Journal of Experimental Psychology: Learning, Memory, and Cognition* 31, no. 6: 1340–59.

Duyck, Wouter, Kevin Diependaele, Denis Drieghe, and Marc Brysbaert. 2004. "The Size of the Cross-lingual Masked Phonological Priming Effect Does Not Depend on Second Language Proficiency." *Experimental Psychology* 51, no. 2: 1–9.

Echaide, Ana Mª. 1984. *Erizkizundi Irukoitza, IKER-3.* Bilbo: Euskaltzaindia.

Elías de Tejada, Francisco. 1948. *Las Españas. Formación histórica. Tradiciones regionales.* Madrid: Ambos Mundos.

Elorza, Antonio, et al. 2006. *La historia de ETA.* Madrid: Temas de Hoy.

Erdocia, Kepa, Anna Mestres-Missé, Itziar Laka, and Antoni Rodriguez-Fornells. 2009. "Syntactic Complexity and Ambiguity Resolution in a Free Word Order Language: Behavioural and Electrophysiological Evidence from Basque." *Brain and Language* 108, no. 1: 1–17.

Escudero, Manu, and Javier Villanueva. 1976. *La autonomía del País Vasco desde el pasado al futuro.* San Sebastián: Txertoa.

Etcheverry, Joannes. (1712) 1976. *Obras vascongadas del doctor labortano Joannes d'Etxeberri (1712).* Edited by Jukio de Urquijo. Bilbao: La Gran Enciclopedia Vasca.

———. ["Sarakoa"]. *Escuararen hatsapenac,* 1712.

Etxepare, Bernat. 1545; 1995. *Linguae Vasconum Primitiae.* Bordeaux; reprint, Bilbao: Euskaltzaindia, in collaboration with the Government of Navarre, the University of the Basque Country, the University of Deusto, and the Public University of Navarre.

Euskal Herriko Ikastolak and Euskaltzaindia. 2010. *Ikastola mugimendua: Dabilen herria; Ikastola eredua 1960–2010.* Bilbao: Euskal Herriko Ikastolak; Euskaltzaindia.

Euskal Herriko Ikastolen konfederazioa/Confederación de Ikastolas. 2009. *Ikastolen Hizkuntz Proiektua.* Bilbao: EHIK.

Euskaltzaindia. 1977. *El libro blanco del Euskera.* Bilbao: Euskaltzaindia-Caja Laboral Popular.

———. 2004. "'Euskal Herria' izena." Regulation 139. Published in *Euskera* 49: 473–77. Available at www.euskaltzaindia.net/dok/eaeb/arauak/Araua_0139.pdf. Last accessed June 15, 2012.

———. 2008–2011. *Euskararen Herri Hizkeren Atlasa.* 3 Volumes. Bilbao: Caja Laboral and Euskaltzaindia.

Euskararen Erakunde Publikoa-Office Public De La Langue Basque (EEP-OPLB). 2004. *Statut juridique.* At www.mintzaira.fr/fr/oplb/statut-juridique.html.

———. 2005. *Diagnostic Quantitatif de l'Offre d'enseignement du Basque et en Basque. Année Scholaire 2004/2005.* At www.mintzaira.fr/fileadmin/documents/Enseignement/F_diagnostic_2004_2005.pdf. Last accessed June 18, 2012.

———. 2010. *Irakaskuntza sailean eraman lanen bilana 2005–2010.* Document supplied by Mixel Esteban, official representative of the Euskararen Erakunde Publikoa-Office public de la langue Basque (EEP-OPLB), June 2011.

Euskera. Volume 1, no. 1 (1920): 61–65

———. Volume 1, no. 2, (1920): 14–19.

Eustat (Basque Statistics Institute). 2010. *Sociolinguistic Survey of Euskal Herria 2006.* At en.eustat.es/estadisticas/tema_99/opt_0/tipo_3/ti_Sociolinguistic_Survey_of_Euskal_Herria/temas.html#axzz1Q7ZIYifO.

Finkbeiner, Matthew, Tamar H. Gollan, and Alfonso Caramazza. 2006. "Bilingual Lexical Access: What's the (Hard) Problem?" *Bilingualism: Language and Cognition* 9, no. 2: 153–66.

Fishman, Joshua A. 1976. *Bilingual Education: An International Sociological Perspective.* Rowley, MA: Newbury House.

———. 1991. *Reversing Language Shift: Theoretical and Empirical Foundations of Assistance to Threatened Languages.* Clevedon, Philadelphia, and Adelaide: Multilingual Matters.

———. 2001. "Why Is It So Hard to Save a Threatened Language?" In *Can Threatened*

Languages Be Saved? Edited by Josjua A. Fishman. Clevedon, UK: Multilingual Matters.

Friederici, Angela D. 2002. "Towards a Neural Basis of Auditory Sentence Processing." *Trends in Cognitive Sciences* 6, no. 2: 78–84.

Friederici, Angela D., Karsten Steinhauer, and Erdmut Pfeifer. 2002. "Brain Signatures of Artificial Language Processing: Evidence Challenging the Critical Period Hypothesis." *Proceedings of National Academy of Sciences of the United States of America* (PNAS) 99, no. 1: 529–34.

Gaminde, Iñaki. 1999. *Euskaldunen azentuak.* Bilbao: Labayru.

———. 2007. *Bizkaian zehar. Euskararen ikuspegi orokorra.* Bilbao: Mendebalde; Diputación Foral de Vizcaya.

García-Sanz, Ángel, Iñaki Iriarte, and Fernando Mikelarena. 2002. *Historia del navarrismo (1841–1936). Sus relaciones con el vasquismo.* Pamplona: UPNA.

Gobierno de España. Instituto Nacional de Estadística (2011): *Censo de 2010.* Internet: http://www.ine.es/ (last accessed June 15, 2011).

Gobierno de Navarra. 1986. Ley Foral 18/1986, de 15 de diciembre del Vascuence. Text published in the *Boletín Oficial de Navarra* (BON), no. 154, December 17.

———. 1988. Decreto Foral 159/1988, de 19 de mayo, por el que se regula la incorporación y uso del vascuence en la enseñanza no universitaria de Navarra. Text published in the Boletín Oficial de Navarra (BON), no. 67, June 1.

———. *Estadística de Datos básicos.* At www.educacion.navarra.es/portal/Informacion+de+Interes/Estadisticas/Estadistica+de+Datos+Basicos.

———. *Guía de estudios.* At www.educacion.navarra.es/portal/Guia+de+Estudios/SistemaEducativo.

Gobierno Vasco. 1983. Decreto 138/1983, de 11 de julio, del Departamento de Educación y Cultura, por el que se regula el uso de las lenguas oficiales en la enseñanza no universitaria en el País Vasco. *Boletín Oficial del País Vasco* (BOPV) de 19/07/1983, 2471-2475. At www.euskadi.net/cgi-bin_k54/bopv_20?c&f=19830719&s=1983108.

———. 1993. *Criterios básicos para la política del euskera.* Vitoria-Gasteiz: Servicio Central de Publicaciones del Gobierno Vasco.

———. 1997–1999. *II mapa sociolingüistico.* 3 Volumes. Vitoria-Gasteiz: Servicio Central de Publicaciones del Gobierno Vasco.

———. 1999. *Plan General de Promoción del Uso del Euskera.* Vitoria-Gasteiz: Servicio Central de Publicaciones del Gobierno Vasco. At www.euskara.euskadi.net/r59-euhadm2/es/contenidos/informacion/941/es_2383/adjuntos/ebpn14gazt.pdf.

———. 2003. *The Continuity of Basque III, 2001: Sociolinguistic Survey of the Basque Country.* Vitoria-Gasteiz: Servicio Central de Publicaciones del Gobierno Vasco.

———. 2004. *Confluencia de los planes para fortalecer el uso del euskera en los centros escolares y de los modelos municipales del Plan General de Promoción del Uso del Euskera.* Vitoria-Gasteiz: Servicio Central de Publicaciones del Gobierno

Vasco. At www.euskara.euskadi.net/r59-738/es/contenidos/informacion/7041/ es_2447/adjuntos/confluencia%20de%20los%20planes.pdf.

———. 2005a. *Level B2 in Basque at the End of Obligatory Education: Summary of the Spanish Version*. Bilbao: Instituto Vasco de Evaluación e Investigación Educativa. At: www.isei-ivei.net/eng/pubeng/b2_english1.pdf.

———. 2005b. *Futuro de la Política Lingüística. Proyecto 2005-2009 de la Viceconsejería de Política Lingüística*. Vitoria-Gasteiz: Servicio Central de Publicaciones del Gobierno Vasco. At www.kultura.ejgv.euskadi.net/r46-17894/es/ contenidos/informacion/hizk_politika_etorkizuna/es_fut_0509/adjuntos/ hp_aurrera_es.pdf.

———. 2005c. *III mapa sociolingüístico*. Vitoria-Gasteiz: Servicio Central de Publicaciones del Gobierno Vasco.

———. 2007. *Nivel B1 de Euskara en Educación Primaria. Informe General*. Bilbao: Instituto Vasco de Evaluación e Investigación Educativa. At www.isei-ivei.net/ cast/pub/b1_castellano.pdf.

———. 2008a. *Fourth Sociolinguistic Survey 2006*. Vitoria-Gasteiz: Servicio Central de Publicaciones del Gobierno Vasco. At www.euskara.euskadi.net/r59-738/en/ contenidos/informacion/inkesta_soziolinguistikoa2006/en_survey/adjuntos/ IV_incuesta_en.pdf.

———. 2008b. *Euskararen belaunez belauneko transmisioa EAEn. Transmisión intergeneracional en la CAV*. Vitoria-Gasteiz: Servicio Central de Publicaciones del Gobierno Vasco.

———. 2008c. *Criterios de uso de las lenguas oficiales en el Gobierno Vasco. IV período de Planificación (2008–2012)*. Vitoria-Gasteiz: Servicio Central de Publicaciones del Gobierno Vasco. At www6.euskadi.net/r59-738/es/contenidos/ informacion/argitalpenak/es_6092/adjuntos/Irizpideakgazt.pdf.

———. 2009a. *IV Mapa Sociolingüístico 2006*. Vitoria-Gasteiz: Servicio Central de Publicaciones del Gobierno Vasco. At www.kultura.ejgv.euskadi.net/r46-17894/es/ contenidos/informacion/argitalpenak/es_6092/adjuntos/MAPAcast.pdf.

———. 2009b. *Basis for a Language Policy for the Early 21st century: Towards a New Agreement*. Vitoria-Gasteiz: Basque Government Central Publication Service. At www.euskara.euskadi.net/r59-738/es/contenidos/informacion/eusk_aholku_ batzordea_nabarmen/es_2009/adjuntos/Maketa-Pacto_Baja-1eng%202.pdf (last accessed June 25, 2012).

———. 2010a. *Evaluación Diagnóstica 2009. 2º ESO. Informe General de Resultados*. Bilbao: Instituto Vasco de Evaluación e Investigación Educativa. At www.isei-ivei.net/cast/pub/ED09_inf_gnal_rdos/ED09_2ESO_inf_gnal_rdos.pdf (last accessed June 25, 2012).

———. 2010b. *Decreto de curriculum de la Educación Básica de la CAPV*. At: www. euskadi.net/cgi-bin_k54/ver_c?CMD=VERDOC&BASE=B03V&DOCN=0000 00460&CONF=/config/k54/bopv_c.cnf (last accessed June 25, 2012).

———. 2011a. *Evaluación Diagnóstica 2010. 2º ESO. Informe General de Resultados y Análisis de Variables*. Bilbao: Instituto Vasco de Evaluación e Investigación Educativa. At: www.isei-ivei.net/cast/pub/ED10_rdosYvariables/ED10_2ESO_ resultadosYvariables.pdf (last accessed June 25, 2012).

———. 2011b. *PISA 2009 Euskadi Informe de Evaluación. Proyecto para la Evaluación Internacional de Estudiantes de 15 años en Lectura, Matemáticas y Ciencias*. Vitoria-Gasteiz: Gobierno Vasco-OECD-PISA.

Goenaga, Patxi. 2000. "Euskaltzaindia eta euskararen arautzea." *Revista Internacional de Estudios Vascos* (RIEV) 45, no. 1: 11–42.

Gollan, Tamar H., and Lori-Ann R. Acenas. 2004. "What is a TOT? Cognate and Translation Effects on Tip-of-the-tongue States in Spanish–English and Tagalog–English Bilinguals." *Journal of Experimental Psychology: Learning, Memory, and Cognition* 30, no. 1: 246–69.

Gracia, Jordi, and Domingo Rodenas de Moya, eds. 2009. Más es más. Sociedad y cultura en la España democrática, 1986–2008. Madrid-Frankfurt: Verveurt-Iberoamericana.

Gràcia, Llüisa, and Miren Azkarate. 2000. "Prefixation and Head-complement Parametre." In *Morphological Analysis in Comparison*, edited by Wolfgang U. Dressler. Amsterdam: John Benjamins.

Granja, José Luis de la. 2008. *Nacionalismo y II República. Estatutos de autonomía, partidos y elecciones. Historia de Acción Nacionalista Vasca: 1930–1936*. Madrid: Siglo XXI.

Green, David W. 1998. "Mental Control of the Bilingual Lexico-semantic System." *Bilingualism: Language and Cognition* 1: 67–81.

Greenberg, Joseph H. 1963. *Universals of Language*. Cambridge: MIT Press.

Gros i Lladós, Miquel. 2007. *Recuperación del Euskera en Navarra*. Bilbao: Euskaltzaindia.

Grosjean, François. 1989. "Neurolinguists, Beware! The Bilingual is Not Two Monolinguals in One Person." *Brain and Language* 36, no. 1: 3–15.

Hahne, Anja. 2001. "What's Different in Second-Language Processing? Evidence from Event-Related Brain Potentials." *Journal of Psycholinguistic Research* 30, no. 3: 251–66.

Hahne, Anja, and Angela D. Friederici. 2001. "Processing a Second Language: Late Learners' Comprehension Mechanisms as Revealed by Event-related Brain Potentials." *Bilingualism: Language and Cognition* 4, no. 2: 123–41.

Hawkins, John A. 1994. *A Performance Theory of Order and Constituency*. Cambridge and New York: Cambridge University Press.

Hawkins, John A., and Gary Gilligan. 1988. "Prefixing and Suffixing Universals in Relation to Basic Word Order." In "Papers in Universal Grammar: Generative and Typological Approaches," edited by John A. Hawkins and Heather K. Holmback, special issue, *Lingua* 74, nos. 2/3: 219–59.

Hernández Abaitua, Mikel. 2008. Ramon Saizarbitoriaren lehen eleberrigintza. Leioa: UPV/EHUko Argitalpen Zerbitzua.

Hidalgo, Bittor. 1994. "Hitzen ordena euskaraz." Ph D. diss. University of the Basque Country.

Hirschfeld, Lawrence A. "The Bilingual Brain Revisited: A Comment on Hagen." *Evolutionary Psychology* 6, no. 1: 182–85.

Hualde, José Ignacio. 1997. *Euskararen azentuerak*. Anejos ASJU, 42. Donostria-San Sebastián: Gipuzkoako Foru Aldundia; Bilbo: UPV/EHU.

———. 2002. "On the Loss of Ergative Displacement in Basque and the Role of Analogy in the Development of Morphological Paradigms." In *The Linguist's Linguist: A Collection of Papers in Honour of Alexis Manaster Ramer*, edited by Fabrice Cavoto. Munich: Lincom Europa.

Hualde, José Ignacio, and Jon Ortiz de Urbina, eds. 2003. *A Grammar of Basque.* Berlin: Mouton de Gruyter.

Humboldt, Wilhelm von. 1904. *Gesammelte Schriften.* Volume 3. Berlin: Behr.

Hurtado, Irene. 2001. *Goierriko eta Tolosalde hegoaldeko hizkerak.* Lazkao: Goierriko Euskal Eskola Kultur Elkartea, Maizpide Euskaltegia, and Lazkaoko Udala.

Ibarra, Orreaga. 1995. *Ultzamako hizkera. Inguruko euskalkiekiko harremanak.* Pamplona: Gobierno de Navarra.

Irizar, Pedro. 1981. *Contribución a la dialectología de la lengua vasca.* 2 Volumes. San Sebastián: Caja de Ahorros Provincial de Guipúzcoa.

———. 1991a. *Morfología del verbo auxiliar roncalés.* Pamplona: Gobierno de Navarra; Bilbao: Euskaltzaindia.

———. 1991b. *Morfología del verbo auxiliar guipuzcoano.* Bilbao: Euskaltzaindia.

———. 1992a. *Morfología del verbo auxiliar alto navarro septentrional.* Pamplona: Gobierno de Navarra; Bilbao: Euskaltzaindia.

———. 1992b. *Morfología del verbo auxiliar alto navarro meridional.* Pamplona: Gobierno de Navarra; Bilbao: Euskaltzaindia.

———. 1992c. *Morfología del verbo auxiliar vizcaíno.* Bilbao: BBK and Euskaltzaindia.

———. 1997. *Morfología del verbo auxiliar labortano.* Bilbao: UPV/EHU and Euskaltzaindia.

———. 1999a. *Morfología del verbo auxiliar bajo navarro occidental.* Bilbao: UPV/ EHU and Euskaltzaindia.

———. 1999b, 2002b, 2002c. *Morfología del verbo auxiliar bajo navarro oriental.* 3 volumes. UPV/EHU and Euskaltzaindia.

———. 2002a. *Morfología del verbo auxiliar suletino.* Bilbao: UPV/EHU and Euskaltzaindia.

———. 2008. *Morfología del verbo auxiliar vasco.* Bilbao: Euskaltzaindia.

Ithurry, Jean. 1920; 1979. *Grammaire basque: Dialecte labourdin.* Donostia: Hordago.

Jáuregui, Gurutz. 1985. *Ideología y estrategia política de ETA. Análisis de su evolución entre 1959 y 1968.* 2nd ed. Madrid: Siglo XXI.

Jefatura del Estado Español. 1979. Ley Orgánica 3/1979, de 18 de diciembre, de Estatuto de Autonomía para el País Vasco, *Boletín Oficial del Estado* (BOE) no. 306, December 22, 1979: 29357-29363. At www.boe.es/boe/dias/1979/12/22/pdfs/ A29357-29363.pdf.

———. 1982. Ley Orgánica 13/1982, de 10 de agosto, de Reintegración y Amejoramiento del Régimen Foral de Navarra. Text published in the *Boletín Oficial de Navarra* (BON), September 3, 1982; corr. err., *Boletín Oficial del Estado* (BOE), August 26, 1982. At www.boe.es/aeboe/consultas/bases_datos/act. php?id=BOE-A-1982-20824.

Kim, Karl H.S., Norman R. Relkin, Kyoung-Min Lee, and Joy Hirsch. 1997. "Dis-

200   *References*

tinct Cortical Areas Associated with Native and Second Languages." *Nature* 388 (6638): 171–74.

Kortazar, Jon. 2005. *Bernardo Atxaga: Basque Literature from the End of the Franco Era to the Present*. Reno: Center for Basque Studies, University of Nevada.

Kotz, Sonja A. 2009. "A Critical Review of ERP and fMRI Evidence on L2 Syntactic Processing." *Brain and Language* 109, nos. 2–3: 68–74.

Kotz, Sonja A., Phillip J. Holcomb, and Lee Osterhout. 2008. "ERPs Reveal Comparable Syntactic Sentence Processing in Native and Non-native Readers of English." *Acta Psychologica* 128: 514–27.

Kroll, Judith F., Susan C. Bobb, and Zofia Wodniekca. 2006. "Language selectivity is the exception, not the rule: Arguments against a fixed locus of language selection in bilingual speech." *Bilingualism: Language and Cognition* 9: 119–35.

La Heij, Wido. 2005. "Monolingual and Bilingual Lexical Access in Speech Production: Issues and Models." In *Handbook of Bilingualism: Psycholinguistic Approaches*, edited by Judith F. Kroll, and Annette M.B. de Groot. New York: Oxford University Press.

Lafitte, Pierre. 1944; 1979. *Grammaire basque (navarro-labourdin littéraire)*. San Sebastián: Elkar.

Laka, Itziar. 1996. *A Brief Grammar of Euskara, the Basque Language*. At www.ei.ehu.es/p289-content/eu/contenidos/informacion/grammar_euskara/en_doc/index.html.

———. 1993a. "Unergatives that Assign Ergative, Unaccusatives that Assign Accusative." In *Papers on Case and Agreement*, vol. 1, edited by Jonathan David and Colin Phillips. Cambridge: MITWPL 18.

———. 1993b. "The Structure of Inflection: A Case Study in X0 Syntax." In *Generative Studies in Basque Linguistics*, edited by José Ignacio Hualde and Jon Ortiz de Urbina. Amsterdam and Philadelphia: John Benjamins Publishing Co.

Laka, Itziar. 2012a. "More than One Language in the Brain. In *Language, from a Biological Point of View: Current Issues in Biolinguistics*, edited by C. Boeckx, M. C. Horno, and J. L. Mendívil, 184–207. Cambridge: Cambridge Scholars Publishing.

Laka, Itziar, 2012b. "Merging from the Temporal Input: On Subject-Object Asymmetries and an Ergative Language." In *Rich Grammars from Poor Inputs*, edited bt R. Berwick and M. Piattelli-Palmarini. Oxford: Oxford University Press.

Laka, Itziar, and Erdocia, K. 2012. "Linearization Preferences Given 'Free Word Order'; Subject Preferences Given Ergativity: A Look at Basque." In *Of Grammar, Words, and Verses*, edited by E. Torrego, 115–42. Language Faculty and Beyond Series, Amsterdam: John Benjamins Publishing Co.

Larramendi, Manuel. 1745. *Diccionario trilingüe del castellano, bascuence, y latín*. San Sebastián: Bartholomè Riesgo y Montero.

———. 1729. *El impossible vencido. Arte de la Lengua Vascongada*. Salamanca: Antonio Joseph Villargordo Alcaráz.

———. 1729; 1979. *El imposible vencido. Arte de la lengua vascongada*. San Sebastián: Hordago.

———. 1756; 1969. *Corografía de la muy noble y muy leal provincia de Guipúzcoa*.

Edited by Tellechea Idígoras. Bilbao: Amigos del libro Vasco; Bueno Aires: Ekin.

Larronde, Jean-Claude. 1977. *El nacionalismo vasco. Su origen y su ideología en la obra de Sabino Arana-Goiri*. San Sebastián: Txertoa.

Legarra, Jose Mª, and Erramun Baxok. 2005. "Language Policy and Planning of the Status of Basque, II: Navarre and the Northern Basque Country." *International Journal of the Sociology of Language* 174, no. 1: 25–38.

Leizarraga, Joanes. 1571; 1979. *Iesus Christ gure iaunaren Testamentu berria*. San Sebastián: Hordago.

Lenneberg, Eric H. 1967. *Biological Foundations of Language*. New York: Wiley.

Levin, Beth. 1983. "On the Nature of Ergativity." Ph.D. diss. Massachusetts Institute of Technology.

López Basaguren, Alberto. 1988. "El pluralismo lingüístico en el Estado autonómico." *Autonomies. Revista Catalana de Derecho Público* 9: 47–84.

———. 2007. "Las lenguas oficiales entre Constitución y Comunidades Autónomas: ¿Desarrollo o transformación del modelo constitucional?" *Revista Española de Derecho Constitucional* 79: 83–112.

———. 2010. "The Spanish Constitution: Problems in Applying the Charter." In *Minority Language Protection in Europe: Into a New Decade*. Strasbourg: Council of Europe.

———. 2011. "Nación y lengua en el Estatuto de Cataluña. Consideraciones sobre la STC 31/2010." *Revista General de Derecho Constitucional* 13: 1–25.

Marian, Viorica, Henrike K. Blumenfeld, and Olga V. Boukrina. 2008. "Sensitivity to Phonological Similarity Within and Across Languages: A Native/Nonnative Asymmetry in Bilinguals." *Journal of Psycholinguistic Research* 37, no. 3: 141–170.

Marian, Viorica, Michael Spivey, and Joy Hirsch. 2003. "Shared and Separate Systems in Bilingual Language Processing: Converging Evidence from Eyetracking and Brain Imaging." *Brain and Language* 86: 70–82.

Mateo, Miren. 2005. "Language Policy and Planning of the Status of Basque, I: The Basque Autonomous Community (BAC)." *International Journal of the Sociology of Language* 174: 9–23.

Mees, Ludger. 2003. *Nationalism, Violence and Democracy: The Basque Clash of Identities*. Houndmills, UK and New York: Palgrave Macmillan.

———. 2006. *El profeta pragmático. Aguirre, el primer lehendakari (1939-1960)*. Irún: Alberdania.

———. 2009. "Visión y gestión. El nacionalismo vasco democrático 1998-2009." In *¿Crisis? ¿Qué crisis? España en busca de su camino*, edited by Walther L. Bernecker, Diego Íñiguez Hernández, and Günther Maihold. Frankfurt a.M. / Madrid: Vervuert.

Mees, Ludger, ed. (2012, forthcoming): *La celebración de la nación: Símbolos, mitos y lugares de memoria*. Granada: Comares.

Meuter, Renata F. I., and Allan Allport. 1999. "Bilingual Language Switching in Naming: Asymmetrical Costs of Language Selection." *Journal of Memory and Language* 40, no. 1: 25–40.

Mitxelena, Koldo. 1978a. "Arantzazutik Bergarara." In *Sobre historia de la Lengua Vasca*. Anejos del Seminario de Filología Vasca "Julio de Urquijo" (ASJU) 10. 1988. Edited by Joseba Andoni Lakarra, with the collaboration of María Teresa Echenique and Blanka Urgell. Donostia: Seminario de Filología Vasca "Julio de Urquijo".

———. 1978b. "Euskararen bide luze bezain malkarrak." In *Sobre historia de la Lengua Vasca*. Anejos del Seminario de Filología Vasca "Julio de Urquijo" (ASJU) 10. 1988. Edited by Joseba Andoni Lakarra, with the collaboration of María Teresa Echenique and Blanka Urgell. Donostia: Seminario de Filología Vasca "Julio de Urquijo".

———. 1981. "Euskal literaturaren bereizgarri orokorrak." In Antonio Tovar, Koldo Mitxelena, et al. *Euskal linguistika eta literatura: Bide berriak*. Bilbo: Deustuko Unibertsitateko Argitarazioak.

———. 1985a. "Las lenguas y la política." In *Lengua e historia*. Madrid: Paraninfo.

———. 1985b. "Sobre bilingüismo." In *Lengua e historia*, 191–212. Madrid: Paraninfo.

———. 1987. "Lengua común y dialectos vascos." In *Palabras y textos*. Leioa: UPV/EHU.

———. 2008. *Koldo Mitxelena: Selected Writings of a Basque Scholar*. Compiled and with an introduction by Pello Salaburu. Reno: Center for Basque Studies, University of Nevada, Reno.

Moreno Cabrera, Juan Carlos. 2007–2008. "Sobre la complejidad y dificultad de las lenguas. El caso del euskera." *Revista de Lenguas y Literaturas Catalana, Gallega y Vasca* 13: 199–216.

Moro, Andrea. 2008. *The Boundaries of Babel: The Brain and the Enigma of Impossible Languages*. Cambridge, MA: MIT Press.

Mueller, Jutta L., Anja Hahne, Yugo Fujii, and Angela D. Friederici. 2005. "Native and Nonnative Speakers' Processing of a Miniature Version of Japanese as Revealed by ERPs." *Journal of Cognitive Neuroscience* 17, no. 8: 1229–1244.

Newmeyer, Frederick J. J. 2005. *Possible and Probable Languages: A Generative Perspective on Linguistic Typology*. Oxford and New York: Oxford University Press.

Núñez, Luis C. 1977. *Opresión y defensa del euskera*. San Sebastián: Txertoa.

Oihenart, Arnaud. 1657. *Les proverbes basques recuillis par le S. d'Oihenart, plus les poesies basques du mesme Auteur*. Paris.

Ojima, Shiro, Hiroki Nakata, and Ryusuke Kakigi. 2005. "An ERP Study of Second Language Learning after Childhood: Effects of Proficiency." *Journal of Cognitive Neuroscience* 17, no. 8: 1212–28.

Ortiz de Urbina, Jon. 1989. *Parameters in the Grammar of Basque*. Dordrecht: Foris.

———. 1988. "Axularren *ezen* konpletiboa eta hizkuntza prozesamendua." In *Studia Philologica In Honorem Alfonso Irigoien*, edited by Itziar Turrez, Adolfo Arejita, and Carmen Isasi. Bilbao: Universidad de Deusto.

Oyharçabal, Beñat. 1993. "Verb Agreement with Non-arguments: On Allocutive Agreement." In *Generative Studies in Basque Linguistics*, edited by José Ignacio Hualde and Jon Ortiz de Urbina. Amsterdam and Philadelphia: Benjamins.

Pablo, Santiago de, José Luis de la Granja, and Ludger Mees, eds. 1998. *Documentos para la historia del nacionalismo vasco. De los Fueros a nuestros días*. Barcelona: Ariel.

Pablo, Santiago de, Ludger Mees, and José Antonio Rodríguez Ranz. 1999. *El péndulo patriótico. Historia del Partido Nacionalista Vasco, I: 1895–1936*. Barcelona: Crítica.

Pablo, Santiago de, Ludger Mees, and José Antonio Rodríguez Ranz. 2001. *El péndulo patriótico. Historia del Partido Nacionalista Vasco, 2: 1936–1979*. Barcelona: Crítica.

Pablo, Santiago de, and Coro Rubio. 2006. *Eman ta zabal zazu. Historia de la UPV/ EHU 1980–2005*. Bilbao: Universiad del País Vasco.

Pablo, Santiago de, José Luis de la Granja, Ludger Mees, and Jesús Casquete, eds. 2012. *Diccionario Ilustrado de Símbolos del Nacionalismo Vasco*. Madrid: Tecnos.

Pagola, Inés. 2005. *Neologismos en la obra de Sabino Arana Goiri*. Bilbao: Euskaltzaindia.

Pagola, Rosa Miren. 1991. *Dialektologiaren atarian*. Bilbao: Gero.

Parlamento Vasco. 1982. Ley 10/1982, de 24 de Noviembre, Básica de Normalización del Uso del Euskera, Boletín Oficial del País Vasco (BOPV), December 16: 3138-3146. At www.euskadi.net/cgi-bin_k54/bopv_20?c&f=19821216&a=198 201955.

Perani, D., E. Paulesu, N. Sebastian-Galles, E. Dupoux, S. Dehaene, V. Bettinardi, S. F. Cappa, F. Fazio, and J. Mehler. 1998. "The Bilingual Brain: Proficiency and Age of Acquisition of the Second Language." *Brain* 121: 1841–52.

Prieto de Pedro, Jesús. 1996. "Artículo tercero: las lenguas de España." In *Comentarios a la Constitución española de 1978*. Volume 1, edited by Oscar Alzaga. Madrid: Edersa.

Pullvermüller, Friedemann. 2002. *The Neuroscience of Language: On Brain Circuits of Words and Serial Order*. Cambridge: Cambridge University Press.

Rijk, Rudolf de. 1969. "Is Basque an S.O.V. Language?" *Fontes Linguae Vasconum* I, no. 3: 319–51.

Rodriguez Ochoa, Jose Ma. 2001. "Aplicación y desarrollo normativo de la Ley Foral del Vascuence en el ámbito de la Administración Foral de Navarra" in "15 años de la Ley del Euskera en Navarra." Special issue, *RIEV* 46, no.2: 545–92.

Rossi, Sonja, Manfred F. Gugler, Angela D. Friederici, and Anja Hahne. 2006. "The Impact of Proficiency on Second-language Processing of German and Italian: Evidence from Event-related Potentials." *Journal of Cognitive Neuroscience* 18, no. 12: 2030–48.

Rubio Pobes, Coro. 2003. *La identidad vasca en el siglo XIX. Discurso y agentes sociales*. Madrid: Biblioteca Nueva.

Ruiz Bikandi, Uri, ed. 2000. *Didáctica de la segunda lengua en educación infantil y primaria*. Madrid: Síntesis.

Salaburu, Pello. 1984. *Hizkuntza teoria eta Baztango euskalkia*. 2 Volumes. Leioa: UPV/EHU.

——. 2005. *Baztango mintzoa: gramatika eta hiztegia*. Pamplona: Gobierno de Navarra; Bilbao: Euskaltzaindia.

———, ed. 2008. *Koldo Mitxelena: Selected Writings of a Basque Scholar*. Reno: Center for Basque Studies, University of Nevada, Reno.

Santesteban, Mikel, and Albert Costa. 2006. "Does L1 Syntax Affect L2 Processing? A Study with Highly Proficient Early Bilinguals." In *Andolin gogoan. Essays in honour of Professor Eguzkitza*, edited by Beatriz Fernández and Itziar Laka. Bilbao: EHUko argitalpen zerbitzua.

Schwartz, Ana I., Judith F. Kroll, and Michele Diaz. 2007. "Reading Words in Spanish and English: Mapping Orthography to Phonology in Two Languages." *Language and Cognitive Processes* 22: 106–29.

Serra, Josep Mª, and Ignasi Vila. 2000. "Las segundas lenguas y la escuela." In *Didáctica de la segunda lengua en educación infantil y primaria*, edited by U. Ruiz Bikandi. Madrid: Síntesis.

Sierra, Josu. 2008. "Assessment of Bilingual Education in the Basque Country." *Language, Culture and Curriculum* 21, no. 1: 39–47.

Siguàn, Miguel, and William F. F. Mackey. 1987. *Education and Bilingualism*. London: K. Page, in association with UNESCO, Paris, France.

Smith, Anthony D. 2009. *Ethno-Symbolism and Nationalism: A Cultural Approach*. New York: Routledge.

Solozabal Echavarria, Juan J. 1999. "El régimen constitucional del bilingüismo. La cooficialidad lingüística como garantía institucional." *Revista Española de Derecho Constitucional* 55: 11–41.

Stuijt, Mark, updated by Daniel Sánchez. 2008. *The Basque language in Education in France*. 2nd edition. Ljouwert/Leeuwarden: Mercator European Research Centre on Multilingualism and Language Learning.

Torrealdai, Joan Mari. 1999. *La censura de Franco y el tema vasco*. San Sebastián: Fundación Kutxa.

Tortosa, Virgilio, ed. 2009. *Mercado y consumo de ideas: De industria a negocio cultural*. Madrid: Biblioteca Nueva; Universidad de Alicante, Instituto alicantino de Cultura Juan Gil Albert.

Trask, R. Larry. 1998. "The Typological Position of Basque: Then and Now." *Language Sciences* 20, no. 3: 313–24.

Txillardegi [pseud. Jose Luis Alvarez Enparantza]. 1978. Euskal herritik erdal herrietara. Bilbao: Gráficas Bilbao.

———. 1984. *Euskal azentuaz*. Donostia: Elkar.

———. 1997. *Euskal Herria en el horizonte*. Tafalla: Txalaparta.

Ullman, Michael T. 2001. "A Neurocognitive Perspective on Language: The Declarative/Procedural Model." *Nature Reviews: Neuroscience* 2: 717–26.

———. 2004. "Contributions of Memory Circuits to Language: The Declarative/Procedural Model." *Cognition* 92: 231–70.

Universidad Pública de Navarra (UPNA). 2007. *Plan estratégico del euskera 2007–2009*. At www1.unavarra.es/digitalAssets/124/124306_Euskararen-Plan-estrategikoa.pdf.

Universidad del País Vasco/Euskal Herriko Unibertsitatea (UPV/EHU). 2007. *Plan director del euskara en la UPV/EHU (2007/2008–2011/2012)*. Leioa: Servicio Editorial de la Universidad del País Vasco. At www.euskara-errektoreordetza.ehu.es/p267-content/es/contenidos/informacion/plan_informa/es_plan/adjuntos/plan_director.pdf.

———. 2010. *La Universidad en cifras 2009–2010*. At: www.ehu.es/p200-shstatct/es/contenidos/estadistica/universidad_cifras_2009_2010/es_cif_2010/universidad_cifras.html.

Van Hell, Janet G., and Annette M. B. De Groot. 1998. "Conceptual Representation in Bilingual Memory: Effects of Concreteness and Cognate Status in Word Association." *Bilingualism: Language and Cognition* 1, no. 3: 193–211.

Van Hell, Janet G., and Ton Dijkstra. 2002. "Foreign Language Knowledge Can Influence Native Language Performance in Exclusively Native Contexts." *Psychonomic Bulletin & Review* 9, no. 4: 780–89.

Van Heuven, Walter, Ton Dijkstra, and Jonathan Grainger. 1998. "Orthographic Neighbourhood Effects in Bilingual Word Recognition." *Journal of Memory and Language* 39: 458–83.

Velasco y Fernández de la Fuente, Ladislao. 1983. *Los Euskaros en Álava, Guipúzcoa y Vizcaya. Sus orígenes, historia, lengua, leyes, costumbres y tradiciones*. Bilbao: Amigos del Libro Vasco. First edition, Barcelona: Imprenta de Oliveres, 1879.

Videgain, Xarles. 1991. "Lexiaren inguruen Euskal Herriko atlas linguistikoaren inkestagintzan." In *Memoriae L. Mitxelena magistri sacrum*, volume 2, edited by Joseba Andoni Lakarra. Anejos de ASJU no. 14. Donostia-San Sebastián: Gipukoako Foru Aldundia.

Weber-Fox, Christine M., and Helen J. Neville. 1996. "Maturational Constraints on Functional Specializations for Language Processing: ERP and Behavioural Evidence in Bilingual Speakers." *Journal of Cognitive Neuroscience* 8, no. 3: 231–56.

White, Lydia. 2003. *Second Language Acquisition and Universal Grammar*. Cambridge: Cambridge University Press.

Yang, Charles D. 2003. *Knowledge and Learning in Natural Language*. Oxford and New York: Oxford University Press.

Zabala, Igone. 1996. "La traducción al vasco de los sintagmas nominales complejos del lenguaje técnico." In *III Congrés Internacional sobre traducció*, edited by Pilar Orero. Barcelona: Universidad Autónoma de Barcelona.

Zabala, Juan Mateo. 1848. *El verbo regular vascongado del dialecto vizcaíno*. San Sebastián: Imprenta de Ignacio Ramón Baroja.

Zabaltza Pérez-Nievas, Xabier. 1997. "El significado oculto de la palabra 'Euzkadi'." *Fontes Linguae Vasconum* 29, no. 74: 77–83.

Zalbide, Mikel. 1998. "Normalización lingüística y escolaridad: un informe desde la sala de máquinas." In "15 años de la Ley del Euskera en la Educación, Administración y Medios de Comunicación," special issue, *Revista Internacional de Estudios Vascos* (RIEV) 43, no. 2: 355–424.

———. 2000. "Irakas-sistemaren Hizkuntz Normalkuntza: Nondik norakoaren ebaluazio-saio bat." *Eleria* 5: 45–61.

———. 2010. *Euskararen legeak hogeita bost urte. Eskola alorreko bilakaera: Balioespen saioa*. Bilbo: Euskaltzaindia.

Zawiszewski, Adam, Eva Gutierrez, Beatriz Fernández, and Itziar Laka. 2011. "Language Distance and Non-native Syntactic Processing: Evidence from Event-related Potentials." *Bilingualism: Language and Cognition* 14, no. 3: 400–411.

Zawiszewski, Adam, and Friederici, A. 2009. "Processing Object-Verb Agreement in Canonical and Non-canonical Word Orders in Basque: Evidence from Event-related Brain Potentials." *Brain Research* 1284: 161–79.

Zelaieta, Edu. 2008. *Baztan-Bidasoako hizkeren azterketa dialektologikoa.* Pamplona and Bilbao: Gobierno de Navarra and Euskaltzaindia.

Zuazo, Koldo. 1988. *Euskararen batasuna.* Bilbao: Euskaltzaindia.

———. 2003. *Euskalkiak herriaren lekukoak.* Donostia: Elkar.

———. 2006. *Deba ibarreko euskara. Dialektologia eta tokiko batua.* Eibar: Badihar-dugu Euskara Elkartea.

———. 2007. "Análisis sobre el origen de los dialectos del euskara." *Gara* (online edition), December 9. At www.gara.net/paperezkoa/20071209/52380/es/Los-euskalkis-actuales-tienen-su-origen-Edad-Media. Last accessed June 18, 2011.

———. 2008. *Euskalkiak, euskararen dialektoak.* Donostia: Elkar.

———. 2010. *El euskera y sus dialectos.* Irun: Alberdania.

Zubimendi, Jose Ramon, and Pello Esnal. 1993. *Idazkera-liburua.* Vitoria-Gasteiz: Eusko-Jaurlaritza.

Further Information Online

Ahotsak, Euskal Herriko hizkerak eta ahozko ondarea (Programme for the Collection and Diffusion of Basque Oral Heritage and Basque Dialects), www.ahotsak.com/english/. Last accessed June 18, 2012.

Eustat (Basque Statistics Institute), "Euskera, cultura y juventud" (Basque, culture, and youth), www.eustat.es/estadisticas/opt_0/id_5/ti_Euskera_Cultura_y_Juventud/subarbol.html#axzz1ZS1bFgFI. In Spanish, last accessed June 18, 2012.

Euskadi.net, "Basque government data on publications regarding the sociolinguistic dimension of Euskara," www.euskara.euskadi.net/r59-738/es/contenidos/informacion/argitalpenak/es_6092/ikuspegi_sozio_linguis.html. In Spanish, last accessed June 18, 2012.

Euskaltzaindia (Academy of the Basque Language), www.euskaltzaindia.net. In Basque, also available in Spanish and French, last accessed on June 18, 2012.

Eustat (Basque Statistics Institute), en.eustat.es/ci_ci/indice.html#axzz1 yAFWtKgy. In English, last accessed June 18, 2012.

University of the Basque Country, Basque language Institute, www.ei.ehu.es/p289-content/en/contenidos/informacion/euskara_inst_sarrera/en_sarrera/sarrera.html. In English, last accessed June 18, 2012.

University of the Basque Country, "Euskalkiak" (Basque dialects), www.ehu.es/seg/doku.php?id=gizt:2. In Basque, last accessed June 18, 2012.

Seaska: Iparraldeko ikastolen konfederazioa (Confederation of Ikastolas in Iparralde), www.seaska.net/web/default.php. Available in Basque, French, Spanish, and English, last accessed June 18, 2012.

Index

List of Contributors

For full biographical information about the contributors, links to their projects, and more, visit www.basque.unr.edu/currentresearch/contributors.

Xabier Alberdi, the University of the Basque Country (UPV/EHU)
Miren Azkarate Villar, the University of the Basque Country (UPV/EHU)
Kepa Erdocia, the University of the Basque Country (UPV/EHU)
Jon Kortazar, the University of the Basque Country (UPV/EHU)
Alberto Lopez Basaguren, the University of the Basque Country (UPV/EHU)
Itziar Laka, the University of the Basque Country (UPV/EHU)
Julian Maia, the University of the Basque Country (UPV/EHU)
Jesus Mari Makazaga, the University of the Basque Country (UPV/EHU)
Ludger Mees, the University of the Basque Country (UPV/EHU)
Pello Salaburu, the University of the Basque Country (UPV/EHU)
Itziar San Martin, the University of the Basque Country (UPV/EHU)
Mikel Santesteban, the University of the Basque Country (UPV/EHU)
Igone Zabala, the University of the Basque Country (UPV/EHU)
Adam Zawiszewski, the University of the Basque Country (UPV/EHU)